Classrooms Without Borders

Using Internet Projects to Teach Communication and Collaboration

Classrooms Without Borders

Using Internet Projects to Teach
Communication and Collaboration

James A. Bellanca
Terry Stirling

Foreword by
David W. Johnson
Roger T. Johnson

TEACHERS COLLEGE PRESS
TEACHERS COLLEGE | COLUMBIA UNIVERSITY
NEW YORK AND LONDON

Published by Teachers College Press, 1234 Amsterdam Avenue, New York, NY 10027

Library of Congress Cataloging-in-Publication Data

Bellanca, James A., 1937–
    Classrooms without borders : using Internet projects to teach communication and collaboration / James A. Bellanca and Terry Stirling ; foreword by David W. Johnson and Roger T. Johnson.
        p. cm.
    Includes bibliographical references and index.
    ISBN 978-0-8077-5209-8 (pbk. : alk. paper)
    1. Internet in education. 2. Project method in teaching. 3. Communication in education. 4. Group work in education. I. Stirling, Terry. II. Title.
    LB1044.87.B425   2011
    371.33'44678—dc22   2010050858

ISBN 978-0-8077-5209-8 (paper)

Printed on acid-free paper
Manufactured in the United States of America

Contents

Foreword

WE LIVE IN A historical period in which knowledge is the most critical resource for social and economic development, and people need to be able to participate in a networked, information-based society. While previously people engaged in manufacturing-based work, wherein they generally competed with or worked independently from one another, people now engage in information- and technology-rich work in which they work collaboratively. People need to be able to work cooperatively in designing, using, and maintaining the tools of technology. The joint use of the Internet and collaboration will play an increasingly large role in most people's lives. Children, adolescents, and young adults have no choice but to develop and increase their collaborative Internet literacy. There is no better place for them to begin than in school. Learning in cooperative groups (both face-to-face and online) while using the tools of technology should occur at all grade levels and in all subject areas. This book provides a valuable resource on how to do so.

The Internet is not the first technological advance to be used in education in the past 120 years or so. In the late 1800s, Thomas Edison was convinced that motion pictures would replace teachers, as one master teacher could be filmed giving a lecture and then that lecture could be mass produced and shown in classrooms all over the world. The same prediction was made about radio in the 1930s and television in the 1960s. These predictions were based on viewing teaching as lecturing. In the 1970s the computer was seen as a way to deliver instruction and assess student learning. Students could watch lectures on a computer as well as read resource materials and do math calculations. Similar to previous technologies, the primary assumption was that each student would work alone. The same assumption could be made about the Internet. Doing so would probably condemn it to be a useful supplement to traditional classroom learning. In this remarkable book, James Bellanca and Terry Stirling have collaborated to cogently present the case that the Internet is different from previous technological innovations in education in that it encourages collaboration among learners (as well as teachers) and expands the possibility of collaborative work with others all over the world. It is the melding of collaborative work and the Internet that promises to change education fundamentally.

The integration of collaboration and the use of the Internet recognizes that learning is inherently social. It does not occur in a social vacuum, but rather in a network of interpersonal relationships. There is overwhelming evidence that the nature of the interpersonal context greatly influences learning. Other people provide the purpose, meaning, and support for learning. In addition, contributing to others' productivity and well-being gives a sense of significance to one's own efforts. It is through interaction with others that an individual's thinking and reasoning is challenged and enhanced, that a variety of perspectives and experiences may be used to examine and solve complex problems, and that students learn to love and value learning for its own sake and take pride in their acquisition of knowledge and skills. The promise of the Internet is that the social nature of learning may be expanded from the classroom to the whole world. It provides an opportunity to create a classroom without borders.

This unique, forward-looking book fills an empty space in the education literature. After defining collaborative work, Jim Bellanca and Terry Stirling discuss the major Internet tools available to students and teachers and how to build international collaborations among classrooms and schools. Their discussion of reverse planning will be very useful to teachers, as will be their discussion of the use of formal cooperative learning to teach interpersonal and small group skills. One of Jim Bellanca's strengths is his longtime championing of the integration of critical thinking and problem skills with collaborative learning. In this book, he and Terry Stirling expand Bellanca's previous work by integrating it with the use of the Internet. Teachers will benefit from their delineation of power lessons, Internet investigations in general, and international problem-based projects—Dr. Stirling's specialty. The authors illustrate how the combination of collaboration and the Internet may change the way classes are delivered, how instruction takes place, and the nature of classroom and school life. Nowhere is that better explained than in this book.

Jim Bellanca and Terry Stirling bring together in one place some of the more thoughtful integrations of collaboration and uses of the Internet. They have written an admirable and much-needed book that advances classroom teaching. It is thus a valuable resource for all educators. It can truly be said that every teacher should read this book and make use of its contents.

—David W. Johnson and Roger T. Johnson, University of Minnesota

Preface

THIS BOOK BEGINS with a metaphor: classrooms without borders. The book is an investigation of the what, the why, and the how of 21st century classrooms that take advantage of the Internet to expand when, where, and how students can communicate and collaborate, not only in their classrooms, but also outside or beyond the borders with students around the globe. Importantly, the metaphor announces a new promise and a new practice for high-quality instruction that "pours and stores" no more.

The book is intended to provide all educators, including parents as the first educators, with a deeper understanding of two key 21st century skills: communication and collaboration. These two skills, part of the Partnership for 21st Century Skills' "4C's," promise to help teachers expand their students' abilities to interact and innovate in the ever-expanding global society. All who recognize the challenges that a global community represents will find this book a practical guide for designing instruction and assessing skills that will enable today's students to thrive in tomorrow's academic and work worlds. It will suggest the practical tools and techniques that allow teachers to transform their instruction from the obsolete pour-and-store methods of the 20th century by adopting those methods already proving to encourage students to learn from doing in 21st century classrooms.

The information in this book is divided into 14 chapters. Each chapter is designed to help the reader gain command of information about two crucial 21st century skills: communication and collaboration. The chapters are designed to move teachers' minds from an exploration of the information about the chapter's topic to an exploration of how to make best use of this information in the classroom. Educational leaders at all levels will find the information valuable as they think about the what, why, and how of integrating these two skills into every school day.

Chapter 1 explores what it is in the global world of the 21st century that makes collaboration and communication important as crucial skills to be purposefully developed. It introduces the key challenges and issues involved with the changes in curriculum, instruction, and assessment when teachers and schools elect to make the changes from the factory models of instruction to technology-infused models that will most enhance the development of students' collaborations inside and outside the school walls.

Chapter 2 defines the key terms *cooperation*, *collaboration*, and *communication*. The chapter provides insights into the connections among the three in the 21st century classroom. The chapter examines the research with a focus on the key instructional tool: cooperative learning. It show how teachers can use this proven instructional strategy to promote the highest levels of collaboration, to enhance communication, and to produce higher yields of achievement and lifelong team skills for all students.

Chapter 3 provides a detailed look at those Internet tools that extend the promise of a classroom without borders. By dividing the array of e-tools into three categories, the chapter enables you to distinguish and prioritize the uses of collaborative e-tools that promote different types of communication skills in the classroom.

Chapter 4 presents the different ways that teachers can use Internet-based collaborative tools to scale classroom walls and take students around the world in their search for informative global learning experiences.

Chapter 5 presents an all-important "how to" for redesigning existing and for creating new lessons and projects that include 21st century skill development. By adapting the backward-design planning model championed by Grant Wiggins and Jay McTighe in *Understanding by Design* (2005), teachers will discover how to take a short cut to standards-aligned lessons and projects that address both process and content outcomes.

Chapter 6 helps teachers understand the practical connection between 21st century skills, the standards, and next generation assessment tools. It shows an easy way for teachers to read a standard (examples are drawn from state and national organizations and the Common Core standards) in order to create enriched learning experiences that include 21st century skills. By distinguishing the content element of a standard (what the students will learn) from the process element (the thinking skill to develop), the chapter shows how to transform a standard statement into outcomes that address both in a single project or lesson.

Chapter 7 attends to the practical skills for deliberate or intentional development of collaboration via cooperative learning. In this chapter teachers will review the advantages of cooperative learning for enriching lessons and projects. Nine productive tactics light the pathway to what research has shown is one of the surest ways to higher achievement by all students. In addition, the chapter leads readers from the use of cooperative learning as a tool for enriching the learning in lessons and projects to the creation of a brightly lit cooperative community that thrives within a collaborative culture.

Chapter 8 takes special note of what is important about the teaching of critical and creative thinking skills in collaborative classrooms. The chapter not only defines the meaning of these terms, but also argues for their purposeful or deliberate instruction as preparation for students' lifelong learning in the 21st century.

Chapter 9 focuses on how to develop sharper minds in all students in a collaborative classroom. The chapter places emphasis on how teachers can ensure that students deepen their thinking skills within the context of power lessons and enriched learning projects.

Chapter 10 introduces the power lesson, a lesson that is designed not only to improve student achievement, but also to develop students' 21st century skills. The power lesson is shown to be a crucial tool for enriching students' learning experiences with technology and with the full array of high-yield instructional strategies.

Chapter 11 introduces the first of three models of enriched learning projects, the investigation model. After defining the model, the chapter provides a sample project using the topic of global climate change. With the model, teachers are encouraged to replicate its key components or to use these components as a springboard to their own innovative projects.

Chapter 12 presents the second model of enriched learning projects, the problem-based project. After distinguishing its characteristics, the chapter presents a sample problem project focused on violence.

Chapter 13 explores the innovative project model. After defining the components that distinguish it from the other models, the chapter presents a project sample that explores innovative solutions to poverty.

Chapter 14 presents a summative framework for teachers to organize their own projects. It reviews guidelines for ensuring that the projects advance collaboration and communication and provides practical tips as reminders to include the key elements that most enrich student learning.

THE END IS THE BEGINNING

The Greeks loved both the literal and symbolic value of the alpha and the omega, the beginning and the end. The end of this book asks you to take the ideas you have gathered and put them in a plan that will start you on a new pathway to 21st century instruction. By making your selection of the ideas in this book that give you new insights into preparing students for 21st century collaboration and communication, you can make better sense of which ideas will work best for you and your students. Whether you select to improve collaboration and communication within the four walls of your classroom or you intend to take your students' hearts and minds beyond the borders, the ideas that you select to add to and refine your instructional repertoire will certainly result in new benefits for your students as lifelong learners in the 21st century.

Classrooms Without Borders

Using Internet Projects to Teach
Communication and Collaboration

CHAPTER 1

New Promise and New Practices in Classrooms Without Borders

Everyone lives downstream from someone else.

—Anonymous

THE INVESTIGATION OF "classrooms without borders" starts with an essential question: What new opportunities does the Internet provide for teachers and students to stretch their learning beyond the traditional classroom walls? To answer that question, this first chapter illuminates the tools and rationale for seeking resources not previously accessible inside the walls. More importantly, it provides a roadmap for adding digital resources in lessons and projects that build the 21st century skills of collaboration and communication.

CLASSROOMS WITHOUT BORDERS?

This book is about classrooms without borders—the promise and the practice. Symbolically, if there are no borders, there is no need to break free. If 21st century learning provides new opportunities, new promises for students to learn beyond the traditional classroom walls in ways that enrich and advance their preparation for a new work world, then it is time to explore the possibilities beyond the limits of the four classroom walls.

"What did you learn in class today?" Mrs. Simpson asked Jo Ellen.

"About the Dali Lama. We talked on Skype with an English teacher and her class in Tibet. They got to practice English and we learned about their everyday lives."

In a classroom without borders, a classroom without walls that limit what and how students can learn, students and teachers gather in a classroom to learn, not only with one another, but also with those outside their classroom walls in other classrooms, schools, and communities around the world. The liberating tool is the Internet.

Because of the Internet's ability to allow our students and us to collaborate and communicate anywhere, anytime, now is the time for us to pass through, over, and around the traditional walls that have isolated classrooms and to cross the world of learning that itself knows no bounds or borders.

It should not be a surprise that we have chosen to focus on two 21st century skills—communication and collaboration—as we envision students leaping over the walls that confined us as students. These two skills, central to the Framework for 21st Century Skills (http://www.p21.org), enable all educators to fly over and beyond their classroom borders in order to facilitate the boundless opportunities for learning that lie outside the brick, wood, and mortar that surrounds their students. Through the use of fast-emerging technologies in 21st century classrooms, the Internet today and cloud computing tomorrow, students not only can better develop their technology skills, but can also learn how to work together and talk with others in ways and places that were never possible in the wall-bound classroom. In addition, these two skills, enriched by other skills such as critical thinking and problem solving, will be re-emphasized in 21st century classrooms. These skills promise to reshape the quality of our professional and personal lives and enrich students' learning in vastly more exciting and productive ways. Through the thoughtful use of available electronic tools, all professional educators have new opportunities to enrich their students' learning as they work with, talk with, and learn with their co-travelers in every corner of the globe.

THE INTERNET: A LOOK BACK

In 1969, there was no official Internet or World Wide Web. The birth of the Internet started with four networked computers that were located at the University of California, Los Angeles and Santa Barbara; the Stanford Research Institute; and the University of Utah, Salt Lake City. The original purpose of this simple network was to communicate and collaborate. As its capabilities expanded, its community of users started to write rules or protocols to govern their exchanges. They didn't have email yet, so they had

> ## WHAT IS A CLASSROOM WITHOUT BORDERS?
>
> A classroom without borders is a learning space in which technology enables students and teachers to communicate and collaborate safely with peers in other schools, towns or cities, states or nations. Walls are no longer the borders that define where the major lessons of the week are taught.

to send the rules around by soon-to-be-old-fashioned mail for comment. If the community liked the rules, the rules became standard.

These rules were not promulgated from above; they were arrived at collegially. Everyone involved had access to the protocols and was able to build on them. This group became the Network Working Group, and today is called the Internet Engineering Task Force. There are now more than 5,000 Internet protocol standards, all available online. The early users were motivated by a desire to make sharing practical. They were not energized by the profit motive and they avoided patents and exclusivity (Crocker, 2009).

Today, mass commercialism has engulfed the Internet. There are subscriptions, memberships, banner ads, sponsored sites, targeted ads, and much more. Nevertheless, an amazing amount of the content and networking capacity of the Internet is free, even as entrepreneurs are fitfully searching to "monetize" their efforts, and the financial world is stymied by attempts to value fast-emerging Internet companies. Whole industries, such as newspaper publishing and retail catalog companies, are losing ground or shifting to Internet-delivered products. The displaced revenue caused by these shifts has yet to be fully realized.

THE WORLDWIDE ELECTRIC COMMUNITY

The Internet has the potential to unite the world. Like the mobile phone, the Internet is literally, figuratively, and educationally bringing together the citizens of the world, the richest and the poorest, in a mass, electronically connected community. Although many barriers and borders remain, language, images, and numbers are universal. English, fortunately for its speakers, is the lingua franca of the digital world.

In 2009, the Internet Corporation for Assigned Names and Numbers (ICANN) voted to allow non-Roman alphabet characters to be used in web addresses, a move that will further level the global playing field (Rhodes,

2009). Poverty and illiteracy also present limitations, but even in the most underdeveloped nations, cell phones and inexpensive notebooks are becoming accessible items that Jeffrey Sachs claims are creating the most massive revolution in history (Sachs, 2005).

The untapped digital possibilities created by the Internet to expand thought and enrich learning are mind-boggling. In some ways, the innovations in Web 2.0, and those emerging in Web 3.0, such as semantic webs, open graph protocols, and artificial intelligence, are coming at such a fast rate that it is difficult to keep pace. Teachers trapped in the sloth-paced change of the educational world find it especially difficult to keep up.

"How do I," asks the overloaded-with-digital-change teacher, "make best use of the Internet in my standards-based curriculum? How can I navigate the vast Internet landscape and direct its potential to the real world of learning by my students? I know my students love these tools; how can I use the tools to enrich their learning? How do I help students expand their world and keep them safe at the same time?" In the best instances, the answers to these questions are merely a matter of time and experience. With proper resources, including supportive professional learning experiences, the answers will come. In the worst instances, when school bureaucracies stick to outdated models of instruction that reinforce the traditional classroom walls or reinforce fears with decisions based on shallow understanding of these technologies, teachers will have to figure out how to overcome mindless obstacles before even thinking about the serious application questions.

Interest from Higher Education

Higher education has traditionally categorized curricula into three basic areas: knowledge, skills, and dispositions. What do colleges and universities expect from the K–12 curriculum? Those who seek well-prepared 21st century students are striving to update these categories. For instance, the Association of American Colleges and Universities (AACU) and their program Liberal Education and America's Promise (LEAP) have developed a listing called The Essential Learning Outcomes (AACU, 2007). These outcomes are what colleges and universities would like to see started in K–12 education, continued in college, and applied in life and the workplace. They include the traditional three areas of the curriculum and add a fourth, "integrated learning," that reflects the fact that most modern situations involve connections drawn across disciplines and rely on complex skills and behaviors.

THE ESSENTIAL LEARNING OUTCOMES

Beginning in school and continuing at successively higher levels across their college studies, students should prepare for 21st century challenges by gaining the following:

Knowledge of Human Cultures and the Physical and Natural World

- Through study in the sciences and mathematics, social sciences, humanities, histories, languages, and the arts

Focused by engagement with big questions, both contemporary and enduring

Intellectual and Practical Skills, including

- Inquiry and analysis
- Critical and creative thinking
- Written and oral communication
- Quantitative literacy
- Information literacy
- Teamwork and problem solving

Practiced extensively, across the curriculum, in the context of progressively more challenging problems, projects, and standards for performance

Personal and Social Responsibility, including

- Civic knowledge and engagement—local and global
- Intercultural knowledge and competence
- Ethical reasoning and action
- Foundations and skills for lifelong learning

Anchored through active involvement with diverse communities and real-world challenges

Integrative Learning, including

- Synthesis and advanced accomplishment across general and specialized studies

Demonstrated through the application of knowledge, skills, and responsibilities to new settings and complex problems

College Learning for the New Global Century, 2007

The traditional concept of integrated learning is reflected in some college curricula. As leading college educators conceive of it, the first 2 years, or 60 semester hours of college credit, are known as "general education." General education is supposed to offer students breadth of learning, or the chance to explore, sample, and, finally, select a major from a wide array of offerings; the major, then, offers depth of learning.

Many colleges integrate courses using common intellectual experiences: the first-year experience concept; learning communities; internships and other experiential learning; and clustered required courses related to a theme, world problem, service learning, civic engagement, and the like. Many of these require students to relate to global, interdisciplinary concepts (Hart Research Associates, 2009).

The list featured here was developed through a multiyear dialogue with hundreds of colleges and universities about needed goals for student learning; analysis of a long series of recommendations and reports from the business community; and analysis of the accreditation requirements for engineering, business, nursing, and teacher education. The findings are documented in previous publications of the Association of American Colleges and Universities: *Greater Expectations: A New Vision for Learning as a Nation Goes to College* (2002), *Taking Responsibility for the Quality of the Baccalaureate Degree* (2004), and *Liberal Education Outcomes: A Preliminary Report on Student Achievement in College* (2005).

Interest from Outside the Education Community

In addition to this 21st century thrust from forward-looking colleges and universities, other groups outside of education are making a push to align 21st century education with the present and future needs of students. Current conceptual frameworks for "21st Century Skills" include those developed by the Partnership for 21st Century Skills (http://www.p21.org/), the Metiri Group (http://www.metiri.com), the Organisation for Economic Co-operation and Development (OECD; http://www.oecd.org), and the Educational Testing Service ICT Literacy Panel (Katz, 2007). Scholars such as Chris Dede (Dede, 2010; Dede, Honan, Peters, & Harvard University Graduate School of Education, 2005) and Henry Jenkins (2008, 2009) have also formulated lists of "digital literacies" that complement reading, writing, and mathematics as core capabilities for the 21st century.

A NEW WORLD BEYOND THE PRINTED PAGE

In the few decades since its birth, the Internet has shown its potential to free teachers and students from dependency on textbooks and other library-bound print resources. If Google and others fulfill their dream of a digitized library of every book in existence, a feat they are moving to accomplish, print books may be as rare as Internet books were a decade ago. Kindles were hardly sent to store shelves when iPads and other promised devices introduced the digital reader with ever-lowering price tags.

The Internet and its fast-maturing offspring, cloud computing, seem destined to render print materials obsolete. Throw in a Kindle and an iPad, or another digital book platform, and the process is accelerated. If this is so, the impetus for teachers and students to be required to gather information from beyond the barriers of the classroom, school, or community library walls—from beyond encyclopedias, thesauri, and dictionaries—the death of print on the paper page will accelerate. Already electronic searches can lead, in a flash, to just the right book, article, website, mentors, or group of other young people interested in the same topic. Already information valuable for secondary, undergraduate, and graduate courses is more up-to-date and economical than the publisher's out-of-date-before-printed, expensive textbooks. As major additional search engines acquire digitizing rights to print publications from libraries around the world, these digital publishing companies will become the quick-access digital library open to all "digital natives" (Prensky, 2006) in any of the increasing number of digital nations. In place of heavy backpacks with their attendant backaches and large textbook bills, how long will it be before we see students toting tablet-sized readers with instant Internet access?

Supreme Court Justice Sonia Sotomayor's mother saved to purchase an *Encyclopedia Britannica*, something that few families had at home in working-class neighborhoods in the 1960s. "She was famous for the encyclopedia," the Justice's aunt recalled (Stolberg, 2009). In her new office, the Justice will find immediate e-access to any law record in the world and e-tools to find the most esoteric tome in minutes.

RELEVANT INFORMATION NOW

The breadth and depth of knowledge available on the Internet provides
another ingredient that makes its information more valuable to teachers
and students: relevance. Recently, a group of young people conducted
an amazing student-led research study in Chicago, a city in which more
than 50% of public school students drop out and minimize their chances
for a bright future (Gewertz, 2008). The students, who attended mostly
low-performing high schools, were trying to determine why high school
students drop out at such an alarming rate. Their first finding was that students internalize the reasons for dropping out and blame themselves for
failing. Their second finding was that dropping out is something that happens slowly and something that isn't planned or expected. The third most
important finding of the study, and the most relevant to this discussion,
revealed that students found relevance lacking in their classes. They did
not relate what they were supposed to be learning in school to reality. They
did not find curriculum that deals with 21st century issues and skills, the
representation of students' cultures and heritage as well as world cultures,
or the connection between their studies and their success in the future of
college and work (Voices of Youth in Chicago Education [VOYCE], 2008).
Students commented on the lack of relevance in their schools based on
their own experience and feelings, not from reading the research reports
referred to throughout this book.

This student project was reinforced by an informal discussion we held
with graduates of an alternative high school in an affluent district. The
graduates, who had become successful classroom teachers, artists, lawyers,
and a newspaper editor, were discussing what the alternative school program had done that was "helpful." After they talked about the personalized
attention, the emphasis on self-direction, and the challenge of learning to
be self-directed, these now 45-year-old adults were asked, "How many of
you had thought of dropping out before you elected this program?" More
than half raised their hands. Their answers paralleled what the VOYCE
students said almost 25 years later. One alternative school graduate made
comments that were especially clear and pointed:

> When I had the opportunity to enter the alternative school, I told my
> parents what I wanted to do. They told me, "No, it will ruin your
> chances for college." I said, "Look at my grades. College is not there.
> I hate school. It means nothing. It is irrelevant with what I want to do
> with my life. In fact, it is irrelevant *period, exclamation point*. All that hap-
> pens is teachers talk and try to stuff our heads with blah, blah, blah."

NEW MODELS OF LEARNING

The Voices project, as well as the growing number of project-based learning sites on the Internet, such as ThinkQuest (http://www.thinkquest.org) and the U.N.'s Millennium Project (http://www.un.org/millenniumgoals), signal a significant change for teaching and learning, a change that can significantly affect the question of meaningful relevance. These projects provide teachers with models that enable them to give up the 20th century models of instruction limited to acquisition of information. They provide opportunities for students and teachers to participate by collaborating and communicating to uncover new frontiers. Yes, acquisition of knowledge is still important and necessary, but it is no longer necessary to limit the students' role to serving as passive, empty buckets. The Internet gives them a tool to seek out information and to develop the quality of their investigative skills. Today's students know that tomorrow they can work and learn with anyone they choose at any location on the globe. They also know that in order to keep pace with the increasingly demanding challenges of formal education that come from around the globe, they can depend on tools that have never before been available at any time and any place for mass learning.

WORDS OF CONCERN AND CAUTION

Some educators have expressed reservations about tapping too heavily into the connectivity of the Internet. They are concerned especially about younger elementary students. These educators see the World Wide Web as an unmanageable world fraught with dragons and demons, a trap woven by deadly spiders. Thus, this may be the place for notes of caution that address the most prominent and often justifiable concerns.

The first addressable concern springs from students' ready access to knowledge on the Internet with many different e-tools. Quick access, critics have noted, results in quick copying. Typically, students in former generations copied from encyclopedias to write school reports. Usually, they were chastised by their teachers and admonished to "use their own words." Today, copying is even easier because of the computer's cut-and-paste functions. And many students believe that teachers won't be able to locate the infraction because the knowledge available on the Internet is so vast.

As with all other advances on the Internet, multiple new tools are available to combat this electronic plagiarism. There are many websites that offer tutorials for teachers on dealing with plagiarism. Many sites include online quizzes; some quiz sites email the teacher when a student has completed a plagiarism quiz successfully. Other sites require that student citations, regardless of form, must provide enough information so that teachers can find and verify the information for themselves. Older students might want to use bibliographic software. Common knowledge and a student's own ideas, are, of course, fair game and, since search tools allow teachers to find many of the sites where students have purloined information and quotations, a little sleuthing pays off. Of course, it is fair to say that teaching students how to gather and cite information is an essential part of the research-learning process. Yes, today, plagiarism is a more challenging problem, but that does not take away the teachers' responsibility to show students the ethical way. It is all the more important that teachers expect students to abide by the code that guides research, on or off the Internet.

A more crucial note of caution relates to how students check the accuracy of information they find on the Internet. Some educators fear that students will download inaccurate information and succumb to electronic biases. "Students believe everything they read," they say.

Resources exist that address this concern. The Internet presents opportunities to foster critical thinking and reading skills in students so that they are adept at analyzing online talk and print, checking for bias, making sound judgments about quoted sources, or evaluating statements from various "experts." One excellent example that teaches Internet research skills is the "All About Explorers" website (http://www.allaboutexplorers.com). This site was created by teachers for teachers to highlight accuracy on the Internet. It enables teachers to make students aware that the sites most likely to contain inaccurate information include those with strong agendas in politics, social views, health claims, and those promoting sales under the guise of information.

Clicking on the "All About Explorers" site yields the information about Christopher Columbus shown in the accompanying box. Because this is a WebQuest site, one of the earliest high-quality, web-based project models

In 1942 Columbus set sail with three ships, the *Niña*, the *Pinta*, and the *Santa Maria*, and about 90 men. The voyage was so much easier than sailing east. On October 12, 1942, Columbus landed on an island southeast of Florida. He claimed this island for Spain and named it the "Indies" since he thought he had landed in India. He named the native people of the island "Indians." The Indians were excited by the newcomers and their gadgets. They especially enjoyed using their cell phones and desktop computers.

on the Internet, the story is only the beginning. In this model, at three performance levels, students are challenged to heed the advice "Just because it is out there, doesn't mean it's good." Students are then shown how to "find the good stuff" as they compare different versions of the story. Eventually, they are aided in drawing their inferences and making certain that their conclusions are logical.

PROACTIVE AND INTENTIONAL SKILL DEVELOPMENT

With the increased misrepresentations that appear on the Internet and in other mass media, there is all the more reason for teachers to develop students' critical thinking skills in an intentional way. Mini-lessons on how to analyze for bias or how to fact check have long been part of English teachers' curricula. In the current digital environment, it becomes all the more important that any teacher who assigns students to do research on the Internet take care to ensure that the students' information-sleuthing skills are at their peak. In addition to teaching mini-lessons on the important thinking skills that improve students' ability to challenge false information, the most effective 21st century teachers coach and assess the development of the skills. Who knows? Students may then use these same skills to question what they see and hear on TV talk shows.

A third addressable concern springs from teachers' concerns for students' safety and security. This is the most important issue that requires teachers' purposeful intervention with the Internet's dark side. Many schools teach students "Internet safety." It is essential that every school have a clear policy regarding student use of sites that might endanger their safety. It is imperative that students be taught to avoid any would-be predators by avoiding posting personal information, contact information, birthdays, and photos on public sites or by answering messages from strangers. They should know not to offer credit information. If they land on a site with inappropriate content, despite filters, they should immediately leave the site. Adults should encourage students to speak frankly about any Internet experiences that make them uncomfortable. Multiple online sites provide educators with the tools and tutorials that address these safety issues. Teachers can access these simply by browsing key words such as *safety* and *security*.

Another difficult issue springs from the power of texting. This is tied into students', especially preteens', increasingly ready access to cell phones. Almost as fast as telecommunication companies upgrade the

HOLD THE FORT!

"I am interested in why your talk about innovative instructional use of technology didn't talk at all about the new web tools or the possibilities of collaborating with students in other schools," the board member asked.

"Oh. We have decided not to allow teachers to use this stuff. They present too many problems," responded the district technology director. "How could we ever control what teachers are doing with other schools on the Internet?"

(Bellanca interview, 2010)

capabilities of mobile phones, young people find ways to use and abuse the new capabilities. Sexting and cyberbullies are today's headaches for parents and teachers. What will tomorrow bring, especially for those students who are the victims of this misbehavior?

Banning messaging to prevent student misuse is a double-edged sword. Yes, the chances of misuse of the tool are reduced, but so are opportunities for students to learn responsible use and for teachers to use texting as a writing tool that promotes succinct and clear thought. At Manor Tech, a New Tech High School in Manor, Texas, the faculty voted to avoid placing any limits on technology. Instead, they wanted to communicate their trust of student's good sense and create the opportunity for offenders to learn a very serious logical consequence—the loss of cell phone privileges in the building. Manor's principal asserts that this particular logical consequence terrifies Manor students, who appear to be physically attached to their phones and who know the importance of Internet access in their daily, project-laden course work. Not only would they lose access to the Internet, the offending students would be severely hampered in their ability to do the large amounts of project research and collaborations required each day.

THE BEST DEFENSE

Young people growing up in this electronic century are little different from their predecessors in recent decades. What does set them apart, of course, is the rampant availability of digital tools. That availability is not going to change. So rather than turning parents and teachers into police on the prowl, warring with the dark side of the Internet, the Partnership for 21st Century Skills (http://www.p21.org/) recommends a different tack. It is a tack in which the best defense is a strong offense.

The partnership, or P-21, contends that the caveats that try to protect young people pale when parents and teachers face the real and increasing need that students express for relevance and meaning in their schoolwork. On the one hand, as they have always done, schools and parents will find the means to control the misuse of technology. On the other hand, P-21 and other groups have identified how the rapid changes in technology and information flow may make schools as we know them a thing of the past, more irrelevant than ever in the eyes of many students. If schools continue on the path of trying to ignore technology or spend all their energy building fences to keep it out of their children's lives and do not attend to making schools more relevant to their students, they will surely lose the game.

P-21 is an advocacy group of leaders in education, business, and public policy from around the nation. Its goal is to bring about policy changes that will enable states and communities to put into place the essential modifications that will encourage schools to return relevance to curriculum, instruction, and assessment practices more in line with the life, advanced learning, and work needs of 21st century students. To this end, P-21 identifies several interdisciplinary themes, in addition to knowledge in traditional core subjects, that students need in order to live successful lives. These include, but are not limited to, global awareness; financial, economic, business, and entrepreneurial literacy; civic literacy; and health literacy. As a pathway to learning this content, P-21 advocates that schools give priority to student development of information processing, media, and technology skills.

As we look at 21st century knowledge and skill frameworks, P-21's framers could only wonder why, for example, the formal study of economics is almost totally absent in the 21st century K–12 curriculum. Likewise, we all have to wonder how long it will take before all students carry wireless digital notebooks or pocket-sized digital readers in place of textbooks and spiral binders. How long will it be before all students learn in such schools—schools in which P-21's conceptual framework of the knowledge, skills, and dispositions provide the educational foundation for today's students? How long before educators realize that the artificial walls they have set up to prevent Internet use in the schoolhouse come tumbling down as soon as students set foot outside the classroom?

SKILLS THAT TRANSFER

Skills form an essential element in any K–12 curriculum. In the 21st century global battle, skills development, especially in the 3R's and the 4C's, will be all the more important. Educational leaders face the challenge of determining how to retain the essential 3R's and add the new essentials of communication, collaboration, critical and creative thinking, and problem solving.

The Internet is proving its capability as an essential tool for teachers who are intent on equipping their students with 21st century skills. The partnership has defined and described these skills in an especially clear and comprehensive manner. According to P-21, students need skills in the broad categories of learning and innovation—which include communication and collaboration skills; information, media, and technology skills; and life and career skills. The P-21 graphic (see Figure 1.1) illustrates the outcome goals and support systems that P-21 has identified for K–12 students.

A FRAMEWORK FOR REFORM

Members of P-21 have striven to establish a broad consensus for a new model of school reform and provide resources for teachers who sense that their school's curriculum is not fully adapted to the 21st century for all students. The depth and breadth of the framework make it a novel approach

Figure 1.1. 21st Century Student Outcomes and Support Systems

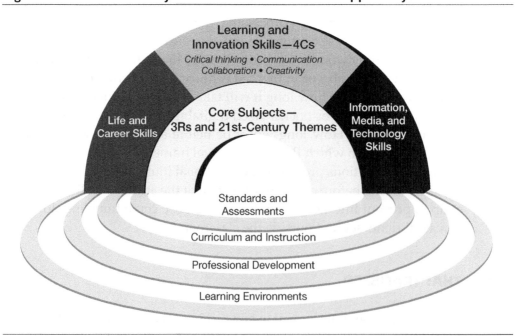

Between 25 and 75% of core academic content curricula explicitly integrate 21st century skills along with global awareness, civic literacy, financial literacy, health literacy, and environmental literacy.
Curricula design processes occasionally follow backward-design principles (e.g., Understanding by Design) that identify 21st century skills as key outcomes.
Between 25 and 75% of instructional strategies utilize a student-centered approach to teaching and learning.

Excerpt from P-21, Curriculum, Transitional Stage, the *MILE Guide* (2009)

to school reform, not only an approach built on a consensus of the school, government, and business powers, but also one that extends into detailed policies and the provision of key resources such as the P-21 MILE Guides. These guides, developed by national professional organizations such as the National Council of Teachers of English (NCTE) and the National Council of Teachers of Mathematics (NCTM), provide detailed curriculum models for easy adaptation by local schools.

SEEKING NEXT-GENERATION ASSESSMENTS

Blocking successful implementation of a 21st century curriculum, such as that presented in the *MILE Guide*, are the current assessment methods. These are focused on teacher accountability. Student performance on standardized tests, the results of which highlight the achievement gap, are increasingly misused as a tool to remove ineffective teachers rather than as a means for improving instruction. These tests measure basic knowledge in limited subject matter and specific types of mental agility. They provide one snapshot in a 200-minute movie. Low-income families and minority groups experience these tests' "disparate effect," the term used by the U.S. Supreme Court. This effect is seen as a major contributor to the achievement gap and as the major force pushing low-level instruction in basic skills.

Although there is nothing wrong with high achievement via test scores, an overdependence on standardized tests of reading and mathematics scores to drive school reform is far too narrow an approach. A curriculum based on these limited tests of limited knowledge and skills is inadequate to prepare American youth for all the avenues of success that will be open to them in the 21st century. Unfortunately, low-performing schools especially tend to rely on a low-level test preparation curriculum that is marginally effective and dispiriting, especially when the research tells schools that "high expectations" are essential while their districts enforce the lowest expectations with a 19th century schooling model. On the other hand, high-performing schools run the risk of using mandates to narrow their curriculum to meet narrow, out-of-date standardized tests (assessment does drive instruction) while relying on parents to supplement their children's education outside of school.

The parent generation knows quizzes, bubble tests, and Scantron. Their 20th century teachers were taught that these were objective measures. These tools were also easier to grade and gave teachers plenty of time to teach. Bubbles don't require essays, blue books, or open-ended questions that were thought to be "too subjective." When parents and many educators hear about 21st century skills being added to the basic 3 R's they wonder how teachers will test and grade their children.

A growing number of revolutionary 21st century schools—the New Tech Highs, the High Tech Highs, the Envision Schools, the Expeditionary Schools—and evolutionary classrooms have successfully adapted other methods of assessments to supplement and even replace the short-answer tests that wallpaper current classrooms. (The term *traditional* doesn't apply. Scantron tests, with their quick bubble answers, didn't become popular until the late 1970s. Their unintended consequence was the almost total elimination of the essay exam.)

For assessing 21st century skills such as communication (including written essays, poems and short stories, presentations and graphics), collaboration (including cooperative learning, teams, technology tools), critical and creative thinking (including their uses in problem-based learning and project-based learning), self-direction (including goal setting, planning, and self-assessments) and responsibility (including the dispositions of responsibility, global awareness, financial accountability, etc.), these innovators rely on teacher-made rubrics, checklists, and surveys.

In any project, teachers provide students with multiple glimpses at the latter's progress by beginning with the students' self and peer assessments of their progress toward predefined and clear outcomes, adding observed indicators of the desired skill or disposition and ending with a summary conference. The emphasis is placed on the students' travel to a desired outcome and the assistance needed to attain the highest-quality result. In this way, assessment is more than a dot on a page or a grade at the end of a course; it is a set of snapshots that show the multiple perspectives of learning that are tied to the development of the skills and dispositions.

REVOLUTION AND EVOLUTION: HOW DO THEY DIFFER?

A *revolutionary* approach to 21st century skills occurs when the method selected to change from the 20th century factory model of teaching and learning is "whole school." The baby is thrown out with the bathwater. A new mission based on 21st century outcomes is defined to fit the vision of what students will need to know and do in order to succeed in the 21st century work world. Instruction becomes 99% project-based; the physical structures are designed to fit the elements of project-based learning; bubble tests disappear and are replaced by rubric-based observations and teacher conferences; collaboration with technology is a norm.

The *evolutionary* change model is a step-by-step change model in which a school or individual teachers adapt new methods for teaching and assessing one at a time. The move to 21st century skills is gradual. One teacher may adopt rubrics and incorporate a critical thinking unit to study mathematics; a science department may adapt the STEM approach; a reading teacher may highlight metacognition with reflective journals on a blog.

Thanks to Bob Pearlman for this distinction. Private conversation, 2010

DISPOSITIONS WE CAN BELIEVE IN

"Dispositions" are a 21st century core concept. The subject of "dispositions" in the curriculum can be a bit tricky because it trespasses on values and beliefs. Dispositions can also be thought of in terms of behaviors or tendencies to act in certain ways. Traditionally, schools have felt comfortable promoting dispositions related to citizenship, patriotism, physical health and culture, competitiveness, obedience, and leadership, among others.

P-21, however, refers to dispositions seen to be more appropriate for the 21st century world: civic literacy, health literacy, social and cross-cultural skills, leadership and responsibility, initiative and self-direction, productivity and accountability, and global awareness. While most educators want students to think for themselves, most would also agree that they would like to turn out students with a multitude of positive behaviors. Yet, since behavior stems from beliefs and, most important, from the worldview and perspective of student's peers, increasing academic performance often rests on students' dispositions, particularly those acquired from their peer groups.

Peer culture is a double-edged sword. On the one hand, peer culture is the best ally that teachers in high-performing schools can have when it comes to maintaining high performance. Our affluent suburbs, with their high-performing schools, are fueled by the majority of their students' acceptance of the academic values that saturate their school culture.

The flip side of that belief in the pre-eminence of high academic performance is the toughest adversary for teachers in low-performing schools. When teens take to texting "mean attacks" because it is the thing to do, or when girls and boys gang up to physically assault kids from different neighborhoods and groups, the power of the peer is even more evident.

Judith Rich Harris, in her landmark work *The Nurture Assumption*, makes a strong argument for the influence of peers (Harris, 2009). Harris lived next to an immigrant family during her childhood and was impressed with how the children spoke and acted like Americans when they left home. She makes an analogy to Cinderella because children, not only immigrant children, tend to act one way at home and another way in public. (Teachers, during family conferences, often wonder if they and the parents are talking about the very same student.) Of course, this makes sense only because children are preparing for the world of the future that will be inhabited by peers; they are not preparing for the world of the past that their parents represent. Harris believes that teachers are in a privileged position to have an effect on students' peer culture because they inhabit the world outside the home. Anyone who doubts the importance of peers on children can witness students' flagrant dependence on cell phones, texting, and social networking.

Of course, we don't mean to diminish the importance of parents. Parents themselves are aware of their limitations in this regard. This is the reason that they move to new neighborhoods or, in some urban environments, make every effort to enroll their children in selective charter or magnet schools, battle with school officials to keep children at high-performing neighborhood schools or escort their children from the home portal to the schoolhouse door. This is the reason parents have always feared that playmates may be "a bad influence."

Sometimes, a few students can constitute a peer group that veers from the common culture—for better or for worse. Sadly, the Columbine massacre comes to mind in the "worse" category. The affluent students who committed the murder/suicides there constituted a peer group that was deviant from the strong primary culture of the school. They lived outside the general culture of the school. In fact, they lived and died to counter that culture.

On the positive side, many have heard the story "The Three Doctors," from a decade ago. Three boys from inner Newark made a pact that they would defy the odds, go to college, and attend medical school. Their books have been read by countless young people and are descriptively titled: *We Beat the Street: How a Friendship Pact Led to Success* and *The Pact: Three Young Men Make a Promise and Fulfill a Dream* (Davis, Jenkins, & Hunt, 2002, 2006).

The three authors have given many inspirational talks to students. On their website (http://www.threedoctorsfoundations.org) they list three key messages: "Never underestimate the power of self-reliance and inner strength, attach a timeline and devise a strategy for achieving your goals, and surround yourself with like-minded people who are in line with your aspirations."

EXTENDING THEORY INTO IMPROVED PRACTICE

Constructivist learning theorists have established worthy arguments on the nature of learning. In their eyes, how students learn is inextricably connected to how teachers teach. When teachers include in their practice those methods that help students construct their learning, build new ideas on old, and transfer ideas to new settings, they match theory and practice. When teachers do no more than talk about the theory and the practice, they provide little help to their students.

Who has not heard that "talk is cheap"? Talk has been the principle barter provided by teachers for students in 20th century schools. Information spills out of the teacher's head into the students who "sit and git." The norm has been for expert teachers to *pour* so that inexpert students could *store* the words in their heads until asked to recite the words back from memory.

In the 21st century, more is required of students than passive acceptance of words and ideas. The constructivist challenge is for the application of new understandings. For this, teaching and learning must go beyond talk about the what—"the character of Hamlet" or "global warming" or "financial literacy"—to discovering how these tools and ideas can promote a more positive world and life for the students.

What will it take for schools to move beyond being places that live and die by low-level information transfer to places that inspire young people to seek out and make sense of new ideas, applying what they have learned in innovative ways? The answers start in the recognition that the many frameworks for 21st century learning, skill development, and knowledge transfer show us different ways to take learning out of the head and outside the borders of students' skulls with the skills marked for the 21st century. With digital tools that are becoming more and more prevalent, teachers can more easily take learning beyond these borders.

Central to all the frameworks are the skills of collaboration and communication, especially within the skillful application of technology. With a relevant and meaningful 21st century curriculum, teachers will be able to take advantage of boundless opportunities to engage students in learning, not only from and with one another in the classroom, but also from and with peers in other classrooms, schools, cities, states, and nations. When they learn how to do this well, the vision of classrooms without boundaries will be transformed into daily lessons.

CONCLUDING THOUGHTS

After Gutenberg introduced his printing press, the information world underwent a remarkable transformation. No longer was information the providence of a select few. Knowledge spread and expanded. In this century, the Internet has initiated a similar revolution, taking knowledge beyond all borders. Not only did the Internet change the amount of information available, it made it clear that knowledge is not enough. Soon, we are told, the Internet will be followed by cloud computing, which will further transform the knowledge landscape and extend the power of constructed knowledge. In that regard, it becomes clearer and clearer that each teacher and each student in each classroom does indeed live downstream from someone else. All our lives and our learning is connected. Through more skillful collaborations on and off the Internet, everyone's communication will affect all our connections faster and faster, deeper and deeper as our new knowledge produces more new knowledge. Will teachers and schools play a part? Will they promote learning without borders? The answers depend on how well they meet the promise and adopt the practices.

CHAPTER 2

Getting Together

Cooperation, Collaboration, and Communication for 21st Century Learning

A mind is a fire to be kindled, not a vessel to be filled.

—Plutarch

THE IDEA THAT the mind is not an empty jar or box into which teachers pour information was stated long before the advent of the 21st century. Throughout history, others have reiterated this point. In the 1960s, American educational reformers such as Arthur Combs and Carl Rogers made this point a central concept in their humanistic theories.

From the first days of the 21st century, advocates for the 21st Century Skills agenda have revitalized the notion of learning as an act initiated and controlled by the learner. They devalued the notion that students had to be passive recipients. As early as the early 1970s, Reuven Feuerstein was spreading the work of his mentor Jean Piaget. Feuerstein's theory of structural cognitive modifiability, an influence on such American psychologists as Howard Gardner, Robert Sternberg and John Bransford, argued for active engagement of students' minds as the most effective means for developing intelligence. The notion that student learning was based on students' ability to be active generators of knowledge rather than passive recipients took firm root.

Foremost among the educators who took to this concept were the advocates of cooperative learning. They laid the groundwork for the development of best practices that would improve student thinking as well as show students how to develop positive peer relationships that were advantageous to their learning of reading, writing, mathematics, and other subjects.

By the end of the 1980s, the word *collaboration* was often used in place of *cooperation*. *Collaboration* became the preferred higher education word for the skills and outcomes of students working together. At the same time, adult educators used *collaboration* to describe the team building they were doing with the corporate world.

How can we synthesize the disparate definitions of the concept "collaboration"? How can we clarify its essential value for 21st century learning and distinguish it from cooperative learning? An understanding of the concept "collaboration" in the context of the emerging culture of the technologically rich 21st century is a touchstone for theory and classroom practices. The range of interpretations of the concept allows teachers to identify how they can best enrich students' development of collaboration and communication skill sets for their students' 21st century learning and work lives. It can also help teachers see the differences and similarities among the three words.

> "It is a giant tree," said the first blind man as he grasped the elephant's leg. "No," said the second, holding the elephant's ear. "It is a giant banana leaf." "You are wrong," said the third, who was feeling the great belly. "It is a wall." The fourth shook his head as he grasped the pachyderm's tail. "You are all so foolish. It is a rope." "How can you think that?" said the fifth blind man as he grasped the elephant's trunk. "It is a large tree limb that curves."

WHAT IS COLLABORATION?

Trying to understand the term *collaboration* in a 21st century context is like watching the five blind men from India trying to identify an elephant. The word *collaboration* is as clunky as their efforts to define whatever it is they think they are touching. Each blind man approaches the elephant from a different angle. Each touches a different part. Each draws a different conclusion. In spite of their limited perceptions, the object the five are touching is an elephant.

In the 20th century, teachers and corporate trainers presented multiple definitions of the concept "collaboration." Each articulated a different point of view about the meaning of this concept. Some argued for the creation of learning-work groups. They hypothesized that collaborative workplaces fit more closely with the needs of corporations by creating learning-work environments that foster innovation, independent thinking, and creative problem solving. These social constructivists limited collaboration to those acts of online decision making that eventually end in a group consensus. Today, some technology advocates describe collaboration as all communication that occurs in the use of digital learning tools. The collaborative skills involved are the skills for using e-tools—such as email, blogs, and wikis—that enhance digital interactions between two or more persons. Other technology advocates take a more narrow view. They may even insist that the mere use of e-tool hardware, software, or Web 2.0 tools is a collaborative act. What matters in this debate is that individuals use e-tools to enhance the communication required.

Increasingly, learning-work advocates see work as centered not on the manufacturing of products, but on a group's generation and refinement of ideas. By implication, learning-work theorists support the creation of new school standards that move away from measurement of content to the encouragement of critical and creative thinking, collaboration, and problem solving. These "new school" promoters adapt the learning-work group's theories as their justification for putting their eggs in the basket of school reform. They see a collaborative physical environment as the foundation for the change that starts with the environment as the primary change agent.

A more learner-centered definition of collaboration comes from cognitive psychologists. John Bransford suggested that collaboration is a problem solving process in which participants work together to arrive at a shared conclusion (Kinzer, Sherwood, & Bransford, 1986). Bransford's cyclical collaboration process passes through five stages: problem agreement, problem definition, solution search, hypothesis testing, and observation of effects. Bransford allows for the teacher to facilitate this group learning process, but highlights the process itself as the chief means of deepened learning for the individual.

Roger and David Johnson, pioneering cooperative-learning researchers and educators, lead the integration of cooperative learning into classrooms. They place more value on the role of the teacher in the learning process than do other constructivists (Johnson, Johnson, & Holubec, 1992, 1993).

The Johnson brothers identify five key actions of teachers as learning facilitators (see box); each action aligns with one attribute in their concept of collaboration. They labeled classroom learning groups as "cooperative learning" groups. These groups differ from traditional, loosely structured learning-work groups in which the only important element is a common task.

According to the Johnsons, cooperative-learning groups require that teachers work as facilitators who structure how students interact in these

JOHNSON & JOHNSON'S
FIVE ATTRIBUTES OF COOPERATIVE LEARNING

Positive Interdependence
Face-to-Face Promotive Interaction
Individual and Group Accountability
Interpersonal and Small Group Skills
Group Processing

Johnson, Johnson, & Holubec, 1993

groups, and facilitators actively develop the interpersonal communication skills and other dispositions that research has shown most help students become more efficient in their learning tasks and achieve to a higher degree.

The Johnsons' description of the "working together" process is similar to the approach of cognitive psychologists in that all members of a group (two or more) work informally or formally to help one another achieve a shared goal. This is the most critical attribute of the concept "cooperative learning." It is essential for defining the term and distinguishing cooperative learning groups from plain "groups" in which two or more persons are doing the same task. Sometimes that goal is the sought solution to a problem; at other times it is the end of a learning task with an agreed-upon product such as a test or essay.

A COMMON GOAL

"And what are you guys going to do?" I asked.

DJ flashed his toothy grin. "We are going to answer these three questions. We have to agree on each answer."

"And what is your goal?" I persisted.

This time Bing answered. "We are going to have one answer that we both think is the best one for each question," she said.

"And how are you sharing the work?"

"We each think of an answer first," Bing said.

"Then we compare our answers," DJ added. "We discuss the differences. If we disagree, we come up with a compromise answer. Otherwise, we pick the best one."

The Johnsons' description of collaboration shares the concept of a common goal espoused by cognitive psychologists. The definition also shares the belief that it is the social interaction that is most responsible for the students' learning. The Johnson definition differs in its emphasis on the teacher's role in using the five attributes as guides for facilitating interpersonal interactions that contribute to attaining the shared goal more effectively. For each attribute, the brothers also identify academic and interpersonal learning tactics for the teachers' use. The tactics are the tools that foster more efficient collaboration, co-laboring usually with technology tools, and more effective cooperation. Together, collaboration and cooperation enhance higher achievement (Roseth, Johnson, & Johnson, 2008).

Unlike the definition of collaboration presented by learning-work researchers, cognition is not mentioned in the Johnson model. In their list of the five defining attributes, the Johnsons do not include cognition. At best, they allow that highly functioning cooperative groups will think more critically and creatively than students working alone.

In the 1980s and 1990s, Bellanca and Fogarty (1991), modified the Johnson model. They added the *purposeful* inclusion of thinking skills as a cooperative learning attribute. This included the explicit integration of higher-order questioning about the core content of a lesson, the use of graphic organizers, and the construction of metacognitive reflections as tactics to close a lesson. From a practical perspective, the BUILD model, developed by their colleagues Susan Marcus and Penny McDonald (1990) is a cognitive-cooperative-collaborative connection, in which the explicit facilitation of cognition and cooperation are connected within the collaborative framework. As a result, Bellanca and Fogarty contend that explicit development of thinking skills within cooperative learning groups leads to students' more effective collaborative learning experiences.

THE COGNITIVE-COOPERATIVE-COLLABORATIVE PROCESS

B = Build In Higher-Order Thinking
U = Unite the Teams with Explicit Tactics
I = Individuate Accountability
L = Look Back and Reflect
D = Develop Skills for Thinking and Cooperating.

Bellanca & Fogarty, 1991

WHAT THE RESEARCH SAYS

The various ways structured teamwork is defined by various advocates, specifically how cooperation and collaboration are alike and different, is somewhat cloudy. In the 1990s, advocates of student interaction at the postsecondary level began to increase the distinction between the two concepts. They noted that the majority of research on cooperative learning was conducted at the primary and secondary levels and looked to study its impact in postsecondary classrooms (Springer, Stanne, & Donovan, 1999). Some higher education users argued that the two most distinguishing factors were the intentional inclusion of critical thinking and a focus on individual performance in collaborative work. However, the majority of articles and books on the subject did little to dispel the fog. The most supportive research for developing collaboration in a classroom comes with the cooperative-learning research. Indeed, it is hard to distinguish the two in practice even in the 21st century when advocates for technology projects in classrooms locked the word *collaborative* onto the less structured and more individualistic teamwork they seemed to prefer.

In spite of the many distinctions that have been attempted in order to distance the two concepts, many years of school-gathered research note that cooperative learning is the most effective means for advancing students' collaborative skill set. It is seen as the most effective goal structure for raising student achievement and for improving lifelong collaborative skills. Although some paradigms such as the Johnsons' do not explicitly include critical thinking, many including the BUILD model do. The same studies indicate that competitive goal structures and individualistic goal structures are less effective than the cooperative structure for enabling high achievement (Johnson & Johnson, 1990).

In 1995, Robert Marzano and his associates at the MidContinent Regional Education Lab (McRel) presented a meta-analysis of the most effective instructional strategies (Marzano & Kendall, 1995). This study ranked cooperative learning as one of the most effective of the top ten. In 2008, Cary Roseth, David Johnson, and Roger Johnson released a recent meta-analysis of cooperative learning's effects. The included studies represented more than 8 decades of research with more than 17,000 early adolescents from 11 countries and 4 multinational samples. This meta-analysis confirmed a basic tenet of social interdependence theory (Johnson & Johnson, 1998). Academic achievement, as well as positive peer relationships, were more strongly correlated with cooperative rather than competitive or individualistic goal structures.

"COLLABORATION IS": A SYNTHESIZED DEFINITION

Collaboration is a process of two or more persons working to achieve a common goal through face-to-face interactions, live or digital, using an agreed-upon problem-solving or decision-making process.

The Johnsons' meta-analysis of cooperative learning is especially noteworthy for its identification of the positive impact of cooperative learning on the outcome most dear to social-constructive theorists: higher achievement associated with positive peer relationships. It also suggests that the teacher may be more important than others would allow. This is because the Johnsons suggest that the teacher is an active *mediator* of peer relationships in the collaborative classroom. Teachers share their knowledge base of cooperative skills with the students so the students may increase their achievement. These teachers do not succumb to show-and-tell; they facilitate and mediate students transforming themselves from passive receptors into active makers of knowledge.

HOW TO ENABLE COOPERATIVE LEARNING TO ENRICH CLASSROOM COLLABORATION

A skilled enabler of cooperative-learning skills is one who is prepared to help students use the key elements of cooperative learning in their collaborative work and their communications with other team members. Some effective facilitator-teachers will build a collaboration rubric based on the five key attributes detailed in the Johnson research. Others will use the BUILD model. Both enable students to assess their own teamwork progress and content mastery. At teachable moments in a unit or project, facilitator-teachers may ask individual students about how they are applying a benchmark, intervene and mediate a more skillful use of cooperative skills when they see a breakdown, and allot time each week for students to check their skills or take feedback from their peer group.

COMMUNICATION INSIDE AND OUTSIDE THE CLASSROOM

Communication is often identified but often overlooked as a 21st century skill. However, it is intractably intertwined with collaboration. With the fast changes, increased interdependence and an information tsunami

SAMPLE COOPERATIVE LEARNING CHECKLIST

Name: _Rosalee Ali_   **Date:** _March 28, 2010_

To what degree this week

_4_   Did I engage my peers in positive face-to-face interactions?
_5_   Did I hold myself accountable for my responsibilities in the group?
_3_   Did I seek multiple points of view on an issue?
_4_   Did I check for group members' understanding of my position?
_0_   Did I review the problem-solving process?
_2_   Did I check for consensus on a group decision?
_2_   Did I check to ensure all voices had the chance to voice an opinion?
_4_   Did I strive to improve my cooperative social skills?
_1_   Did I assess how our group was working together?

My summary: I think I am really trying. I keep reminding myself that we are all in this together. I need to improve my checking.

predicted for the 21st century, high-quality communication skills will play an ever more prominent role in the enrichment of skillful collaboration. In addition, communication skills are often associated with using digital tools that call up ever more sophisticated communication skill sets face-to-face within the classroom and via the Internet around the world.

Email notes, tweets, blogs, and wikis are the most prominent digital tools that connect collaboration and communication. These are prominent, word-intensive e-tools that allow for one-way messages and two-way conversations near and far. However, 21st century digital communication does not end with print. As Web 2.0 tools proliferate, students have easier access to more and more video and audio tools for streaming everything from still pictures, to slideware combinations, to multimedia presentations.

Already many Web 2.0 tools have crossed the line from "artwork" to basic communication tools. Although many of these e-tools are one-way communicators that do not require overt responses from those who "see" the messages, their creation often requires collaborative effort by a team of "makers" and can generate responses from viewers. In either case, students with a high-level communication skill set in multiple modes will be better prepared to collaborate with others within and without the borders of the classroom.

The advent of digital tools that enrich students' communication possibilities with audiences near and far complicates the teacher's role. What was once a simple curriculum based in an English or language arts print-centered classroom, development of multimedia digital communication skills brings new challenges and new possibilities for teachers in every subject area.

The Written Word

Even though some may forecast the death of the written word in the next few generations, especially if school budgets eliminate writing exams and professional development, it makes little sense to throw the baby out with the bathwater. Yes, budgets are tight. Yes, online communication via visuals has increased rapidly. Yes, writing is not easily measured by bubble tests. Yes, the act of writing may depend more on digital tools than on paper-print. None are significant justifications for abandoning the written word.

Emails, wikis, blogs, and even tweets are totally dependent on the "written" word, be it printed in block letters, scrolled in Palmer method on an interactive whiteboard, or tapped out on a digital keyboard. Research reports still depend on the written word, as do essay questions, poems, and presentations guided by a shared slide. Written summaries remain a high-effect learning strategy that is usable with any of the tools. Letters still demand composition skills, if not just a little thinking. Given the amount of communication we do on a page, digital or paper, is it not reasonable to conclude that, somewhere in the curriculum, teachers can help students learn sentence construction, paragraph logic, expository format, research style, and all the other conventions of skillful written communication?

It would be naive to assume that students using e-tools to write or show their ideas and feelings will do so without learning the grammar, syntax, and logic rules of effective language use. Email letters will still require students to know how to punctuate, structure sentences, and build paragraphs that make sense to the reader. Research summaries still require a strict expository format with footnotes that follow American Psychological Association (APA) or other guidelines. Summaries still require a strong thesis sentence and logically aligned details.

The Visual Word

Visual communication is the most prominent emerging literacy for the 21st century. As with the written word, there are quality standards that guide the construction of quality still and live media presentations. At the very least, teachers will have to develop rubrics to guide students in assembling collages, designing shareware, editing multimedia demonstrations, developing podcasts, and creating films that communicate the thoughts and feelings they intend others to see and understand in a visual language that extends beyond the classroom walls.

The Digital Word

Communicating in digital formats has lead to a new technological literacy. Not only do students need to master the hardware used for communicating but they must add in the skilled use of software and Internet tools. Each of these has its own communication rules, some derived from the traditional writing curriculum and others, such as Twitter, evolving from the nature of the tools themselves. In addition, the digital word requires digital etiquette. How will teachers best enable their students to recognize different value sets? How will teachers develop students' online respect for others' thoughts, values, and beliefs?

NEW FRAMEWORKS FOR COLLABORATIONS

Two frameworks for enabling collaboration are making their way into schools in the 21st century. The first targets faculty members in Professional Learning Communities (PLCs). The approach advocated by Richard and Becky DuFour and their colleagues drawn from practitioners coast to coast is designed to facilitate teachers' use of data in order to improve student achievement, especially by those students who often fall between the cracks. Small groups of six to ten teachers meet, review data on student performance, and then assist one another in developing plans to address the needs of the targeted students. By working in a collaborative framework, these PLC groups also break down the traditional professional isolation that has been a consequence of the factory school model. In that model, most teachers close their doors, work long hours with students and seldom have a formal structure, other than the occasional Individualized Education Plan (IEP) conference, to collaborate.

A second structure, the Critical Friends group, is common practice in many of the innovative schools that intentionally develop 21st century skills. The New Tech Highs are especially committed to the Critical Friends approach, not only for faculty-faculty collaboration, but in many of the schools, as a student-student framework. Some of these schools combine the student use of Critical Friends with formal instruction in cooperative learning. Mike Morrison, former principal of Napa Valley's New Tech High and a lead trainer in the New Tech University, insists on the importance of using such high-effects instructional strategies and intentionally teaching the skills of cooperative learning. He also believes that by embedding formal cooperative learning in the Critical Friends approach so that teachers and students are always addressing significant, authentic, and relevant issues, the school's collaborative outcomes are more readily apparent.

A key attribute that differentiates Professional Learning Communities from Critical Friends is the role of the facilitator. A Critical Friend is a facilitator of the group process. Unlike the PLCs, in which the teacher group is self-facilitated and focuses on a *task* (reviewing and using data), the Critical Friends group is more intent on learning the collaborative *process* from a specially prepared "leader" who guides the group's interactions. That "process focuses on developing collegial relationships, encouraging reflective practice, and rethinking leadership" (http://www.depts.washington.edu/ccph/pdf_files/CriticalFriends.pdf). In this context, the word *critical* highlights the facilitator as (1) necessary, (2) prepared to guide the group in constructively confronting key issues, and (3) capable of providing crucial feedback in such a way that words are taken seriously and lead to change.

Each of these frameworks has been adapted in a variety of ways. Both share the common goal of bringing traditionally isolated faculty together on a regular basis. They also share the common interest of bringing change to practice, and many of the strategies used overlap. What both frameworks and their offshoots provide for 21st century schools is an active professional collaboration in which communication by faculty and students is actively and intentionally addressed.

CONCLUDING THOUGHTS

An understanding of the concept "collaboration" in the context of the emerging culture of the technologically rich 21st century shows it as the mortar that binds together the most desired student skills for working together. Newly developed e-tools enrich opportunities to engage students in learning and thinking tasks with other students, wherever the different students are physically located. As distinguished from collaboration, cooperative learning, the interpersonal side of the collaborative coin, is a necessary ingredient for helping students become more effective and efficient in their use of collaborative tools.

CHAPTER 3

Internet Tools for 21st Century Classrooms

I think it's fair to say that personal computers have become
the most empowering tool we've ever created. They're tools of
communication, they're tools of creativity, and they can be shaped
by their user.

—Bill Gates

I N 1952, ILLIAC, the first computer built and owned entirely by an educational institution, began operation. It was 10 feet long, 2 feet wide, and 8½ feet high; contained 2,800 vacuum tubes; and weighed 5 tons. This electronic giant paved the way for an ever-increasing number of smaller and smaller computers. The use of computer chips in other electronic devices followed, until today, new tools are ready for any individual to connect to the Internet; collaborate with colleagues on the other side of the globe; and communicate with family, friends, and fellow workers in whatever country they find themselves. The greatest boon, however, has been the availability of digital tools for the classroom. Less than a century after ILLIAC's birth, teaching and learning is undergoing an electronic revolution. Already, whole schools are abandoning the print-and-paper world to construct electronic learning communities that know no paper.

THE PAPERLESS CLASSROOM

For 21st century students, it is hard to imagine a classroom without paper. Shin Le's classroom was just that before the invention of paper (see sidebar). It may not be long before classrooms again are paperless classrooms without books.

Before paper, how did people write their ideas? The Sumerians carved into heavy clay tablets and carried them from place to place. Other civili-

Shin Le smiled. "This thing you call paper is wonderful. It makes my writing assignments so much easier than those bamboo sticks."

"Yes," affirmed her tutor. "And it is also less thick and coarse, made from our hemp scrolls. I found the uneven texture of the hemp unsuitable for brush writing."

"What is it that makes this paper?" Shin Le asked.

"I believe that Cai Lun uses bark, hemp, rags, fishnet, and some silk. He is trying to add more silk to his mix."

Shin Le nodded. "Those materials make this paper so much lighter. Even though the paper is thinner, it is harder to rip with my brush. That used to be so frustrating."

The tutor smiled. "Yes, I agree. You are producing so many more pages now. I can see more of your best ideas. And I bet your parents are happy. Fewer pages wasted is a considerable savings for them."

Adapted from Chinese Culture,
http://www.chinaculture.org/gb/en_aboutchina/2003-09/24/content_26514.htm

zations drew on cave walls. The Chinese of the Western Han Dynasty used pounded hemp to make paper. Not until 140 BC did Cai Lun discover how to pound multiple ingredients into paper like Shin Le was using.

If Shin Le's classroom had kept up with the world outside her castle, she might have found a world that was ready to give up all paper, not because it was hard to write on, but because it was obsolete. If she had traveled through time like Dr. Who, she might have seen an event as important in history as Cai Lun's invention of paper. She would have stopped in the Middle Ages and met a man named Johannes Gutenberg, who was about ready to mass print paper with a new press.

If her time machine had stopped in Urbana-Champaign in the mid-1950s, Shin Le might have enrolled in a class at the University of Illinois, where she would have used punch cards on the giant computer housed there. If her first stop were this year, she might enter a classroom with students sitting at a computer with an electronic printer and perhaps a fax machine or smartphone. In place of a blank wall on which to hang her hand-painted papers, she might have seen an interactive whiteboard or discovered a digital notebook or Kindle. If she traveled for another 10 years, she might not even recognize these early 21st century innovations.

As the 21st century moves forward, more and more teachers and their students are finding shiny new tools for their home- and schoolwork.

Many students are already familiar with more e-tools and apps than most teachers and administrators. Many already use these e-tools as well as new software programs, applications, and websites, which have the potential to transform teaching into a much more effective interaction with students. As teachers discover the instructional value of these e-tools, they find students more and more expectant about doing more and more difficult learning tasks with ever more sophisticated e-tools for completing their classroom work. In future months and years, they can expect many more.

NEW TOOLS FOR DIGITAL LEARNING

In the last years of the 20th century and into the first decade of the 21st, teachers gradually uncovered a treasure chest of digital tools that could enrich teaching and learning experiences in ways that would boggle the minds of their 19th century counterparts. As use of these tools has expanded in general society, so too have the examples of their effectiveness in the classroom begun to grow in number. More important is the developing notion that these same tools may better prepare 21st century students to work and learn in the ever-changing brave-new-technology world students will face after graduation. If nothing else, having learned how to evaluate the e-tools that line store shelves today, students will be better positioned to judge the value of those e-tools yet to be invented.

Digital tools that enrich student-learning experiences come in many shapes and forms. Like the various roles in a stage drama or film, these e-tools play different characters and have different lines to enunciate. First, there are those e-tools in the lead parts, the star players who take up most of the play's time on the big stage and headline the production. These major leads, the blogs and wikis, play the dominant roles that are most able to foster communication and collaboration in- and outside the classroom. Second, there are the e-tools that fill the supporting roles. These are the e-tools that help teachers prepare lessons, units, and projects that increase collaborative learning and communication among students. Among these are interactive whiteboards and content management systems such as Moodle, Blackboard, and Wet Paint, as well as social network sites such as Ning. Finally, there are the mini-tools that fill out the cast such as Flickr, CMaps, and other electronic graphic organizers; Glogster; Wink; podcasts; and various types of shareware.

GROUP 1: THE HEADLINERS

In this first group, two digital tools have earned marquee recognition as the "stars" of the show. The blog and the wiki receive headline attention because they anchor what can happen with advanced technology in the classroom. They are sine qua nons, those e-tools teachers cannot do without if they are going to take a systematic approach to the integration of technology into their classrooms. Blogs and wikis facilitate that integration in multiple ways. They are helpful for organizing, managing, and enhancing communication and collaboration among all the classroom players, especially when teachers make learning plans that are project centered. Blogs and wikis also make the task of the teacher, the learning production's director, easier.

The Blog

A blog is a type of website. Blogs are frequently integrated into a larger website. Picture a blog as an online journal or an Internet log. In the classroom, a teacher or all students can maintain individual blogs. When starting classroom blogs, it is most practical for teachers to keep the control in a single classroom blog. In this way, they can set standards and etiquette, control entry and comments, and prepare students to set up their own blogs. As students become more adept at blogging within lessons, teachers can prepare students for integrating blogs into classroom projects that communicate with peers in other towns, cities, or nations.

Many students will come to class with prior blogging experiences. They already will have home blogs set up for tracking movie stars, playing games, watching TV shows, and the like. More sophisticated students will participate in sports, news, or political blogs. They already know that blog entries are posted in reverse order with the requirement of a public signature. They also may have some familiarity with blog etiquette and know how to integrate photos and RSS audio with text entries.

Once teachers have tapped into students' prior knowledge about technology with an advance organizer such as "learning links," a KWL (what I Know, what I Want to know, what I Learned), or other prior knowledge graphics, they can explain their intentions for setting up a classroom blog and explain its value within the classroom. At this time, teachers can highlight the blog as a classroom information-management tool or as an instructional tool. Using a direct-instruction lesson that identifies how they

A SAMPLE BLOG

This fifth-grade teacher collected answers and ideas about a story just read by students. She broke the blog into four sections: characters, theme, plot, and setting. Here are sample entries regarding her posted questions about character.

Friday, February 11, 2005

Character

Who are the main characters and how are they realistic?

posted by cordle | 10:57 a.m.

Akin said . . . The main characters in this story are Anna, Papa and Caleb. They are realistic because they talk, walk and cook. They also drive a horse, know how to plow a farm and write. They are real people in the story but the story is fiction. February 17, 2005, 2:27 PM

Sarah said . . . You are right. We are as real as characters get. So what do you think about my situation? February 22, 2005, 10:20 a.m.

cordle said . . . The main characters are Sarah, Papa, Anna, and Caleb. The characters are realistic because in the story they do things that real people would do. Sarah is coming from Tennessee to be a new mom. The kids tell stories to each other. The Papa sang to the kids in front of the fire place. February 22, 2005, 10:29 a.m.

rholsman said . . . We think Sarah's situation would be hard because she doesn't know the new kids, and you have never met them before. It would also be hard because it would be hard to replace the mom who had passed away. February 24, 2005, 8:48 a.m.

Katrina said . . . The main characters in the story are Sarah, Papa, Anna, and Caleb. Although set in a different time, the characters are very true to life. They are a family. They work together, they talk to each other, they deal with situations together. Things happen to them that they must deal with, just like real people do everyday. March 4, 2008, 4:40 p.m.

Kajal said . . . The main characters of the book are Sarah, Anna and Caleb because they are the ones who are usually talked [about] in the book. March 9, 2008, 7:40 p.m.

http://my-ecoach.com/online/webresourcelist.php?rlid=4992#2
This site also provides tutorials and links about blog use.

MAKE LEARNING LINKS

Put students into cooperative groups of five. Establish roles and rules. (See Chapter 2.)
Give each student a strip of paper, 1" x 12".

- For all to see, show the word *blog*. Ask students to write all they know about this word in sequence on their strips. Use single words only with commas.
- Give each group a tube of paste and instruct them to interlock their completed strips. This should produce a linked chain in each group. Instruct the groups to review the links, cross out duplicates, and discuss each word.
- Rotate the chains around the groups. Each group that discovers a new word on a received chain can circle it and check its meaning with the sending group if necessary.
- On the board, ask each group in turn to add a list of unduplicated words about blogs.
- After a word's discussion, ask a student to place the word into one of the following categories that you have identified for all to see: "communicate," "collaborate," "innovate," "think critically." Discuss each item so that all in the class are familiar with the terms.

Bellanca, 2009

will use the blog or, with an online tutorial, teachers can create a level playing field for students without prior blogging experience. At this point, the blog becomes a tool that allows teachers to manage and guide differentiated instruction.

For both classroom information management and instruction, teachers will find that blogs help in many additional ways. Teachers can select the blog uses that will best facilitate the many management, information, and instruction tasks that spring up in a classroom.

Wikis

A wiki is the second e-tool that merits a lead role in the 21st century classroom. In classrooms, teachers can use wikis to facilitate collaborative communication more easily than with any other e-tool. Because it is an

Figure 3.1. Triple T Chart

Differentiating Instruction with a Classroom Blog		
Individual Work	**Small Group Work**	**Large Group Work**
Summary of day's work	Jigsaw research	Class instructions
Guided individual practice		
Solo product	Pair products	Class examples
Silent reading tasks	Paired partner	News for home
Personal log entry	Reading	Quiz for all
Private reflective	Lab notes	Announcements
Journal entry	Team product	Assignments
Solo research task	Group investigation	Parent notes
Solo graphic organizer	Team C-map	Online etiquette

open-source collection of web pages, a wiki allows equitable access to anyone who wishes to contribute to its content. Simple markup rules and a code of etiquette directs anyone who accesses a wiki to modify the content already posted. The most well known public wiki, Wikipedia, encourages guests to add to any encyclopedia article. Wikipedia has been adding more controls and review panels to discourage abuse of its open invitation to share knowledge.

Wikispaces for Teachers

Important online support for introducing wikis into the classroom comes from Wikispaces for Teachers (www.wikispaces.com). Wikispaces is a free wiki site for educators. To make a wiki most practical in a classroom, Wikispaces encourages teachers to control entry and exit to posts on the site. Wikispaces recommends that only pin-coded students or their parents be allowed to enter a specific site and see the posts. Teachers can customize their classroom wikis and use them with no limits on the number of student users, pages, or edits of existing files. Wikispaces provides its basic site "advertisement free" to teachers.

USES FOR BLOGS

a. Provide the unit, lesson, or project-launch question or loosely structured problem scenario.

b. Provide lesson or project objectives and rationale linked to standards.

c. Retain products such as tests, essays, multimedia presentations, and book reports. Keep each student's work separate.

d. Post rubrics for grading products and processes.

e. Post criteria for grading products, collaboration, and content.

f. List members of cooperative learning groups.

g. Make a commentary on the subject matter.

h. Give instructions or feedback for specific groups or individuals.

i. Give instructions for student journals or diaries: text only or with streamed audio or visual entries.

j. Post instructions for student reflections.

k. Store class notes (one note-taker per day for absentees).

l. Cross questions from students with other students' answers.

m. List reflection prompts, dialogue starters for write-pair-share, or end-of-class wraparounds.

n. Post plans for group debates on a single topic.

o. Give all class feedback to students.

p. Post summaries ("I learned . . .") of responses to launch question.

q. Publish sample student letters, essays, stories, and nonprint work.

r. Make a lesson or unit vocabulary list.

s. Post online resources and reference list with links.

t. List teams for field trips.

u. Post the class newsletter.

v. Post project summaries.

w. Ask for student responses to a thoughtful question.

x. Show samples of graphic organizers.

y. Store all student products in individual files.

Wikispaces does the most of any wiki site to facilitate teacher-beginner collaborations in the wiki universe. Since 2006, Wikispaces has given away hundreds of thousands of sites to teachers. These free sites have been a prime mover for helping teachers get started with classroom wikis.

For K–12 teachers anywhere in the world, Wikispaces also provides free support services. Services include dedicated blog webinars, tutorials for starting and using best practices with a wiki, and stories of success from

21ST CENTURY TECHNOLOGY TERMS TO KNOW

Asynchronous time: Unscheduled time. Students go on the blog at will.

Avatar: An imaginary or substitute identity that stands in for a real person. First developed for computer games, avatar sites now allow users to create an alternate online identity.

Bookmark: A tag that helps the maker find related words, topics, articles, or ideas by browsing. Computer users make their own bookmarks.

Cloud computing: A new generation of off-site information storage able to perform the functions that were traditionally done with software installed on an individual computer. Web cloud services such as Flickr, Google Docs, JING (video screen capture service) are early iterations of cloud storage systems.

Open source: A new computer development approach that allows multiple access points.

RSS feed: Stands for Really Simple Syndication feed. A family of web formats used to include updated works—such as blog entries, news headlines, music, audio, and video. Moves in a standardized format onto a personal site on a regular schedule. This is a subscription service.

Synchronous time: A scheduled time during which everyone is on the blog at once.

Tag: A key word indicator that the tag-maker applies to connect concepts or facts without needing to make a subordinated category for the key word in a document.

Template: A preformatted outline that allows teachers to "fill in the blanks," especially when making a plan.

Tutorial: An online site that provides one-on-one instruction in how to use a tool or site.

VOIP: An online phone system that allows seeing and hearing, or just hearing, as students talk to one another through their computers with the "voice over Internet protocol." Skype is the most popular VOIP and a *free* system, if both parties are registered users. Skype is limited to one-on-one video conferencing, though multiple computers can be connected for voice only. NEFSIS, a pay system, is a VOIP that can handle one-to-many video conferencing. Hinc is a system that allows for multi-way video conferences with up to 1,000 sites.

Web 2.0: A platform that allows for increased collaboration on the Internet. Blogs, pods, wikis, and social networks, video-sharing sites, mashups, and folksonmies are specialized Web 2.0 tools. (For more complete explanations of these specialized tools, browse the name.)

Web 3.0: The latest web platform that provides tools to integrate and understand web information. Tools include semantic webs, micro formats, natural-language searches, data mining, machine learning, recommendation agents, and artificial intelligence. (For more complete explanation of these specialized tools, browse the name.)

peers. Teachers can use classroom wikis to build and track community service projects, provide advance organizers to motivate student interest in upcoming lessons, construct all-class vocabulary cluster maps, and foster collaborative note-taking. Most commonly, teachers use wikis as a brainstorming tool that produces multiple ideas. Sometimes the brainstorming occurs as an advance organizer for a lesson or project; however, it is just as likely that teachers facilitate brainstorms when students are gathering information about a topic or generating many possible solutions to a problem.

Addressing Concerns with Added Security. For schools that are especially concerned about safety and security, Wikispaces provides a fee-based upgrade, Private Label, as an extra-secure block to e-invasions. With the Wikispace Private Label, a school or district can set up its in-house wiki community separate from Wikispace. This arrangement allows the schools to connect to public wikis such as Wikipedia while it keeps private wikis used only by pin-coded teachers. This arrangement also gives the district the most security control over the sites in its private network.

Multiple Uses for Classroom Wikis. The creativity of a teacher is the driving force of a classroom wiki. Wiki use follows no formula. Its varied uses fall into several categories that are relevant to 21st century skill development.

Getting Started with Wikis. In the first months using one of these e-tools, teachers help students become wiki masters by keeping the tasks simple and short. For instance, a best practice for the first month of novice use is to limit time. A daily prompt-response ("Today, I learned . . ." or "My question today is . . .") is a good starter. From this, teachers can scaffold use of student reflection to complete summaries, brainstorm lists, or create other more complex entries.

Wet Paint

Another helpful wiki starter site for teachers is Wet Paint. Wet Paint (www.wetpaint.com) is a prize-winning free wiki that helps nontechnical teachers or students create a classroom wiki in a quick three-step process. This site is eminently readable and easily used. When having teachers or students design their own wikis, Wet Paint provides clear and succinct material, more like guidelines than specific procedures. By going to Wet Paint Central, teachers will find tips "for a successful site." The list begins with this simple value statement: "The more unique content your site has about

WIKIS IN MY CLASSROOM: WHAT TEACHERS SAY

Wikis promote positive relationships inside and outside the classroom.

"My students answer a list of questions about their interests and talents. They post these and look for other kids in the class with similar interests" —**D.S., Milwaukee, WI**

"When I have a child out sick, the class sends happygrams and get-well cards on our wiki." —**M.G., Ocean City, NJ**

"I ask students to write a one-page autobiography to share." —**T.O., Gainesville, FL**

"The wiki is my motivation for students writing to pen pals. I joined Interpals (www.interpals.net) and picked the forum I wanted." —**S.T., Missoula, MT**

Wikis extend assignments outside the classroom walls.

"My students write essays and post them on the wiki for feedback from a peer team. The author selects the focus of the feedback (content, form, critical thinking, etc.)." —**R.S., Springfield, IL**

"I list the vocabulary words for the week. Students look up the definitions for homework and post these. We discuss the differences." —**M.W., New York**

"I post weekly assignments in math. Students put answers on the wiki. Parents have access too." —**J.M., Albany, GA**

"I ask my English classes to do a deep reflection on how the material we read that week affected them or changed their beliefs. Posts are anonymous if they want." —**T.S., San Francisco**

"We have a weekly debate on a science issue like 'Should evolution be taught?' They post their different points of view on the site first, then we debate in class." —**A.B., Philadelphia**

Wikis stimulate critical and creative thinking.

"I start every lesson in my history classes with a problem. I make the problem up from the textbook topic. On the wiki, the kids post their solutions. Then we start the lesson." —**J.G., Christchurch, NZ**

"Each student in my chemistry class works with lab partners to make a question about something they don't understand in the lesson. The other teams answer on the wiki." —**S.B., Bay City, MI**

"We brainstorm the ways we can use media tools to end our projects." —**S.F. Bath, ME**

WIKIS IN MY CLASSROOM: WHAT TEACHERS SAY *(continued)*

"When we are studying a novel like *To Kill a Mockingbird,* my students fill out a CMap on the wiki." —**N.S., Elgin, IL**

Wikis improve communication skills.

"I ask my students to write short stories and post them on the wiki. Other students post their critiques of the writing style or the story elements." —**G.B., Wilmington, DE**

"Each week, I ask each student to assess what they learned that was most helpful in communicating their ideas and feelings." —**K.S., Austin, TX**

"I post one essay a week after I have fouled up its grammar and punctuation. They post their corrections." —**D.R., Indianapolis, IN**

"My students worked in groups to tell a story in pictures. They used sequence charts to get the order of the story. The other teams had to put the story into words and post it with the picture story." —**D.B., Birmingham, AL**

Wikis develop cooperative learning skills.

"My AP Biology class uses the wiki to post summaries of their experiments. They post their assessments of how they worked cooperatively. I insist that every assessment start with a description of their individual accountability." —**M.D., Fargo, ND**

"I use the wiki to give students feedback on how I observed them working in cooperative groups." —**M.G., DeKalb, GA**

"Students post their research jigsawed group summaries. I provide feedback." —**T.T., Appleton, WI**

"My students do their think-pair-shares on the wiki. It promotes their working together." —**R.S., Newark, NJ**

---

your topic, the more visitors you will attract. Make it easy for them to explore your content." It follows with a list of links to pages that explain each topic in depth:

- Write unique content
- Create a strong homepage
- Design it to attract interest
- Organize your content
- Use site templates
- Get some ideas and inspiration

THE WIKI STORM: A SAMPLE STARTER ACTIVITY

1. Post a question (e.g., How many ways can this geometry problem be solved? If you were faced with traversing the Donner Pass, what ways would you consider to get over the mountains? What guidelines should we consider that show good manners on a wiki? What are your questions about the meaning of Mobius?).
2. Instruct students how to post their responses. Give a time limit.
3. At the end of the time, ask students to review all responses and make notes on why they like one or two.

Under each topic, the Wet Paint authors practice what they preach. They show how-to examples for all steps. On the "organize your content" page, readers see an organized page that starts with a title, two sentences on why an *organized* page is important, tips, and samples of finished projects.

GROUP 2: THE SUPPORTING CAST

Very rarely is a cast limited to two characters. *South Pacific* featured Nellie Forbush and Emile as its main characters. The musical added the supporting characters of Bloody Mary, Lt. Joe Cable, and Billis. This supporting cast helped the leads develop their "personas" and carry out the themes and conflicts that draw the audience into the story. In the tech-enriched classroom, teachers use a variety of e-tools to support the star blogs and wikis. Interactive whiteboards and content management systems play strong supporting roles on the technology stage.

Interactive Whiteboards

Interactive whiteboards are electronic versions of ye olde chalkboard. Whiteboards are linked to a computer and projector. Instead of writing on a chalkboard, a projecting screen, or a large sheet of newsprint to present information that all students need to see, teachers can turn to the more versatile interactive whiteboard that invites student engagement.

Teachers can use the whiteboard just as they would a chalkboard in a standard lesson: write the words, make the lists, or ask a student to solve a math problem for the whole class to see. The whiteboard, however, encourages teachers to do much more. Teachers can make a media presentation on the whiteboard, post an electronic graphic organizer, or connect to a school network wiki or blog to show visual material posted by other students. If teachers have a whiteboard that keeps digital files, they can save all the posted material.

Teachers who use whiteboards to manage projects can increase their management of multiple teams in doing projects. Teachers can prepare instructions that all students need to see on their own computers and then

---

SAMPLE INTERACTIVE WHITEBOARD
USES FOR LESSONS AND PROJECTS

Show outcomes:

- Ask open-ended launch question
- Display materials lists for selection by students
- List key elements of the problem scenarios
- Brainstorm process sequence for an inquiry
- Build rubrics and checklists with students
- Challenge students to sequence task instruction
- Brainstorm lists of ideas
- Display inside pages of books and ask for critiques

Assign students to

- Build and complete a graphic organizer on a topic
- Complete stems or prompts
- Show streamed video or slide show
- Create interactive graphs and charts
- Have teams map sequence of events
- Have students use RSS feeds for storytelling or biographies
- Create class story or cartoon story
- Display student project products with student presentations
- Make videos of favorite stories
- Trace explorations
- Explain steps in a science experiment
- Demonstrate solutions to a math problem
- Map connections among characters in a story
- Display summaries of a lesson or project
- Illustrate ideas in a visual way
- Make a map to show a journey taken
- Explain the steps in completing a project
- Use a rubric to guide assessment of a project by the rest of the class

communicate these instructions as needed. In addition, as students complete their projects, teachers can call them to the whiteboard and have the students project their final reports or make presentations with inserted multimedia.

Teachers with interactive whiteboards can easily fall into a trap. The trap is using it as just another blackboard, albeit one that uses brightly colored markers, or as a projection screen. The word *interactive* indicates the main purpose and value of the whiteboard: to stimulate student interaction. The most effective uses of the interactive whiteboard occur when teachers' lesson designs call on students to use their creativity to present project results with charts and graphs they make, to complete concept maps while brainstorming new ideas and revealing new insights, to visualize character traits, to tell stories they have written in multimedia, and so forth. The list of possible activities to promote interaction on the whiteboard is long. Its potential, however, is wasted if teachers ignore the tool's capacity to engage students in meaningful activity.

The *better* and *best* uses of digital whiteboards are not those that simply replace the conventional blackboard and create a short-lived "awesome" or "cool" factor that soon wears off. The better uses come when teachers use whiteboards as a creative tool that allows students to show products, make presentations, blog, build a public wiki, and show *their* media work. As the above list shows, the only limit to what students can create with a whiteboard is the teacher's readiness to use this tool to encourage students as creative and innovative thinkers who will better recall and understand key concepts because of the interactive experience than if they are simply passive heads to be filled with information. In short, the interaction with the whiteboard as a creative tool turns them into active makers of knowledge.

Course Management Systems

Course management systems help teachers manage the learning in their classrooms. A course management system is a software application for the administration, documentation, tracking, and reporting of classroom and online events, e-learning programs, and course content.

The most recognizable course management system name is Blackboard. All over the world, especially in universities that specialize in distance learning, professors use Blackboard to design their courses. In addition, many professors, instructors, classroom teachers, and business-world trainers have adopted Blackboard to organize their courses in the classroom.

DIFFERENTIATING INSTRUCTION OUTSIDE SCHOOL WALLS

- Provide e-pal access to students in need of writing practice.
- Allow each student team to select a different topic to investigate with global classroom partners in other countries.
- Select and tailor individual assignments from the Human Rights Resource Center.
- Connect teams with the UNICEF Voices for Youth Program.
- Generate essential project questions according to students' readiness to work on a project.

Course management systems allow teachers to teach their classes in whole or in part online. The systems provide more equal access for all. They also allow teachers to increase contact with persons outside the classroom, including K–12 parents. A content management system promotes collaboration and communication by making it easy for teachers to differentiate instruction with planned interactions inside and outside classroom walls.

In addition, the systems allow teachers to keep a record of all contacts made by students on blogs, in chat rooms, or in discussion forums.

Classroom-management systems expand the possibilities for professional learning experiences within a district or among districts. These systems free teachers from synchronous presentations where teacher trainers continue to talk at them with frontal lectures. Instead, teachers can elect when and where they are going to use self-selected course work that allows them to be active collectors of information from many modes of presentation. With an asynchronous schedule, teachers can also decide how they will make sense of what they are learning and how to use these ideas with their students.

A rising competitor to Blackboard is the open-source (free) content management system Moodle. This easy-to-use system was created by educators for educators' use in the electronic age. Moodle prides itself on the ease of access to information and to rapid communication among teachers, parents, administrators, and students. MoodleRooms, the online company that created this online platform, provides teachers with low-cost special services, including increased controls for safety and security, permanent interaction records, and yearly learning plans. Compliant with the standards for distance learning called the Shareable Content Object Reference Model (SCORM), Moodle lets teachers connect their classrooms to forums, chat rooms, and blogs and to make international connections as well as use the secure parent portal. Moodle provides on-demand professional development so that teachers can take advantage of all the Moodle features as they build collaborations inside and outside their classrooms (www.moodlerooms.com).

GROUP 3: THE BIT PLAYERS

The third player group on the digital classroom stage features the bit players. These characters have minor roles, most of which help carry the story forward with important tasks such as comic relief; Yorick in Shakespeare's *Hamlet* is a good example. These tiny parts are essential. Each has a specialized use.

An ever-expanding list of *specialized* e-tools provides teachers with practical support for technology-enriched lessons and projects. Like the bit parts in a play, these e-tools have a very specialized use. As teachers and their students become more comfortable communicating and collaborating in the classroom with their blogs and wikis, all can begin to add these special purpose tools to their e-tool repertoires.

E-Tools Just for Teachers

Some of the most specialized e-tools are designed to help teachers perform redundant tasks. These tools include grade books, electronic lesson planners, and digital quiz and survey makers.

E-Gradebooks. Managing student grades is a time-consuming task in any classroom. Electronic grade books make the task easier for teachers in several ways. First, teachers can enter and manage grades from wherever they are located: at home, on the train, or in the teachers' lounge. They no longer have to worry about making hand calculations in order to weigh the value of different grades for different tasks. Nor do they or their students have to inquire over and over about missing work. On predetermined dates, teachers can have their grades automatically calculated. Missing assignments and extra credit are handled by the software. Teachers can also transmit grades immediately to parents and students through the Internet.

E-Lesson Planners and Project Planners. Systematic planning prior to a lesson, unit, or project permits teachers to shorten instructional time. On his website (www.jaymctigh.com), Jay McTighe (Wiggins &

McTighe, 2005) provides templates and tutorials for educators adopting the backward-design process. Adobe (www.adobe.com) and others have developed free online lesson plans and tutorials. Additional plans have been developed as part of www.tryengineering.org, a resource for students, their parents, their teachers, and their school counselors. Each lesson plan is tied to education standards and includes teacher summaries, student worksheets, and activities.

E-Quizzes and Tests. When teachers want to collect information from students or parents or when they want students to collect information for their research projects, they can select a free survey e-tool. The same tools often help them make quick quizzes to check students' understanding of key ideas and grasp of facts.

E-Templates. Google Docs is the most easily accessed source for templates that make collection of information practical in the classroom. After registering at Google Docs, teachers can easily prepare students to use selected formats located in Google Docs (http://www.docs.google.com), where they will find a collection of more than 300 templates. Google Docs provides free tutorials and other services that protect, and defend against misuse of, student work. When students want to connect with peers in other schools or nations, they can use simple email as the contact tool.

Other E-Tools for Teachers and Students

Other e-tools benefit both teachers and students in their collaborative communications. They include email, Twitter, e-journals, e-portfolios, VOIP, RSS feeds, podcasts, shareware, electronic graphics, Flickr, and other multimedia tools. Teachers can select which of these tools they want students to use well to support off-line lessons and projects or integrate into learning work that is strengthened by online tools.

Email. Teachers can start email communication as soon as students begin to identify words. As students progress in their ability to write phrases, clauses, and sentences, teachers can advance both reading and writing skills that highlight clear and succinct messages in an email format. From a cheery introduction, "Hi, my name is Sarah," to a respectful closing, "Thanks for your interest," primary students can expand their messages with word lists, summaries, and personal reflections. As they learn to compose, they increase their communication skills as well as learn the most basic technology skills. In addition, students increase their readiness to attach surveys and other forms within their communication with peers in other groups in the classroom and with new friends outside the classroom borders.

Twitter. For emails, the 140-word (more or less) format can help students learn how to communicate complex ideas in a tight format. Teachers can start "tweets" with short prompts or stem statements, such as "Today, I learned . . . ," or "I wonder why . . ." that students can store in online journals or send to a blog at the end of a class period, lesson, or activity.

Delicious. This is a tagging site that allows teachers to classify documents by means of a key word (http://www.delicious.com). If a history teacher is preparing to teach the Holocaust as a project, she can call up and preview online articles she wants students to read and post them for the class. If a 5th-grade teacher wants to identify sites for a biology field trip, she posts "biology," searches, and is presented with an array of possible sites that meet the criterion.

E-Journals. Journals fit well on blogs or as stand-alone entries that are available only by pin to the teacher or the student. E-journals store daily tweets, summaries of student discussions, analyses of key readings, personal reflections, goals and plans, and assessments or concept maps that students use to trace their thinking connections throughout a lesson or project. Teachers schedule 5 minutes or more for students to go online and compose their entries. If time allows, teachers may invite students to share journal entries with other students online or by reading to the entire class. Teachers can set up individual student blogs as a home site for students' journaling activities.

E-Portfolio. Teachers help students gather artifacts of their work in a collection and think reflectively about their work. Artifacts may include personal information, goals and plans, essays, journal entries, tests, products from a project, feedback from the teacher or peers, and other entries selected by the teacher or the student that connect to student learning. Students can use graphic organizers such as the CMap (http://www.cmap.org/) or a problem-solving chart to trace their learning journey. E-portfolio entries, controlled by pin access for security, may include work from a single project or lesson, or through a given period of time such as a marking period or semester. When teachers must provide a grade for portfolio work, it is best that they provide students with a rubric that will guide the works they include.

The site "E-portfolios" (www.eportfolio.org) provides a student-centered platform for use by schools. The portfolio is augmented by a project builder and an assessment module. Students control what goes into the portfolio and who may see it. Neither teachers nor students needs to be a programmer to use the site, which is maintained 24/7.

Multimedia Tools. When it comes time for students to communicate their ideas or show what they have learned from a project or lesson, the Internet provides a plethora of visual, audio, text, and interactive forums. Students can mix and match the tools to create ever more complex and engaging presentations via mixed media.

VOIP. Voice Operated Internet Protocol is an Internet-connected phone system. One company, Skype, provides free calls between registered customers around the globe. Students in upstate New York classrooms can call to Australia, New Zealand, or Florida with Skype and talk without hindrance (other than too narrow a bandwidth) as long as the receiving students have Skype connections. (Other VOIPs charge for the connection, as does Skype if both parties are not registered.)

If students have camera capability built into their computers or a low-cost camera, they may also see the person. The visual VOIP allows students to view the work-learning environments, make formal visual presentations to students far and near, and show samples of their work. Skype provides free tutorials for the setup and operation of this communication system (www.skype.com).

RSS Feeds. Wikipedia defines an RSS feed as "a family of web feed formats used to publish frequently updated works—such as blog entries, news headlines, audio, and video—in a standardized format."

Teachers can use RSS feeds (a document feed through the web in voice or print text) to gather up-to-date information or news on a topic that they want to review on a regular basis. For instance, social studies teachers may want to tap into a feed for up-to-date posts on a current issue the class is studying. Teachers may link their class into several feeds so they can follow the latest information from multiple points of view.

Podcasts. Technically, a podcast is a digital media file that allows users to see, hear, and store broadcasts that they download for off-line

MORE E-TOOL FREE ADDRESSES FOR SPECIAL USES

www.scribbler.com:	free downloads of formats for greeting cards, letters
www.wordle.net:	free word cloud maker
www.slideshare.net:	presentation sharing community
www.C41pt.co.uk:	a Twitter tagging mechanism
www.eluminate.com:	e-learning and collaboration software

use. Teachers may download a podcast such as the most recent State of the Union address or a Beethoven symphony. They then can include the audio file as part of a presentation to the class. Teachers can also prepare students to download video broadcasts, edit them, and include the cuts in a shareware presentation or video strip.

Shareware. Copyrighted software that helps classroom teachers provide templates that students can use to make agendas, certificates, calendars, resumes, and design slides. The most well known shareware is the copyrighted PowerPoint from Windows. Teachers can have students use the PowerPoint or other open-source software usually without incurring charges. Other shareware is offered "on a trial basis." This trial software requires payment at the end of a set time period. PowerPoint is popular because of its ease of use for designing presentations. If students are going to use PowerPoint, teachers can take advantage of the many design options built into the program. Teachers' greatest challenge will be to limit students' creative output.

Starting with the three-by-three-by-one rule, teachers can encourage students to limit their presentations to three points, one visual, or both, on a maximum of three slides. Instruction in the making of PowerPoint slides as the skeleton of a succinct presentation will advance students' precision and accuracy.

Two sites, interact4 classrooms.com and awesomebackgrounds.com, provide free basic shareware tutorials. Teachers can use these tutorials to help themselves or they can use the tutorials with older students.

E-Graphic Organizers. Visual or nonlinguistic representations have become popular tools for helping students organize, understand, and communicate information. The key to the most effective use of graphic organizers, whether in an electronic form or sketched by hand, is in making the correct mind-picture connection. Each organizer facilitates a specific thinking operation (e.g., Venn = comparing; web = brainstorming; fishbone = cause-effect analysis). Students learn to use visual organizers best when teachers start with a nonrelated example, model the thinking needed, and then allow students to practice the thinking process with the organizer. After giving corrective feedback, teachers can ask students to use the organizer with content they are studying. Free graphics at C-map.com provide tutorials and samples for the free electronic concept map.

Flickr. When students want to embed photographs into a PowerPoint presentation or integrate a video into a multimedia presentation, they use Flickr. This is a website that hosts photograph collections (including the students' own) that students can use to illustrate their presentations.

WebQuests. Bernie Dodge and Tom March introduced WebQuests in the mid-1990s (http://www.webquest.org). WebQuests are multivalue Internet applications that have caught the attention of many teachers. WebQuests encourage teachers to introduce students to inquiry projects while using the Internet to gather information in answer to a question, to draw conclusions, and to make a presentation. On the WebQuest home site at San Diego State University, teachers can locate all the information they need and join hundreds of thousands of teachers around the world in using WebQuests as a coherent entry to the world of Internet collaborations (www.webquest.sdsu.edu). Included on the WebQuest site are pages and pages of WebQuest examples sitting on the Internet.

ThinkQuest. ThinkQuest may be the most friendly website on website creation on the Internet. It hosts an international webpage competition sponsored by the Oracle Education Foundation, provides many of the important tools such as a blog maker, and maintains a library of award-winning websites created by students from around the globe. With the site, teachers can organize student teams to create websites on a free, protected, online platform for teachers and students. In the ThinkQuest project environment, students and teachers can create online projects on pages where they post text, photos, multimedia, message boards, and polls; collaborate with students in other countries; and find a collection of award-winning websites. Its friendliness allows students to create projects across all borders or to stay within the classroom. Teachers can integrate the quest projects into their daily curriculum and use the tool to promote 21st century skills (www.thinkquest.org).

EXAMPLES OF WEBQUEST INTERNET PROJECTS

Topic Hot List—compilation of key works or resources, ideally a webpage with hyperlinked bookmarks

Examples:

- China on the Net: http://www.kn.pacbell.com/wired/China/hotlist.html
- Crool Zone- School Safety Issues:
  http://www.kn.pacbell.com/wired/nonviolence/hotlist.htm
- Especially Español:
  http://www.kn.pacbell.com/wired/espanol/index.html#hotlist
- Science Hot List: http://sln.fi.edu/tfi/hotlists/space.html
- Space Hot List: http://sln.fi.edu/tfi/hotlists/space.html

Multimedia Scrapbook—links to photos, maps, stories, facts, quotes, audio clips, virtual tours, etc., to explore important aspects of a topic

Examples:

- Donner Online: http://www.kn.pacbell.com/wired/donner/index.html
- Exploring China:
  http://www.kn.pacbell.com/wired/China/scrapbook.html

Knowledge/Treasure Hunt—list of web pages and questions for gathering up-to-date information and knowledge

Examples:

- Banana Quest: http://www.biopoint.com/banana.html
- Black History—Past to Present:
  http://www.kn.pacbell.com/wired/BHM/bh_hunt_quiz.html
- Wonders of Science CyberBee: http://www.cyberbee.com/scihunt.html

http://www.mtwp.net/~jane_glass/wqsmore.html#

NEW TOOLS, NEW TECHNIQUES

Computer technology is renowned as a rapid generator of new tools for gathering information and communicating ideas. Every year new tools appear in abundance. From the days during World War II when a team of scientists and engineers at the University of Pennsylvania invented a general-purpose electronic digital calculator, know as ENIAC (Electronic Numerator, Integrator, Analyzer, and Computer), change was the name of the game. ENIAC was the first modern computer. It was made up of 18,000 vacuum tubes and weighed 30 tons. Just over a half century later, Apple advertises a superlight in-your-pocket phone, the first smartphone, which lets users manage their bank accounts, monitor gasoline costs, locate favorite haunts, find an apartment, track personal phone numbers, and on and on. Technologists have reduced once-giant, superheavy computers to a few ounces and a few inches that give information unheard of even a decade ago.

With today's children growing up speaking a new and different language, the international technology language, they understand learning-data and use them in new ways. To adapt to 21st century children's new language and learning patterns, schools too are exploring how new technologies can enrich instruction. In the 1960s, teachers in training were often required to take a course in audiovisual aids. They learned about slide projectors, tape recorders, and movie projectors. By the beginning of the 21st century, technology courses were highlighting the use of laptops and phones packed with dozens of digital applications. Today, special video projectors and interactive whiteboards, Web 2.0 open-source software coupled with notebook-sized computers that fit inside students' knapsacks, and parent portals are transforming classrooms from passive learning habitats to enriched environments where parents, students, and teachers collaborate not only within classroom walls but also beyond the borders of the school property.

PROMISES OF THE FUTURE

What new tools will further advance how teachers teach and how students learn in the next few decades? Major trends suggest that increased bandwidth will allow schools to host 3D video, complex educational games, and virtual realities to teach complex abstractions. Emerging terms such as *netbooks*, *push notifications*, *Ning*, *cloud-based technology*, and *nanotechnology* will join daily vocabulary lists as e-theories are turned to e-practices that have broadened e-classroom implications.

The transformation process is already intense. A recent study at Harvard Medical School (Kerfoot, Masser, & Hafler, 2005) indicates the interest in applying new technologies for the enhancement of instruction. In this project, students were asked to assess how two new technologies, plasma screens and broadband Internet access, assisted their problem-based learning groups.

A STUDY OF TECHNOLOGY IMPACT

Purpose: Computers with 50-inch, wall-mounted plasma screens and broadband Internet access were installed in all small group tutorial rooms at Harvard Medical School (Kerfoot et al., 2005). This study examines how the introduction of this educational technology affected the problem-based learning tutorials.

Method: A total of 37 tutorial groups, stratified by year of student, were observed at separate time points (autumn 2002, spring 2003) to document the patterns of use of the technologies. Based on these observations, end-of-course surveys were developed and distributed to students and tutors. Observational field notes and open-ended survey responses were qualitatively analyzed for themes.

Results: Using a 5-point rating scale, both students and tutors indicated that the technologies had a positive impact on their tutorials. In autumn 2002, plasma screens were used for an average of 17.8 and 22.1 minutes per 1-hour observation in Year 1 and 2 tutorials, respectively; in spring 2003, usage declined to 6.9 and 5.9 minutes, respectively. Resources used included Internet sites (54% total use time), PowerPoint presentations by students (22%), and course-specific postings (24%). Marked course-specific variation in usage was noted. Observational and survey data revealed that the technologies interrupted the flow of tutorial discussion. Students and tutors expressed concerns that the plasma screens might be altering the process of problem solving in the tutorials.

Conclusions: Both students and tutors reported that the introduction of computers and wall-mounted plasma screens had positively affected tutorials. Questions were raised about how this technology might alter tutorial dynamics. Further research will be needed to investigate these pedagogical concerns.

THE IMPACT OF SOCIAL NETWORKING

At a time when educational researchers are focusing more and more on how Internet tools and other technologies can create more effective learners, two practices stand out: Web 2.0 tools and social networks.

Social Networking

Who has not heard of Facebook, YouTube, and the many smaller social networks that are popular especially with young people? Early social networks evolved from computer networks. They took users beyond the collaborative work world into a new world where people are linked socially in communities. Some communities are purely social; others are learning communities for students and professionals. Unlike other e-tools, social networks are still developing as instructional tools. Groups of teachers with common interests such as early childhood development or special-needs children are forming professional learning communities. Some colleges and universities are experimenting with social networking among teachers who are interested in a common field of study and searching how to best sustain new practices.

Ning is a social networking tool that competes with large social sites like MySpace and Facebook. It allows teachers, administrators, professional developers, and others who want to create a social network related to a special common interest to build their own network. Eventually, some innovator may invent a classroom use for Ning so that students can build their own school, district, state, or international common-interest network.

Web 2.0

Web 2.0 is the second tool of high impact to educators who are integrating Internet tools into the classroom. Web 2.0 is a universal platform that facilitates the use of free open-source tools. Teachers do not have to worry about paying special fees to make use of the many options that Web 2.0 provides. As a result they are far more eager and ready to increase the collaborative communication, information sharing and idea generation that the Web 2.0 tools provide when using the Internet. In a few short years, Web 2.0 concepts have led to the development of web-based communities, hosted services, and applications such as social networking sites, video-sharing sites, wikis, and blogs. In the classroom, Web 2.0 tools have accelerated a multitude of different applications so that teachers can enrich student thinking and learning.

CONCLUDING THOUGHTS

E-tools have demonstrated their ability to help teachers enrich collaboration and communication in lessons and projects and enhance student learning in many ways. For the Internet tools that are the foundation of Internet activity, teachers can make a plan for the particular uses that fit their students. For those e-tools that play more of a supporting instructional role, brief descriptions and online tutorials will help teachers use these more specialized tools. Finally, as teachers take a look at future trends, they can see that the rapid flow of new e-learning tools will not abate soon. Instead, students of the 21st century will have the opportunity to expand the catalog of e-learning tools with which teachers can further enrich students' thinking and learning.

CHAPTER 4

Is Anyone Out There?

How to Communicate and Collaborate Beyond Classroom Borders

Internet-savvy students rely on the Internet to do their schoolwork.
—Pew/Internet Project

WHO HASN'T HEARD the phrase "guide on the side"? School consultants have tossed it around for decades. Yet why is it so uncommon to see a classroom with a teacher working *among* groups of students, observing and assessing, coaching and conferencing? Why is it still so common in this first quarter of the 21st century to see teachers, apparently oblivious to some of the strongest research yet obtained for what works to produce the highest achievement yields, for teachers to be standing in front of the classroom talking to students who are entrapped in "sit and git"? When will it be possible for students to shout, "Pour and store is no more"?

This chapter examines what teachers can do to work as the guide on the side, not only to promote face-to-face student collaboration, but also to encourage Internet collaborations beyond classroom walls. It discusses how teachers can design collaborative lessons and projects so students can communicate with peers through in-school networks or talk with new friends in other schools and states or around the globe.

In this chapter, teachers are guided through a backward-planning process and introduced to resources that make international projects a worthwhile approach to teaching and learning beyond classroom borders while addressing learning standards for rich 21st century content.

IT'S ABOUT TIME

When Christopher Columbus sailed the ocean blue in search of the new world, his sailors counted the many months needed to connect and

"It is a great idea," Mr. Lanahan declared. "I think we all agree that an Internet investigation would raise the ante on our projects. And we also agreed that the kids would love them. But Internet projects are not practical."

"I don't know what you mean by 'practical,'" responded Ms. McGuire, the English department chair.

"Where will we ever find schools across the ocean that want to work with us?" asked Mr. Lanahan.

"I don't see that as a problem," interjected Mr. Pink, the department's youngest member. "Lots of kids do it on their own. MySpace goes worldwide."

"MySpace is not for schools," countered Mr. Lanahan.

"Right," said Mr. Pink, holding his own against the senior department member. "But there are a good number of online sites where they will make the connections for you."

communicate with the new world's inhabitants. When the first transcontinental flight passengers flew from New York to San Francisco in the early 1950s, they scheduled a multiday trip. By the mid-1960s, the first astronauts were taking that same amount of time to reach and step onto the moon. Today, a student in Missoula, Montana, can press a keyboard letter and instantaneously talk with another student in Sydney, Australia, or Cape Town, South Africa.

PARTNERSHIPS BEYOND CLASSROOM BORDERS

The first task for teachers who want to make Internet connections beyond the borders of their classrooms with students in other schools, districts, states, or nations is to search for like-minded teachers. "How do I start this search?" a teacher must ask. "How do I search without spending gobs of money and long hours?" "Where do I find teachers who share my vision?"

Five easy steps shorten the process:

Step I: Target the big questions that you want to ask in your project

Step II: Make a systematic plan for securing connections outside your classroom borders

Step III: Identify established e-networks

Step IV: Prepare students with etiquette

Step V: Outline the project logistics in detail

Target the Big Questions

Before thinking about ways to find colleagues in other countries who may be willing and able to have their students collaborate across fields and continents, it is recommended that teachers first identify the big issues and key questions that underscore their own standards-based curriculum. Rather than continue to look at their course of study through a sequential series of textbook chapters, well-prepared teachers who know their course content can select big issues that are major concerns of the times and connected to their state's prescribed learning standards. The wider the scope of the issue, the easier it will be to build student interest and to find teachers and students in other schools with a similar interest. The goal is to hook all students together and keep them engaged in a study that is important to them even though they come from different cultures and may live on the other side of the globe.

With issue-oriented Internet collaborations, teachers have a second advantage: They can connect their students' studies to standards in a single discipline such as history or science or to multiple disciplines. To make interdisciplinary connections meaningful and relevant, teachers can construct content studies aligned with the various disciplinary standards. For instance, an Internet investigation that focuses on a significant health and disease question could challenge students to address standards in mathematics,

---

SIGNIFICANT ISSUES, MAJOR CONCERNS

- Poverty
- World Hunger
- Immigration
- Women's Rights
- Health and Disease
- Environmental Destruction (e.g., rain forest destruction, diseased water)
- Global Finance
- Religious Bias
- Racial Conflict
- Human Rights
- Senior Citizens
- Safety and Security
- Equal Education Access
- Stem Cell Research

biology, chemistry, sociology, and literature. A problem-based scenario that starts with a loosely structured problem describing various situations in which religious bias has led to war and ethnic cleansing can include standards of literature, political science, economics, mathematics, and art.

All teachers may not have the opportunity or the desire to create *interdisciplinary* studies or tackle the most significant issues that have a global reach. These teachers can create significant Internet studies outside their borders with a content area focus. In these cases, teachers can have the most success with Internet connections and collaborations by having students tackle significant issues inside a single discipline. Yes, there may be the global reach, but the intent is not global studies per se. The intent is the extended connections that the Internet facilitates whether with a classroom down the hall, in another school in the same district or across North America, or with a classroom in another nation.

Such projects are appropriate for any grade. Consider these examples that start with standards-connected launch questions about big ideas:

STANDARDS AND ISSUE SAMPLES

Course: Middle Grade Language Arts
Standard 14: Students will identify, analyze, and apply knowledge of the themes, structure, and elements of poetry and provide evidence from the text to support their understanding.
Issue: *American Themes:* What does the poetry of Robert Frost teach us about the important themes of American poetry?

Course: High School Language Arts
Standard 16: Myth, Traditional Narrative, and Classical Literature. Students will identify, analyze, and apply knowledge of the themes, structure, and elements of myths, traditional narratives, and classical literature and provide evidence from the text to support their understanding.
Issue: *The Heroes Speak:* Compare how modern TV heroes speak to us and carry forward the messages of ancient Greece's tragic heroes.

Course: High School Technology and Engineering
Standard 3: Explain engineering control volume concepts as applied to a domestic water system. Does the amount of water entering a residence equal the amount of water leaving a residence?
Issue: *Water Conservation:* Predict what would happen if a city established volume controls in order to better conserve its water supply in times of drought.

By identifying big issues with significant launch questions as the start of a collaborative Internet study, teachers who are novices to Internet teaching, especially when they take the project beyond their own school walls or plan an interdisciplinary study, jump-start their students' connection-making thought patterns and make the project more likely to succeed. When the issue is a global one, it is more likely that students in potential partner schools will have a stronger interest in participating. Clarity on preferred issues will also allow teachers in search of partner schools to communicate with more confidence. It is also advantageous when partner teachers plan what it is they want from each other so that potential partners are clear on the project's goals as it relates to their own students' learning goals. With Skype and other VOIP networks, teachers across borders need only their minicams and headsets to talk with each other with no fees for as long as they want. (Go to Skype online for the discussion of inexpensive VOIP hardware.) Some "help sites" such as E-Pals or GlobalKidsNet contend that students from different cultures find their own ways to overcome language barriers. Other sites provide free translation services. Where VOIP networks don't work, email is a worthy substitute. In any case, many teachers in schools that are continents apart manage to overcome the concerns and issues involved with joining students in collaborations across great distances. Where there is a will, there is a way.

Make a Backward Plan

Very few teachers have the time to take on a collaborative project with other schools that does not fit in both teachers' curriculum goals and standards. Thus, it is important that teachers who are hoping to launch a collaborative Internet study initiate a backward plan that will carry them forward to clear, standards-based outcomes. Step II in the "getting ready" process, therefore, starts with the learning standards that define what students will know and do as a result of the proposed collaboration.

In effect, beyond-the-borders teachers will use an *understanding by design* process. They will start their planning by identifying the projects' results (Wiggins & McTighe, 2005). After teachers know how the project will line up with the standards, they will think about how they will judge whether students have attained the desired results and then can "guesstimate" the classroom time that the collaboration will take and what specific products will tell them that their students have accomplished the proposed goals and answered the launch questions (see Chapter 5 for a more explicit exposition of the backward-planning model). With these final thoughts answered first, interested teachers can design the flow of the project. This design will include checking and using prior knowledge during the first days of the project, developing relevant background knowledge, firming expectations for cross-cultural etiquette, providing small-group and individual coaching and ensuring that students reflect on what they learned, how they used their thinking skills, and how they collaborated with their teammates and their new friends in other lands. Teachers cannot forget to plan how they will use formative assessment of the standards involved with the project and how they will make the summative assessment. When they view this task as a developmental opportunity, rather than as a mathematical exercise designed to produce a precise and accurate grade, they will find themselves constructing the type of feedback that is most helpful for students.

Use Existing Resources to Locate Possible Internet Partners

The place to start the actual search for Internet school partners is the Internet. Using the web for Step III is a good idea for two reasons. First, it keeps the search for collaborators in the teachers' hands. It doesn't require that a school have a specially paid technology specialist. The search is as easy as the use of a free search engine such as Firefox or Google to seek out schools in the ever-expanding universe of Internet-connected schools. Online sites are ready with information that will facilitate making these connections, locally, nationally, or globally. Second, Internet use saves time in finding organizations that promote Internet connections outside school borders and provide coaching and other resources. After two or three clicks, teachers can be at any of the sites that will help them with a connection to a possible partner school.

The initial stage of searching for partners in a multischool collaboration requires the most patience. Once teachers locate willing partners, they will have the contact set for many years. However, teachers must do the first search-work to find and select the best possible partner schools. These criteria will make the start of the search smoother, faster, and simpler.

- Assuming that their own district has no objections, teachers' first criterion for a partner school is the quality of its Internet access. Although individual students may have such access, it is important for safety reasons that projects go through the school with a careful checkup of the potential partner schools safety and security practices

ONLINE SCHOOL NETWORKS FOR GLOBAL INVESTIGATIONS

1. Global School Network
2. Europa Twinning Network (Europe)
3. Calibrate
4. Community Learning Network (Canada)
5. World Kids Network
6. School Network Africa
7. World Links Organization
8. The Global Teenager Project
9. The Infundo Project
10. The World Bank
11. UNESCO
12. National School Network
13. Europa Network
14. European Commission (Finland)
15. Greek School Network
16. AT and T Education Network
17. GLOBE (environment)
18. Ed.Gov (international collaborations)
19. iEARN USA
20. Department of Defense Schools
21. The Heifer Project
22. People to People International's School and Classroom Program
23. Sister Cities International/Sister Schools
24. International Studies for Indiana Schools
25. UNICET Voices of Youth Program
26. Taking IT Global
27. The Global School Net
28. Edutopia

- The second criterion is that administrators in potential partner districts or schools approve their students' participation. Policies in these schools may also require parental permission.
- The third criterion requires that the teachers in the partner classrooms understand what is involved and what the collaboration will require from the students in each school. Just as is the case in in-school teaming, collaborative pre-talk is essential.

Use-Established Online Networks

Many teachers start the partner-school search by going to websites that identify existing national and international school networks. These sites provide leads to Internet-linked networks of schools in many states and countries. In addition, teachers can browse other search engines to identify schools in the United States that have advanced Internet capabilities or may have advice and connections to international schools. By looking under the search phrase *Internet school networks*, teachers will find U.S. districts that have posted their Internet rules and etiquette or announce network membership. Two of the most helpful starter networks to browse are iEARN (http://iearn.org/) and kidsnet (http://www.kidsnet.org).

A Contact Protocol. Teachers interested in finding international partners for an Internet project can email the potential district or school with a letter of query. When teachers are in districts that do not allow for collaborations with out-of-district partners, but do allow partnering with schools in their own or nearby districts, teachers should contact a potential partner district's chief academic officer or chief technology officer. They can check the willingness to collaborate and identify potential schools and teachers by email address. Follow-up email to the school's principal and possible teachers will describe the project and its expectations. Follow-up emails may also share the launch teacher's plan.

In several of the model collaborations outlined in this book, sample letters are provided. Teachers may adapt these for contacting potential school partners. These letters, however, only lead to the first conversations. It may take many emails to firm up the final agreement.

When two teachers agree on partnering their students for Internet collaboration, they compose a simple letter of agreement. This letter would best contain the following points:

- Who is involved (school names, teacher names, grade, students)
- Parent permissions (if required by school policy)
- What electronic tools students will use
- What global issue students will discuss
- What the teacher's role is
- Timelines for the project
- Guidelines and etiquette
- Other expectations

Over and above the basic protocol, teachers can take advantage of practical suggestions for online collaborations that engage students from diverse cultures.

Online Common Sense. Parents and teachers have rightful concerns when students get on the Internet. If a school does not have set policies and procedures that prevent Internet mishaps or abuses, teachers will have to lay the appropriate groundwork. Most importantly, they must prepare their students to prevent problems related to intellectual property rights and predator prevention.

Safety and Security. Horror stories about predators on the Internet hit the news daily. One TV network features a weekly show dedicated to catching predators. In spite of school policies, teacher admonitions, or parent supervision, some students continue to put themselves at risk. The battle is unending, but it is necessary protection if students are going to reap the advantages of learning online and meeting new friends in new countries.

Before teachers start with Internet collaborations, they should attend to the following safeguards:

- What are the school district's policies and practices regarding student projects on the Internet? At a minimum, policies should designate which search engines are permitted for student use, what Internet-use practices are recommended and which are frowned upon, and what parents must know about their role.
- If a district does not have policies in place, teachers have two choices. First, they can delay the start of the Internet investigation and advocate with administration and the school board for policies. Or they can go ahead with the project, but carefully work with students to prepare them to defend themselves.

Safety Check. The Media Awareness Network (http://www.media-awareness.ca) provides a number of free online game tutorials for younger students such as "Privacy Playground," "Cyber Sense and Nonsense," and "Jo Cool or Jo Fool." In addition, it licenses "Reality Check," an interactive tool to teach high school students how to evaluate online information.

All these tools help teachers build their students' understanding that ultimately they are the ones most responsible for policing their own safety and security online.

TIPS FOR TEACHERS FACILITATING
INTERNATIONAL INTERNET PROJECTS

1. Learn the rudiments of the partner school's language. Even if you have selected a school in which teachers and students speak some English, as a courtesy, study the basics of their first language. E-Pals is a website that does provide students' translation of English into seven languages. Other sites offer translations for adults. In the same vein, U.S. teachers need to prepare their students for metric conversions. Teachers and students can go to www.sciencemadesimple.com for an easy-to-use converter.

2. Know where the partner school is located. The National Geographic site will show students the location of the partner school. With that "global" picture, teachers can enrich the learning experience by spending time to learn about the region's geography, economy, history, and the like. Going a step beyond, teachers can take extra time during the first phase of learning in an investigation so that students can chat with students in another land about these topics.

3. After teachers have received the districts' OK to proceed with an international investigation, they will contact the partner teacher. Teachers should spend several weeks communicating via email to learn as much as possible about each other's schools, communities, and students.

4. Take additional time to investigate the cultural uniqueness of the partner school. Encourage students throughout the project to do this as well. A large Venn diagram on the class bulletin board can highlight the cultural similarities and differences found by the students. Be especially aware of any religious differences and values. Students may want to discuss such differences. Encourage them to do so, but with respect.

No Matter What. Teachers can never take too many precautions when it comes to online safety. It matters little what the school policies are or what other precaution the teachers take if they do not bring parents into the loop. No matter what, it is imperative that teachers keep constant communication with parents, soliciting their support and emphasizing their responsibility to look out for their children online. Teachers should not only inform parents of the general practices and policies regarding students' Internet use in the classroom and outside, but also provide information about every project.

TIPS FOR TEACHERS FACILITATING
INTERNATIONAL INTERNET PROJECTS *(continued)*

5. Investigate similarities of popular culture between the two countries. Encourage students to go beyond the superficial similarities (e.g., Chicago, guns and Dillinger, Mickey Mouse, McDonald's) to discuss significant cultural issues.
6. Set up agreements for technology use between the two schools and monitor how well students abide by these rules. Some schools have to pay for time spent online or to be a consortium member. This means they may have to use less email. Honor the needs.
7. Connect to an embassy website for the country of the partner school. This site will keep you and the students up to date on the news of the day from the partner country.
8. Watch the time. Remember that the schools are in different time zones and perhaps hemispheres. Use www.kidlink.org for a dual clock, holiday schedules, and so on. Remember also that many countries will use a 24-hour clock and write day, month, and year in that order. Encourage students to write out the words and numbers of dates rather than use the typical U.S. month, day, and year sequence.
9. Encourage everyone to identify him- or herself during initial introductions as male or female.
10. Encourage students to keep language simple. Use short words, simple sentences, and literal phrases. Avoid big words that need a dictionary, slang, or abbreviations.

Adapted from ed.gov's guide to collaborations on the Internet
(www2.ed.gov/teachers/how/tech/international/index.html)

Prevent Plagiarism. For students who want to plagiarize, plagiarism is much easier online than it ever was off-line. That ease changes what teachers must do to prevent plagiarism in all aspects of a project. To better prevent online plagiarism, teachers can turn to new Internet tools as their aide. In addition, teachers can help themselves by communicating more forcefully what uses of Internet material (or any print material) are acceptable and which are unethical.

The first line of defense is for teachers to let students know they will be using online resources or software to check for plagiarism. With this

A SAMPLE NOTICE

We, _____, a ____ grade teacher at _____
School in _____, and_____, a _____grade
teacher at _____ School in _____, agree that our
students listed by name on the attached page will participate in the Internet
project _____.

This project will focus on the issue of _____. Students may
communicate with each other as long as they follow the policies of our schools
for student-to-student conversations (attached).

Teachers will supervise the students' correspondence and communicate
with each other to uphold academic standards and electronic etiquette.
Students in the classes will develop an agreement on the etiquette they will
follow. Look for your child to bring home that agreement within the next week. It
will ask you to discuss its points with you and to follow the guidelines at home as
well as at school when completing this project.

This project will take place between _____ and _____ with contact
on a _____ basis. All students are expected to make email responses to the
sender in the project within one week of reception.

warning, teachers can add the consequences of those who violate the
principles and practices. Some secondary teachers require students to do
their own checking prior to sharing their final work with the teacher or
other audiences, certifying that they have checked for compliance.

- www.turnitinsafely.com
- www.easyrater.com (a free site)
- www.efufy.com

In addition to these check sites, teachers can turn to www.plagarism.
org, a free site that presents information on when students need to cite
sources, how to cite sources, and why. Teachers use the site to prepare students. Better yet, with older students, they can assign students to study the
information themselves.

The most effective prevention tool, however, is the assignments that
follow mini-lessons on plagiarism. It is important that teachers construct
projects that don't invite students to plagiarize. When students are drawing

information from Internet sites, teachers must insist on 100% citation use as well as readiness to explain how they avoided mere copying. Open discussions on this topic will help students develop the clarity and integrity to avoid taking short cuts with another author's ideas.

Prepare Students' E-Netiquette

To help students better understand e-netiquette, teachers can send students to World Kids Network (www.worldkids.net). It provides advice for students of all ages on how to use email, blogs, chat rooms, bulletin boards, and other Internet tools safely. Teachers can enhance the pages of this site by holding structured discussions that encourage students to take care with Internet use inside and outside the classroom. By using such graphic organizers as the web, the newspaper grid, or the agree/disagree chart, students can gather information from the site as preparation for small- or large-group discussions about caring for themselves online. Such tools become handy devices for students to share with their parents what they are learning and to engage parents in understanding their role in e-netiquette.

Most school districts have adopted policies and provided procedures and forms for student use of the Internet. If a school needs to set such a policy or add the forms, administrators can use Internet resources such as the Virginia Department of Education, Division of Technology, site.

In the model projects presented in this book, teachers will find samples of letters to parents. The parents' role is to supervise Internet use outside the classroom. The letter home is the minimum teachers should do when engaging students in an Internet investigation. The letter not only informs the parents of an exciting learning project, but also alerts them to the responsibility for monitoring Internet use at home.

If teachers choose, they can also inform parents how to access the guidelines from the World Kids Network or provide parents with a booklet outlining guidelines. Going a step beyond, teachers can conduct workshops for parents. Examples of parent workshops on Internet etiquette are available from organizations such as the Media Awareness Network, Netsmartz Kids, Children's International Network, and the Global School Network.

As new tools are developed for student use of the Internet, teachers can set as a selection criterion that the new e-tool or e-site has built in the most cutting-edge controls. These should provide teachers with the means to set permissions and retain absolute control over who is allowed access to the site and how students use the tool or site to talk with others online.

Plan Logistics to Avoid Problems

When launching Internet collaborations, teachers may encounter three logistical problems. First, scheduling problems can frustrate students who are not familiar with time zone and hemisphere time differences. Second, teachers must align project time with the other work in their classrooms. Third, in schools with limited computer stations, teachers may encounter difficulties with computer availability.

1. Because email will provide the most frequent means of contact, students need to remember which time zones and hemispheres are different for each school. It matters little when they send their messages to countries in different time zones and hemispheres. However, if they do want their peers to receive messages for early morning, students will have to watch the clock.
2. A second important logistical element is the teachers' decision for integrating Internet collaborations into the daily schedule. The first issue with the daily schedule is how much time to allow for the Internet connection.
   a. In the elementary grades, there are the widest options.
      i. Integrate the project into the daily schedule dedicating 30 minutes to 1 hour per day to 3 to 5 hours per week.
      ii. Set aside a 4-week unit or allocate more hours per day.
   b. In the middle and upper grades the options are more restricted. Upper grade teachers can
      i.   Schedule project work daily for the entire class period for 4–6 weeks.
      ii. Schedule two days per week for the entire class period for 10–12 weeks.
      iii. Schedule 1 day per week of the entire class period for 10–12 weeks plus out-of-class assignments. Allow 5 days in the final weeks for reports to the class.
3. Limited computer stations with Internet capability can compound the access problem. The ideal scenario provides one station for every two students. One station for three students is a livable adjustment. When this 1:2 or 1:3 ratio is not possible, either in the classroom or a computer lab, teachers will have to "stretch out" the time for the project or allow more "homework" time when students can work on the project out of class. The ultimate solution, which is coming closer every day, is for schools that are replacing

computers or buying new stations to turn to netbooks for students. These small basic computers and new versions that promise to be tiny enough to carry in a pocket allow every student to have a computer with Internet capability.

RESOURCES FOR GLOBAL CONNECTIONS

In addition to the sites listed below of organizations that will help teachers make school-to-school contacts, there are a host of other resources teachers can use to help them connect their students with students at home and around the world. Sites provide help with project lesson plans, forums, chat rooms, expert interviews, case studies, and lots of data. Teachers may use their browsers to identify the addresses for these sites and others related to them.

1. **World Wise Schools (http://www.peacecorps.gov/wws/).** This great site matches Peace Corps volunteers in the field with teachers. Teachers can sign up for a 2-year conversation based on the volunteer's direct experience in a country. World Wide Schools provides a handbook of ideas that makes the exchange rich and informative.
2. **Worldwide Global Concerns Project (http://orgs.tigweb.org/concern-worldwide-global-concerns-project).** Schools can sign up for print and online information about a critical global topic. Discussions focus on multiple points of view and provide up-to-date information for teachers and students. Projects emphasize critical thinking and debate.
3. **Human Rights Resource Center (http://www.hrusa.org/)** provides K–12 online units with a student-centered classroom focus. Many resources are provided on a wide range of current issues.

For the specific collaboration projects in this book, the following e-sites provide additional help as teachers plan collaborations on the Internet around significant issues:

A. **Poverty**
Population in Perspective: http://populationinperspective.org/
KIDS Can Make a Difference:
http://www.kidscanmakeadifference.org/

B. **Education**
   UNICEF Voices of Youth Program: http://www.unicef.org/voy/
   Beyond the Fire: http://www.itvs.org/beyondthefire/
   Fire and Ice: http://www.elluminate.com/fire_ice
   E-Pals: http://E-pals.com
C. **Global Warming**
   The Learning Web: http://www.thelearningweb.net/
   GLOBE: http://www.globe.gov/
   Global Warming 101: http://video.nationalgeographic.com/
      video/player/environment/global-warming-environment/
      global-warming-101.html
D. **Health**
   YouThink: http://youthink.worldbank.org/issues/education/
   Feeding Minds, Fighting Hunger:
      http://www.feedingminds.org/
E. **Multiple Issues**
   It's Your World: http://info.iiepassport.org/studyabroadguide/
   ICONS Project: http://www.icons.umd.edu/
   VIDEA Global Citizens:
      http://www.videa.ca/global/citizen.html
   UN Works: http://www.un.org/works/
   The CyberSchoolbus: http://cyberschoolbus.un.org/
   The Patel Center: http://patelcenter.usf.edu/
   Outreach World: http://www.outreachworld.org/

CONCLUDING THOUGHTS

Finding school and teacher partners willing to share in Internet collaboration outside classroom borders can prove daunting. However, if teachers
take a no-frills approach by using the Internet itself to locate the many
free sites that are related to Internet collaborations, they will find the best
and fastest answers. If teachers plan carefully before they go in search of
possible national and international partners, and if they take advantage
of the many existing global school networks, they can make a quick and
relatively painless start. As they proceed in the initial conversations with
possible partners, teachers can avoid future headaches by obtaining formal
written agreements and by attending to safety and scheduling issues. By
recalling that the first outside-the-walls project is like any new endeavor,
teachers can look to the future knowing that the first time is the most challenging and time consuming.

CHAPTER 5

Last Things First

Putting Backward Planning to Work

Enduring understandings go beyond discrete facts or skills to focus
on larger concepts, principles and processes.

— Jay McTighe

IN ARTHUR MILLER'S play *Death of a Salesman*, Biff tries to turn Willy
Loman's life around. Willy, a longtime salesman, had lost his touch. His
life was going backward.

Willy's backward walk took him off the track he wanted to follow.
The backward-planning-design process, an educational best practice articulated by Wiggins and McTighe in *Understanding by Design* (2005), encourages teachers to turn their thinking around. Instead of the normal
sequence of events that they were trained to follow when planning a lesson, going forward piece by piece from the beginning of the lesson to its
end, this approach asks teachers to think in reverse. The backward design
asks them to walk backward on purpose by starting with the outcomes
or results they want to see from a lesson or project. Like a jockey who is
told that he or she will have to run the Preakness from the finish line back
to the starting gate or a writer whose publisher tells him or her to submit
the last chapter first, most teachers find the challenge to design lessons
backward a formidable task. Walking backward is not easy to do.

Backward design focuses on outcomes. It encourages teacher designers
to take a close look at the results they want to see from a lesson or project.
What do those results look like? What precisely will the students know
about the drama they are going to read or the experiment they are going to
conduct? What precisely will they be able to do after they put their knowledge to use, transfer new ideas, or practice a skill?

Outcomes take on special significance when teachers have to think
about the transfer of knowledge. More and more, teachers are expected to

produce students who can show that they can transfer. If they are learning to add whole numbers, can they show that skill in a carpentry class? In a meal they are cooking? In how they measure chemicals? If students learn the lessons of the importance of family love from a novel they read, will they be able to transfer that learning to their daily lives? If students discuss the importance of voting for maintaining a strong democracy, will this carry into their own habits?

To increase the odds that outcomes are the focus of learning designs that strengthen collaboration, the backward-lesson-design approach starts "at the end" of the planned lesson, be it for a class period, five class periods, or a multiweek unit. With the backward format, the teacher thinks backward from the answer to a launch question: "What do I want my students to know and do when the lesson is over?" "Do I want them to develop their cooperative skills so I can see those skills applied in my classroom lessons or in a project done with peers?"

This design identifies what students will know and do as a result of the organized instruction. It will show that students *know* the cooperative roles and guidelines. More than that, if the transfer has been planned for, the teacher will be able to observe students performing the role in team tasks. He or she will see students behaving according to the guidelines and be able to mark his or her observations on a checklist or rubric.

In their backward planning, after establishing and identifying the answer to a launch question such as "How well will students show collaborative behaviors in their technology teams?" and matching the response with standards, teachers prepare the outcomes and the assessment tools they will use. They design tests, rubrics, or checklists that will guide students through their collaborative learning tasks. Because they know what the collaborative behaviors look and sound like, they know they must design the lesson with those behaviors as the expected outcomes. For instance, if they select the DOVE guidelines as the behavior pattern they want to see, they will not only teach the guidelines, but will also prepare the assessment tool that will help the students know they are accountable for demonstrating the behaviors each day.

Only after they are clear on the outcomes and measures do teachers select the instructional strategies they will use to help students reach desired outcomes. On the first day of the lesson, after presenting information telling students what they will be expected to know and to do as a result of their learning experiences, teachers help students make informed choices about individual learning goals.

DOVE GUIDELINES:
MODEL GUIDELINES FOR COOPERATIVE GROUPS

D = Delay judgment. Listen to the full explanation of an idea.

O = Opt for the Original. Seek many different ideas and different takes on one idea.

V = A Vast number of ideas is helpful. Explore multiple points of view.

E = Expand by piggybacking on others' ideas. Make others' ideas larger, deeper, more robust by adding your best thinking.

THE DOVE RUBRIC

In a cooperative lab group, to what degree does the student:

Delay Judgment

/ ————— / ————— / ————— /
   Not at all   Sometimes   Regularly   Habitually

Opt for the Original

/ ————— / ————— / ————— /
   Not at all   Sometimes   Regularly   Habitually

Give Multiple Ideas

/ ————— / ————— / ————— /
   Not at all   Sometimes   Regularly   Habitually

Expand by Piggybacking

/ ————— / ————— / ————— /
   Not at all   Sometimes   Regularly   Habitually

Adapted from Bellanca & Fogarty, 1991

Ms. Swartz: Yesterday, I told you about the Internet project I am planning for this quarter. I saw lots of eyes light up. This will be different from the way I usually ask you to work.

You are going to be collecting ideas and opinions from students in different countries all over the world. Each of you will be dealing with a different country and we will be putting what you learn together.

Sheila: That sounds complicated. Can't we just talk to them?

Ms. Swartz: You could, but if that is all you do, you won't be learning very much that is really important.

Annabelle: Why are we doing this?

Ms. Swartz: Good question. I like "why?" questions best. You just got me ready to talk about the purpose of this project. So take a look here at this chart. To get everyone started on an equal footing, we will start by discussing these objectives. They show what you will have to understand at the end. It also shows you what is most important to understand and what is just nice to know. So, let's start at the back end and talk about what I want you to learn. That will make the project a lot easier.

THE END IS THE BEGINNING

Novice gardeners often start the growing season with a packet of seed or a potted plant. They go out into the garden, find an empty square of bare earth, turn the ground, and bury the seed. Each year they repeat these steps, then wait for the seedlings to sprout, bloom, and attract bees. This seems a sensible sequence. Like the "do-re-mi" lyrics from *The Sound of Music*, these gardeners start at the beginning and follow the same steps to the end before "ti" takes them back to the start the next year.

In most classrooms, students follow a similar start-to-finish pattern. This is what McTighe and Wiggins imply is a "forward lesson" format. It marches the class from start to finish in a prescribed time. The teacher starts each lesson by telling students what they are going to learn in a lesson. A sequence of tasks follows. If the lesson is in the direct-instruction model, the teacher walks students through a sequence of steps, varying the order to fit the situation. At the end, students take a final exam. In between, students run the lesson's course, gathering bits and pieces of information, as the teacher checks for understanding at various spots. In many lessons in the lower grades, the teacher talks; the students listen, memorize facts and figures and fill in work sheets. After guided practice to reinforce the concept or skills, the teacher assigns homework as independent practice or gives the final test. In the upper grades most teachers lecture about a topic and end with a final test to see who is ranked first, second, or third. Sometimes, upper-grade teachers may add a lab to the lesson. For instance, in biology, students will have a special class period called "lab" two periods per week added to the lecture periods. In lab, the teachers will show students how to find the parts of a flower or worm. The students will dissect the flower or worm and label the parts to match a diagram. They may have a lab practicum to check that they can identify the parts. In the end, the students will take a final exam for the total lesson that sometimes includes what they saw during the dissection.

In a growing number of 21st century classrooms, teachers take an alternative path. If they are doing a project, especially an interdisciplinary project or one that integrates 21st century skill instruction with content, it is advantageous to replace the traditional start-to-finish lesson design with a backward format. These teachers are more like the gardeners who start the spring planting by sketching a design that shows what the mature garden will look like at harvest time. Over time, the design may become more complex, but the start of any year's garden is a map that will dictate which results the gardener will reap in which location. The gardeners think about past experience with color, texture, height, shape, light needs, water needs, bloom schedule, and other factors. These will dictate what plant goes where, what watering and fertilizer happens when, and how the garden will grow. They do not cast seeds willy-nilly into the wind. They plan which silver bells will blossom in which row. Having carefully considered many options, often using a sketchpad or large map of the garden to make

Figure 5.1. Contrasting Lesson Design Formats

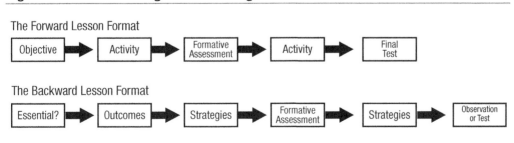

their determinations, they know what to expect each month. In short, these gardeners picture the end result they want before they plant their first seed in the ground.

Many business executives employ a similar backward-thinking process. In a recent conversation among educators and business leaders on the Illinois Consortium for 21st Century Skills Board of Directors, a seasoned school administrator asked this question: "With the heavy requirements for accountability for student outcomes emerging in this state, it is easy to see how we can determine outcomes for basic skills, especially in reading and mathematics. However, for 21st century skills, there are few assessment tools for identifying outcomes for such things as critical thinking or collaborating. There certainly is a dearth of quantitative measures to tell us when students have produced these outcomes. How do you do it in the business world?"

The answers from several of the executives were similar. First, they agreed on using the essential critical thinking skill of "analysis" as their exemplar. "Everyone in my bank," stated a bank president, "needs to develop and use analytic thinking skills. This doesn't mean they have to define it. It means they have to show they can analyze their work: a business plan, a balance sheet, a portfolio, and so on. They have to defend their analysis when they are asking for money. Since I have done all those things myself, I know what degree of skill is needed and whether a person is using that skill well. I have a checklist in my head."

A telecommunications consultant added her thoughts. "I have to analyze documents and interactions every day. It is the most important skill in my job. I have checklists that guide my analysis of a task or a product. These tell me how well I did and remind me what to do differently. I guess you would say that these experiences are my tests. 'Can I do what I am supposed to do?'"

A third executive, the director of a large not-for-profit arts agency, added that when analysis is a key tool for her staff, she watches not only how they analyze but what results come from the analysis. Did they have the data to accept or reject an application? If so, how did they interpret that data? Were the interpretations logical? Based on data? Biased? "In the end," she said, "I look to see how well they can take a task apart and put the pieces back together. What was the result? The result is what matters."

These responses from the business world, the world that schools are preparing students to enter, pointed out several keys that apply to backward lesson design. First, assessment is both formative and summative.

Second, the most common assessments do not have to be quantitative, but the person doing the assessment of thinking has to know what cognitive behaviors or other results to look for. Third, the end result is more important than the pathway to that result.

BACKWARD DESIGN: A VALUABLE TOOL FOR TEACHERS

The reverse-planning concept enables teachers to be more thoughtful about all aspects of instruction. They can more easily make a systematic lesson plan or a project plan that will guide students in their learning quests toward mastery of a skill such as analysis or deeper understanding of a concept, such as fractions. Backward design is especially appropriate in classrooms where teachers are investigating how they can best integrate successful instruction of 21st century skills within a curriculum already bursting at the seams with an overabundance and often increasing amount of content knowledge.

BACKWARD DESIGN: A VALUABLE HELP FOR STUDENTS

The backward- or reverse-design process also has advantages for the students. First, this process brings an end to the random "what's on the test" guessing game in which scarce time that students need for systematic study and deep understanding of content is given over to off-center concerns about the superficial elements of the course content. It is hard for many students to distinguish the most important concepts when they are left to guess about the expected results of a lesson.

Every lesson in which students waste time trying to guess what questions to study, not knowing beforehand what will be on their final exam, detracts from a rich or a rigorous learning experience. In the 21st century, effective teachers must help students understand the essence of what they are required to study by distinguishing key concepts from supporting facts and sub-ideas. Yes, these teachers will be saying, "I am going to help you learn for the test by telling you that I am teaching to the core *concepts* that will be on the test." This style of teaching to the test is different from what is usually meant by that term. "I am posting the road signs that key you to the most important stops on a family trip," the backward-design teacher says. "From those, we will work together to see what material will best help you enjoy those stops."

When working with a backward design, teachers can take the opportunity to produce understandings and improve skills that are always forecast at the lesson's start. They also can more easily integrate the plethora of 21st century skills into content in rigorous and rich lessons. Thus, rather than cram critical thinking, innovation, and collaboration and communication activities into a tightly scheduled lesson, they can design the lesson so that the goals are integrated.

In the *Understanding by Design* model, teachers begin by deciding what will be most important for students to understand and do as a result of the lesson. The students' final understandings will align with the class's content standards; the skills will align with high-effects strategies that strengthen students' collaborative and critical thinking skills and the results planned from the start will answer significant questions about the content. These teachers can select the instructional strategies they will use to accomplish these predicted outcomes and move students to the outcomes as predicted.

When initiating a mindful, collaborative-learning lesson using this design process, teachers can prevent students from becoming mired in details and procedures, clicks and links. By focusing students' attention from the beginning on what they will have to show they understand and can do as the final result of their collaborative efforts, teachers raise the stakes that all students will achieve *significant* outcomes. When students all know what they must learn from their studies before they start, teachers level the playing field. Success does not depend on the ability to guess what is important or to work by trial and error. Like a parent who announces the destination and reasons for a long car trip as the family loads the car, teachers can set up a roadmap that has a clear end in mind: "We are *all* going over the river and through the woods to your grandmother's house for Thanksgiving dinner."

Teachers who want to show students where they are traveling, what path they are taking, and why they are taking the trip take advantage of providing early in a lesson the signposts that reinforce the direction they are taking to the final result. In this regard, rubrics and other assessment tools are presented during the first days of the unit or project. These tools are like GPS maps that a driver turns on at the beginning of a trip. Teachers who adopt the backward-planning model use the maps to show students where they are going and the roads they will take to "Grandma's house." They share their assessment tools so that their students will understand those key concepts and principles that McTighe and Wiggins call "enduring."

ENRICHING LESSONS WITH COLLABORATION

Understanding by Design lessons are strengthened when teachers enrich the lessons with a collaborative overlay. Rather than asking students to work alone, teachers design these lessons or projects with teamwork in mind. The reasons are clear. Research studies have consistently shown that structured collaboration produces higher achievement results than learning tasks in which students work alone (Johnson, Johnson, & Smith, 2007). Not only does structured collaboration in a lesson heighten the chances of raised achievement results, it provides 21st century teachers with the opportunity to teach the collaborative skills that the work world is demanding. With the well-documented methods of cooperative learning so readily available, teachers can teach collaborative skills simultaneously with content and critical thinking. Many birds are slain with a single stone.

Most students in this millennial age prefer working together. The tools to make that task more effective come from the well-established cooperative-learning tool kit. To start, teachers need only set "collaboration" in place as the expected work method. As in business and industry, teachers, the managers of instruction, can select the collaborative method most appropriate for a task with the knowledge that they are increasing the effects on learning in an environment that reinforces strong relationships among the students. While this interactive mode might not "fit" the learning style of every student, it does fit the task needs of a collaborative project. As students will discover when they arrive at the adult work world, collaboration is an expected work mode. It is not likely that students will be given a choice to work in their own individualistic styles when they arrive in the workplace.

After considering the achievement research, the existence of proven instructional tools, and the increasing use of collaborative groups in the workplace, it only seems sensible and practical that 21st century teachers will take advantage of collaboration as an essential design element in their lessons.

The next generation is not being adequately prepared for the jobs it will inherit. . . . Workforce entrants are caught between an educational system that teaches—and measures—one set of skills and a rapidly evolving workplace that demands another.

Susan Stewart, "Will You Want to Hire Your Own Kids? (Will Anybody Else?)," 2009, p. 1

WHAT DOES AN UNDERSTANDING BY DESIGN COLLABORATIVE LESSON PLAN LOOK LIKE?

Lesson Title: The Illinois Constitution
Level of Difficulty: medium
Grade: 7 or 8
Schedule: May 1–12

Launch Question: What are the major impacts of the Illinois Constitution on our daily lives?

Outcomes:

1. Students will show an understanding of how the constitution organizes and affects state government.
2. Students will show an understanding of their rights and responsibilities as Illinois citizens.
3. Students will make a collaborative visual presentation of their analysis of the constitution in respect to its effect on their rights and responsibilities.
4. Students will provide an assessment of their improved knowledge, critical thinking, and collaborations during their examination of the Illinois Constitution.

Evidence:

1. A knowledge test regarding the Illinois Constitution
2. An individual essay discussing citizen rights and responsibilities provided by the Illinois Constitution. Rubric to show application of grammar standard, expository organization standard, and personal example use.
3. Rubric to assess team CMap of Constitution
4. Rubric to assess analysis of Constitution
5. Rubric to assess collaboration

As this sample lesson illustrates, teachers can teach the required content, the Illinois Constitution, simultaneously with critical thinking, collaboration, and communication. The focus is on the Constitution and its applications to the students' rights and responsibilities. However, instead of just asking students to read and explain the meaning of the sections in the Constitution or memorize key information on the final test, the teacher uses a backward design to increase the likelihood that the students will take away not only their understandings, but also the sharpened skills. This carefully calibrated design suggests that the "how" of teaching has a

---

WHAT DOES AN UNDERSTANDING BY DESIGN COLLABORATIVE LESSON PLAN LOOK LIKE? *(continued)*

Strategies:

1. KWL as advance organizer: What do you know about your rights and responsibilities under the Illinois Constitution? Think-pair-share.
2. Jigsaw intro: Review of rubrics, tasks, and timelines. Assignment of teams. Team rubric review.
3. Jigsaw reading with CMap: The Illinois Constitution.
4. Essay assignment on rights under the Constitution: Content rubric review.
5. Discussion of analysis: Team jigsaw analysis.
6. Jigsaw presentation by teams: Check for understanding Q and A.
7. All-class discussion: Venn diagram regarding KWL list versus Know list regarding rights and responsibilities.
8. Journal entries: Summary of comparisons. Read and feedback.
9. Teams design and present CMaps: Check for understanding.
10. Constitution Test.
11. Essays submitted.
12. Completion of all C rubrics: two-four-eight strategy.
13. Summary of Illinois Constitution study.

---

direct relation to the content being taught. Starting with the essential question, every ingredient in the plan is *intentionally* included.

THE ESSENTIAL LAUNCH QUESTION

The first step that teachers take when preparing a collaboration-in-reverse plan is to select the essential launch question. The essential question takes students immediately to the standards-based enduring principles or concepts students will be expected to understand at the study's end. What will the students understand and be able to do at the end of this collaboration that they did not understand and do at the start? In this lesson, will the students understand their state's Constitution and its application to their lives? From other *Understanding by Design* lessons, will students understand the causes of a historic event such as the fall of the Berlin Wall, a literary tragedy such as *Romeo and Juliet*, or a social issue like immigration? Will they understand why and how human decisions often have unintended consequences as occurred in the Gulf of Mexico with the oil rig explosion? Will they understand how to multiply fractions or to solve a complex calculus problem? Will they understand how to perform a scientific investigation with algae or prepare an analytic research paper comparing blue- and red-state issues? Will they understand the differences and similarities between cultures in South Africa and Bosnia?

Beyond the content study, when teachers use collaboration lessons to develop specific cooperative skills or to promote improvement of students' critical thinking skills, they add these sets of desired results to the expected content outcomes. More questions are raised. "What collaborative skills will students demonstrate?" "How will students show their increased ability to use critical thinking skills to deepen understanding of the content?" "How are they improving their listening skills in the groups or learning to stay on focus?"

To help students focus on the core and enduring concepts and the lasting skills that they will improve by the end of a collaborative, learning-enriched lesson, teachers must think from the start about the standards-aligned *assessment* tools that they will ask students to use. In this third step, teachers have many choices, including rubrics, checklists, and observation charts. Their selection depends on determining how far all students have advanced in their content understandings, well as in their use of collaborative and critical thinking skills.

The first example shows a minirubric made for a study of Egyptian culture. It presents benchmarks that demonstrate what students must understand from this study in answer to a standards-aligned launch question. The benchmarks ask students whether they can identify the distinguishing features of a pyramid, stipulate the historic context that may explain why the Egyptians built the Pyramids, and recall how they built them. Teachers can extend the rubric by adding benchmarks for the "why" and the "how" so they can use the tool for formative assessment. As a result, the assessment tool becomes a roadmap to guide students as they distinguish between the labor used and the mathematics used to build the pyramid. Teachers can use the same tool at the end of the lesson as the summative or end assessment.

ASSESSING THE THREE C's:
CONTENT, COLLABORATION, AND COMMUNICATION

In addition to assessing the core content throughout the collaborative lesson, teachers with high expectations can assess the other C's integrated

---

A MINIRUBRIC SAMPLE: EGYPTIAN CULTURE

I am able to identify the distinguishing features of a pyramid.

Identify what characteristics make it special or unique.

/————————/————————/————————/
Not Yet   A Little   A Great Deal   Everything

Explain why the Egyptians built the pyramids.

/————————/————————/————————/
Not Yet   A Little   A Great Deal   Everything

Explain why the pyramids were important in the Egyptian culture.

/————————/————————/————————/
Not Yet   A Little   A Great Deal   Everything

Tell the innovative methods they used to build the pyramids.

/————————/————————/————————/
Not Yet   A Little   A Great Deal   Everything

Tell the challenges they overcame in building the pyramids.

/————————/————————/————————/
Not Yet   A Little   A Great Deal   Everything

Tell why the pyramids became important in history.

/————————/————————/————————/
Not Yet   A Little   A Great Deal   Everything

My Evidence for High-End Assessments:

---

in the lesson: Collaborative e-tool skills, Communication skills, and Critical thinking skills. Students can keep the rubric handy to guide them through the lesson. At select times, teachers can stop and review the students' progress.

A SAMPLE RUBRIC: USING E-TOOLS

E-Tool: *Class Literature Blog*
My Name: *Viviana Pokorny*   **Date:** *May 1*

I know the procedures for correct use of this e-tool.

/————————/————————/————————/
Not Yet   Somewhat   Fairly Well   Expert

I know the appropriate places to use the tool in a project.

/————————/————————/————————/
Not Yet   Somewhat   Fairly Well   Expert

I use the tool appropriately.

/————————/————————/————————/
Not Yet   Somewhat   Fairly Well   Expert

I can explain the tool's appropriate use to others.

/————————/————————/————————/
Not Yet   Somewhat   Fairly Well   Expert

Comment: This was the first time I used it to answer the questions Ms. Small asked about the characters in the story. I could follow the directions. I can't yet do it on my own. vp

---

Assessing Critical Thinking Skills

Assessment rubrics, checklists, and observation charts are tools that communicate the highest expectations when they require students to show the quality of their thinking operations throughout a lesson. From an achievement perspective, research informs teachers that the more purposefully students think about mental operations such as finding similarities, developing and proving hypotheses, making generalizations, comparing, sequencing, making connections, drawing conclusions, and summarizing core ideas, the better they will learn the material. Mind and brain literature reaffirms the superior instructional value of intentional development of thinking skills and cognitive habits of mind over the laissez-faire

---

SAMPLE CHECKLIST: ASSESSING CRITICAL THINKING

Name: _Amit Shahst_   **Date:** _September 6_

_X_   I saw you stop and think before you raised your hand.
___   I saw you make a plan before you did the math problems.
___   You told me what you need to do to make sure you are not jumping to conclusions.
_X_   I saw your journal entry in which you thought about the pluses and minuses of your thinking today.

Comments: Your plus-minus chart was very complete with good examples. I liked the three examples you gave to back up the point that you are trying to be less impulsive when doing your math problems. I am hoping you are ready to make that into a plan.

---

notion that improvement of thinking skills happens best without teacher mediation. When teachers provide early notice that students will have to reflect on their own thinking and assess its efficiency against cognitive standards that indicate how well they are using the cognitive operations to solve problems or answer the key question, they further advance student achievement. Teachers do this by challenging students to reduce episodic and impulsive thinking; by building students' ability to work with

---

THE COGNITIVE FUNCTIONS IN THE PHASES OF LEARNING

Gathering Information	Making Sense	Communicating
Labeling	Defining problems	Projecting virtual relationships
Systematic searching	Comparing	Giving thoughtful response
Precise collection	Summarizing	Explaining
Accurate collection	Arranging logical evidence	Using metaphor
Finding clues	Connecting facts and ideas	Transferring concepts
Focus	Analyzing for bias	Explaining
Using multiple sources	Analysis for cause and effect	Demonstrating
Grouping and labeling	Sequencing	Constructing
Making a hypothesis	Integrating ideas	
Making a plan	Synthesizing ideas	
Seeking others' point of view	Analyzing points of view	

Adapted from Feuerstein, 2001

SAMPLE OBSERVATION CHECKLIST: INDEX CARD

Name: _Susan Morrison_   **Target Skill:** _Sequencing_

Date	Comment
January 3	Completed sequence chart of story. Three items out of order.
January 17	Revised sequence chart. All in correct order
January 24	Completed second chart. All items in order.

---

multiple sources of information; and by coaching them in how to anticipate errors, be precise and accurate, and decipher similarities throughout the project. When all students, especially those who struggle to learn efficiently, increase the quality of these cognitive functions, they become more effective learners (Feuerstein, 2001).

Observation checklists are tools that teachers can adopt when assisting students in the formative assessment of communication skills being developed in a collaborative experience whether on the Internet or off-line. Checklists precede summative rubrics and written summations. They are an easy-to-use tool for teachers to note what students are doing and thinking as they work to answer the launch question. Checklists also inform teachers what these students can do better before the students arrive at the end line in collaboration with their peers. The tools' positive effect is compounded when teachers show students the content of the checklists well before students start their active search for answers to the launch question or problem solution.

One way for teachers to increase their effective use of observation checklists is to prepare index cards, one for each student. Each card identifies one student and the 21st century skill to which that student is attending. At the end of a marking period, the teachers transfer the card's information to a scoring rubric.

Teachers may assess collaboration in several dimensions as all students work in well-structured, mixed-ability learning groups. In these groups structured for teamwork, each member agrees to achieve a common goal with shared equipment. Sometimes the shared task is concrete: Assemble these documents. At other times, the task is more conceptual and challenges the group to solve a problem such as "How does the company improve its customer service image?"

Teachers can construct simple assessment tools that will help students pay attention to their improved collaborations by purposefully attending to the improvement of social skills, participation, and leadership in helping the group work together. Each dimension of group cooperation can have its own benchmarks for improvement announced to the students at the start of the lesson. As with early announcements of expected content results and improvements in critical thinking, students hear the expectations for working together from the start of the lesson.

A SAMPLE RUBRIC FOR SELF-DIRECTED LEARNING

Assessor: _Mr. Barney_   **Date:** _Oct. 18_   **Function:** _Intern_
Student: _Mark Simpson, Period: 3_

Student sets realistic weekly goal.

/——————— /———————/——————— /
Not Yet   Now and Then   Most of the Time   Always

Student asks for feedback on progress.

/——————— / ———————/——————— /
Not Yet   Now and Then   Most of the Time   Always

Student reviews weekly outcomes.

/——————— /———————/——————— /
Not Yet   Now and Then   Most of the Time   Always

Student tracks own progress.

/——————— /———————/——————— /
Not Yet   Now and Then   Most of the Time   Always

Student reflects on progress and marks changes.

/——————— /———————/——————— /
Not Yet   Now and Then   Most of the Time   Always

Comment: Mark has improved this week. His goal was more doable and he kept daily track of progress. He asked his support team for feedback on how well he kept his commitments. Mark still needs to work on the depth of his reflections.

1. **Social Skill Development:** The student listens, shares, clarifies, encourages.
2. **Small Group Participation:** The student follows guidelines, assumes roles, contributes to collaboration.
3. **Leadership:** The student models, helps, supports, facilitates, checks for understanding about role as leader.
4. **Self-Direction**: The student sets reasonable and achievable goals, looks for outcomes, picks appropriate strategies, and gathers feedback.

Assessing the Communication Element

Communication is a natural part of collaboration. In fact, it is the glue that binds a significant collaboration together. As soon as one student sends an email message to a second student, writes a blog paragraph or contributes to a wiki, participates in a think-pair-share dialogue, or talks to others in a group, that student is sending and receiving messages—the essence of communication. A message may go to the other side of the classroom or fly through virtual space to peers in China, Colombia, or Zimbabwe. The message may be in words, pictures, or symbols.

Collaborative lessons provide multiple teachable moments for teachers to develop students' communication skills in writing, speaking, and listening. By teaching students how to write with tweets, emails, blogs, and wikis and to speak with podcasts in a lesson, they integrate conventional language arts instruction into learning experiences that make the communications tasks authentic and meaningful to students. When a student is sending an email message to a peer, that sending student has more motivation to proof the copy and check that meaning is clear than the student who is assigned to write an essay on a topic that the teacher has invented.

A SUMMATIVE RUBRIC FOR AN *UNDERSTANDING BY DESIGN* LESSON

In addition to the formative assessments selected within an *Understanding by Design* lesson, teachers help the students by showing and discussing each lesson's summative assessment. This assessment will show the students how the various expectations are connected and that every piece of learning need not be separated into little boxes. The summative rubric integrates content, collaboration, and cognitive outcomes.

A SUMMATIVE SELF-ASSESSMENT SAMPLE

Name: _____   Date: _____

My Summary:

States the big idea.

/——————/——————/——————/
  Strong   Average   Weak   Not Yet

Answers the essential question.

/——————/——————/——————/
  Strong   Average   Weak   Not Yet

Includes logical sub-ideas.

/——————/——————/——————/
  Strong   Average   Weak   Not Yet

Provides accurate details to illustrate or prove each point.

/——————/——————/——————/
  Strong   Average   Weak   Not Yet

Includes multiple sources of information.

/——————/——————/——————/
  Strong   Average   Weak   Not Yet

Shows precise use of spelling, grammar, punctuation, and sentence structure.

/——————/——————/——————/
  Strong   Average   Weak   Not Yet

Synthesizes key ideas in response to question.

/——————/——————/——————/
  Strong   Average   Weak   Not Yet

Grasps key concepts in content.

/——————/——————/——————/
  Strong   Average   Weak   Not Yet

Shows increased ability to collaborate.

/——————/——————/——————/
  Strong   Average   Weak   Not Yet

Comments:

CONCLUDING THOUGHTS

Learning designs start "at the end" with teachers' identification of what is most important for students to know and do as a result of their thinking, interacting, and learning in the lesson. For each element that teachers identify for students to learn about or do, the teachers assign a value. In a like manner, they think through each task that they will assess and create value-differentiating rubrics that will guide students through their work. After being presented with the information telling them what they will be expected to know and to do as a result of their collaborative learning experiences, students can make informed choices about what they individually will emphasize as they actively engage themselves in the collaborative effort.

CHAPTER 6

How Do Projects Say Yes to Standards?

"Cheshire Puss," asked Alice. "Would you tell me, please, where I ought to go from here?"

"That depends a good deal on where you want to go," said the cat.

"I don't much care where," said Alice.

"Then it doesn't matter what way you go," said the cat.

—Lewis Carroll, *Alice in Wonderland*

"WHAT IS AVAILABLE to help teachers know where they ought to be taking students in their lessons?" is a question that parallels the Cheshire Cat's. The Partnership for 21st Century Skills' framework provides a partial answer. For the first time in American educational history, schools have a public document that they can adopt as the "big picture frame." The framework suggests values and actions that schools can adopt 100% or adapt as their compass for learning.

The second answer comes from state and national standards. These provide schools with road markers that select out for them socially accepted norms for learning, at least in a minimal way, what the state or national organization, such as the National Council of Teachers of Mathematics (or Science or English), has declared "important to know and do." Rather than leave decisions to teachers about what is most important to teach in a subject area, the state standards say, "This is it."

There is no shortage of standards for a teacher to follow. Standards abound, most notably in the content arena. Although some state content standards are too watered down to effectively guide teachers and students toward the goal of effective communication and collaboration, there do exist sets of usable national standards.

By paying attention to standards statements that include the two 21st century outcomes, collaboration, and communication, along with clear

"What are you reading?" Mr. François asked his daughter.

"*The Wizard of Oz*," the girl answered.

"I never read it, but I love the movie. Is there really a yellow brick road in the story?"

"Of course. It is a very important part of the story. My teacher says it is a symbol."

"Oh?" responded Mr. François with a slight raise of his left eyebrow. "For what?"

"Well, Dorothy and her friends get to follow the yellow brick road to Oz. It symbolizes a path to an important goal. With the road signs, you get help to walk the road to your goal. For Dorothy and her friends, it was a guide to get them all to Oz safely, everybody helping everybody."

benchmarks to guide teachers and students, teachers can know that they are teaching to 21st century standards. Their students will benefit by knowing what they are expected to know about the content and to apply the key concepts and skills in other situations.

INTENTIONAL COLLABORATION AND COMMUNICATION

When teachers add outcomes for collaboration and communication to the classroom agenda, they up the expectations ante. First, they provide students with new tools to learn. They introduce a new set of skills. And they ask the students to use these tools and skills to develop a new disposition, working with peers.

Teachers, however, cannot just hope that students collaborate and communicate because the students are given these collaborative tools. Just as Dorothy developed the love, smarts, and courage of her three friends as they walked along the yellow brick road toward Oz, teachers advance students' communication and collaboration skills and dispositions by teaching their students how to collaborate more efficiently and communicate more effectively.

For students to become highly functioning collaborators and communicators in the 21st century, there are ample tools and tactics teachers can select to make this happen. One strategy calls for explicit instruction of collaboration and communication skills. Traditional courses on logical reasoning are built on the explicit instruction of skills. University professors analyze the skills needed for logical thinking. They rely on direct instruction to inform students about the principles and practices of reasoning. Their belief is that logic is its own content and is best learned free of distractions from the application disciplines such as law or science. After students have mastered the skills of logic, free of distracting content, they learn how to bridge the new skills into many other content areas and life situations arguing with logic. In some cases, the professors may use strategies such as debate, case studies, essays, and arguments to build the bridges. This, the advocates of explicit instruction contend, is the most effective way to produce students who reason with logic. The same methods, advocates of this approach hypothesize, will be most efficient for teaching other 21st century skills.

A second theory calls for teachers to "catch the students" collaborating in their daily lessons. The advocates of this theory argue that when science teachers hear an illogical argument, when English teachers notice that students are making weak comparisons, or when social studies instructors hear arguments supported by weak data, they make an intervention at the "teachable moment." They provide immediate feedback that explains to the student what he or she had just done with the logic: "That was a first-class syllogism, Michael. Your conclusion was very logical." Likewise, when teachers observe conflict in a cooperative group or see students frustrated in their online search for information, they intervene on the spot. The intervention may be one-to-one mediation that notes the ineffective communication or collaboration and indicates a more effective path. The intervention can also be a mini-lesson dropped into a unit or project. With a mini-lesson, teachers identify the "what" and "why" for the intervention, model skilled use of the targeted skill, and then provide ample time for the students to practice the skill within their content.

The third theory is strategic and eclectic. Its advocates take the position that there is no magic formula for developing 21st century collaboration and communication. However, there are best practices that scientific research suggests will most enable teachers to increase content achievement through improved cooperative skills. Teachers can add these practices to their instructional repertoire. Depending on the situation, teachers can elect which of the collaborative-communications strategies they will pull from their toolboxes. In one class, they may use formal cooperative learning; in a second class, a graphic organizer; in a third class, a combination of the two in an inquiry project.

A TEACHABLE MOMENT

"What seems to be the difficulty here?" I asked the two students hunched over their computer. "Am I hearing a dead-end argument?"

"No. He won't let me correct the email. It doesn't make sense," responded the first student.

"It doesn't make any difference. What I mean is clear. If the other kids want to answer us and say it is not clear, OK, OK," interjected the second.

"I see the problem. Actually, several," I said. "First, you are disagreeing about the spelling of your email. Let me ask a question about that. When the class discussed the standards for email, what did we say about spelling?"

"Bad spelling looks bad and can confuse the reader?"

"Right," I answered. "So, John, how does Scott's answer apply in your disagreement?"

"I guess he's right. We have to correct the spelling," John said.

"Now, what does this example teach you about communication?" I asked.

"It is better to resolve our disagreements by checking the facts against the principle," John offered.

"And what does that mean here?" I asked. "Scott."

"The principle is 'check spelling before sending an email.'"

"That is a good answer," I said. "You not only follow the principle by doing what it says, you avoid the dead-end argument."

"And," smiled John, "it helps us stay together."

To apply the strategic approach to the development of collaboration and communication skills, teachers first target the specific cooperative skills they want their students to master. As in all backward planning (see Chapter 2), teachers focusing on students' collaboration and communication skills will spotlight what specific skills the students will show they can perform. Effective teachers do not want to throw eggs randomly into a pan and wait to see what comes out. They are very intentional in saying, "I want scrambled eggs" or "I want my eggs over easy and this is how I plan to do it."

Teachers' intentionality is as essential when strategically developing students' collaboration and communication skills as it is in their attempts to make sure students grasp the full meaning of a core concept in the curriculum or think more critically. For this, seven principles can guide teachers' decision-making processes as they plan their strategy:

1. Identify the relevant standards for collaboration and communication
2. Identify the specific behaviors for the targeted skills
3. Engage the students in a mini-lesson from which they can learn the skill by guided doing
4. Mediate the students' understanding of the skill and its appropriate uses
5. Provide ample opportunity to develop the skill with intentional practice
6. Give constructive feedback during student practice
7. Enable the students to learn from the "doing" experience

When creating their strategic plans for developing collaboration and communication, teachers can draw on the best-practice research. This research enables them to select the strategies and tactics that are most powerful in producing achievement. It also provides them the opportunity to model for students the use of these tactics in combinations that increase the strategies' effects.

When putting the nine strategies into practice, teachers can allow about one class period per month to focus students on a selected collaborative skill, such as maintaining individual and team accountability, modeling best use of the skill in the collaborative task, making regular connections of the skill to the standard, or identifying the specific behaviors that support that skill. Then, they guide students to integrate and practice the skill

---

NINE CLASSROOM STRATEGIES THAT MOST INCREASE ACHIEVEMENT

1. Identifying similarities and differences
2. Summarizing and note-taking
3. Reinforcing effort and providing recognition
4. Homework and practice
5. Nonlinguistic representations
6. Cooperative learning
7. Setting objectives and providing feedback
8. Generating and testing hypotheses
9. Cues, questions, and advance organizers

Marzano, Pickering, & Pollock, 2001

in daily lessons. Teachers ask students, at least once a month, to assess the quality of their skill applications. By referring to a checklist, teachers can double-check their focus on the chosen skills.

Getting to the Standards

Whichever of the theories teachers may select as a ground for their instructional approach, it is a good idea to align curriculum and instruction with legally mandated standards. Some advocates of 21st century skill instruction are unhappy with existing state standards. Their calls for standards that do a better job at targeting 21st century skills, such as those enunciated by the Partnership for 21st Century Skills (http://www.p21.org) or the National Council of Teachers of English (NCTE) (http://www.ncte.org), will allow for the more universal inclusion of collaboration standards that will provide more accurate roadmaps and stronger motivation for getting students where they want them to go more efficiently.

Most state standards as well as the standards promulgated by national professional organizations, such as the National Council of Teachers of Mathematics (NCTM) (http://www.nctm.org) or the International Society for Technology Education (ISTE) (http://www.iste.org), in the major subject areas are sufficient in number and quality to guide the development of 21st century skills. When it comes to the promotion of students' collaboration and communication skills, all organizations could benefit

---

SAMPLE CHECKLIST FOR COLLABORATIVE SKILL DEVELOPMENT

___ 1. I have aligned my course curriculum with ISTE's technology standards for collaboration.

___ 2. I have targeted specific collaborative skills by observing my students.

___ 3. I have selected a "collaborative skill of the month" on which I will focus students' attention by giving them an initial experience to analyze.

___ 4. I have a plan for integrating the target skill into each day's lesson using combinations of the high-effect strategies.

___ 5. I give students a weekly opportunity to assess their improved use of this skill.

___ 6. I am prepared to give feedback on students' development of the targeted skill.

___ 7. I have linked the skill development to students' use of e-tools.

SAMPLE ISTE COMMUNICATION
AND COLLABORATION STANDARD

Students use digital media and environments to communicate and work collaboratively, including at a distance, to support individual learning and contribute to the learning of others. Students

- interact, collaborate, and publish with peers, experts, or others employing a variety of digital environments and media,
- communicate information and ideas effectively to multiple audiences using a variety of media and formats,
- develop cultural understanding and global awareness by engaging with learners of other cultures, and
- contribute to project teams to produce original works or solve problems.

their members by increasing the sparse number of benchmarks for these two prominent skill sets.

When aligning instruction with collaboration and communication standards, teachers can turn to their national organizations or their state departments of education. The first place to turn may well be the NETS standards prepared by the ISTE.

Teachers can find similar standards statements to guide their integration of the 21st century collaboration and communication into the curriculum from national professional organizations in the various content areas. For instance, NCTE calls for "students' use of a variety of technological and information resources (e.g., libraries, databases, computer networks, video) to gather and synthesize information and to create and communicate knowledge." NCTM aligns its various standards at all grade levels and provides links to helpful websites for examples of best practices that integrate technology into daily mathematics instruction.

State boards of education are starting to add technology standards to their frameworks. In 2008, Massachusetts added its technology standards. The standards are intended to guide teachers as they address the specific 21st century skills with the aid of technology.

The Partnership for 21st Century Skills' standards for communication and collaboration are a starting point for school teams wishing to identify how they can adjust their current curriculum. Although these statements do not drill down to each grade level, it should not be difficult for school or district teams, organized by grade level, subject, or both, to identify when

SAMPLE STATE STANDARD FOR TECHNOLOGY

Standard: Demonstrate the ability to use technology for research, critical thinking, problem solving, decision making, communication, collaboration, creativity, and innovation.

This standard

- focuses on applying a wide range of technology tools to student learning and everyday life;
- aims to ensure that students will be able to use technology to process and analyze information;
- is to help students develop skills for effective technology-based communication;
- includes the use of technology to explore and create new ideas, identify trends, and forecast possibilities; and
- aims to provide students with an awareness of how technology is used in the real world.

Communicate Clearly

- Articulate thoughts and ideas effectively, using oral, written, and nonverbal communication skills in a variety of forms and contexts
- Listen effectively to decipher meaning including knowledge, values, attitudes, and intentions
- Use communication for a range of purposes (e.g., to inform, instruct, motivate, and persuade)
- Use multiple media and technologies and know how to judge their effectiveness as well as assess their impact
- Communicate effectively in diverse (including multilingual) environments

Collaborate with Others

- Demonstrate ability to work effectively and respectfully with diverse teams
- Exercise flexibility and willingness to be helpful in making necessary compromises to accomplish a common goal
- Assume shared responsibility for collaborative work and value the individual contributions made by each team member

and how in the curriculum teachers can integrate instruction that promotes development of these skills. With such a revised curriculum prepared, the same professional learning teams can work with each other to develop their readiness to use the modified approaches.

Target Crucial Learning Behaviors

The partnership's standards for communication and collaboration enable teachers to highlight those crucial learning behaviors that make most sense to students. Teachers select from the standards relevant skills such as "articulate thoughts through written communication" or "listen effectively." Using cooperative teams, they can engage students in the 5- to 10-minute creation of T-charts or other visual organizers that identify what each of the selected skills looks and sounds like. After student teams generate their charts with the behaviors organized visually, teachers can facilitate the creation of a master list. If teachers have made wikis available to students, students can take 15 additional minutes with the class wiki to create the master list.

Develop Understanding of the Targeted Skill

Following the creation of a T-chart, web, or brainstormed list, teachers can launch a complete lesson that will deepen students' understanding of the targeted skill. Using a think-pair-share, the easiest of the collaborative tactics with which to start, teachers can pose a series of questions about the chart. In one class period, the pairs can define the skill, decide why it is important, and when they think it might be most appropriate to use its behaviors in a collaborative classroom. For each round (what, why, how), students write their own answer to the question, share it with a partner,

Figure 6.1. T-Chart Sample: Shared Responsibility

Looks Like	Sounds Like
Pairs	"Let's double-check our jobs."
Groups of three	"You do #1 and #2. I will do #3 and #4."
Role for each posted	"I agree on our list. Our shared goal is . . ."
Balanced assessment rubric by role	"My job is to record. Your job is to present on each."
List of responsibilities for each person	"Let's make a responsibility checklist."
Equal airtime	"Let's time each report (5 minutes)."

and then participate in an all-class posting. Teachers can post the pair ideas for all to see (chalkboard, whiteboard, newsprint) or invite students to use the wiki. After all ideas are listed, the class can eliminate duplicate ideas.

Crystallize the Targeted Skill

For at least a month, it is helpful for teachers to keep students' attention on the targeted skill. What this accomplishes is similar to what happens when a chemist is growing a crystal. New pieces adhere to the basic piece. As a result the skill becomes larger and more complex. Teachers can crystallize a skill in a variety of ways.

a. Once a week allot 5 minutes at the start of a class period for students to write in a journal or make a blog entry describing one of the behaviors that they are working to improve. "Yesterday, I made sure that I involved my partner by turning over the computer role to her and coaching her on the search skills that scared her."

b. Wander among the teams and listen or look for the desired behaviors. Make a verbal compliment or hand out a sticky-note compliment.

c. On Monday mornings, ask each student to use his or her blog to make a plan for improving the targeted skill for the week. Which skill? Which behaviors?

d. Invite each team to make a PowerPoint picture, print it out, and post it for all to see. The picture should represent ways they are attending to the targeted skill.

e. Invite each team to print out and hang a banner ad that celebrates their use of the targeted skill.

f. Have students tweet each other with an "I am proud" statement that focuses on the targeted skill.

Encourage Self-Assessment and Give Constructive Feedback

In spite of what some bean-counting psychometricians might desire, there is little evidence to support the notion that a quiz or a test to determine the students' knowledge about these skills will provide meaningful formative assessment. There will be a much more powerful impact on students' ability to use these skills appropriately if the feedback starts with the students themselves, for themselves. Students can use blogs to make weekly entries that assess their skill development. (If the classroom lacks the proper technology, the old-fashioned paper journal will work just as well as the recorder of feedback). Teachers allot 5 minutes at the end of the week and provide a tactic such as a write-pair-share or a stem starter to initiate the self-talk. Students reflect on the targeted collaborative or communication skills and make their entry. When time allows, teachers can ask students to share their entered assessments with their teams of the entire class. To ensure equitable time to all students, teachers can prompt short responses with a stem such as "This week, I am pleased that I . . ." and allow each student a chance to complete it without comment from others.

There are also useful self-assessment sequences that teachers can use on a regular basis. First, they put the tactic such as Ms. Potter's questions or My Summary online so that the students can copy the form. After students send the completed assessment to the teacher, the teacher can read it, make a comment with edit tools, and then deposit it in an electronic binder, such as the open-source freeware live binder. Or the teacher can ask the student to make the deposit so that students can practice their categorizing skills.

SELF-ASSESSMENT TACTIC I: MS. POTTER'S QUESTIONS

Targeted skill: _Taking self-responsibility_   **Date:** _April 1, 2009_
Name: _Morpheus Matt_   **Teacher:** _Ms. Moldano, Period: 7_

What did I do well this week? I double-checked at the end of each class to see that everyone had a copy of my notes in their inbox.
What can I improve? I need to make sure that my notes always follow the outline format that Ms. Moldano taught us.
What help do I need? I need my teammates to give feedback on my format.

SELF-ASSESSMENT TACTIC 2: HOW I DID SUMMARY

Targeted Skill: _Taking self-responsibility_   **Date:** _April 27_
Name: _Morpheus Matt_   **Teacher:** _Ms. Moldano, Period: 7_

This week was a good and bad week. The good was Mary, our team leader, commented on how my notes were getting better. This was the first time that the outline was perfect. The bad news is that it's taking me too much time. I have to figure a way to shorten the notes so I can get them done at the end of the period. Mary is going to help me. We're meeting tomorrow in study hall.

To enrich students' self-assessments, teachers take every opportunity to provide constructive feedback targeted specifically at the skill of the month. There is no desk sitting by the teacher while the students work in cooperative teams in lessons and projects. The teacher's primary role, as students attend to their collaborative tasks and communicate with one another, is to observe as they walk among the teams, listen and watch what students are doing, and note how they are using the targeted skills. At opportune moments, the teachable moments, teachers can quietly intervene in a group task and share their observations about the group's collaboration or an individual's skill use. "I noticed that this group is helping Morpheus with his notes." "I am pleased to see that Morpheus is being precise with his note-taking. Let me suggest that at the end of class, you each tell him what you liked." At the end of the week or the skill-month, teachers can summarize their observations on the blog or verbally share the observations with the entire class. As researchers have noted, this positive approach to feedback shows the strongest effect-size data.

Integrate E-Tool Use

E-tools can play a major part in facilitating development of targeted collaboration and communication skills. As noted in examples above, blogs and wikis provide rich opportunities for students to receive and give feedback, complete self-assessments, and ask for specific types of help. If teachers prefer to use pods, they can record podcasts that give feedback to the entire class or are made available for specific groups.

There are multiple benefits to using the e-tools as feedback tools. First, they enable teachers to be more systematic in their feedback. Second, students can receive personal feedback in greater detail from the teacher. Third, students can share constructive feedback more easily and privately with one another. Fourth, students can keep the feedback in a folder for use later in a summative assessment. Fifth, the tools provide an easy way to promote dialogue between teacher and student that is highly individualized. Sixth, the e-tools facilitate the students' development of their own capabilities, aided by their peers' and their teacher's feedback, in a learning environment that the teacher has made safe and secure for all.

Make Proactive Interventions

When the development of 21st century skills is encased in a constructivist learning plan, teachers transform from being storehouses of knowledge

Trust. This school is about trust. Without trust there is no Manor Tech.

—Principal Steven Zipkes, Skype interview, June 15, 2010

and the primary source of information to being facilitators of collaboration and mediators of critical thinking. In this role, they are responsible for five "jobs": (1) planning the classroom interactions that improve students' skills for collaborating and communicating effectively, (2) establishing a climate in which students can trust their peers as they share important ideas about the content with one another, (3) facilitating group cooperation, (4) integrating skill development with the tools that will help all advance their abilities to use the targeted skills to more effectively master the prescribed content, and (5) guiding assessment of the outcomes both formatively during the lesson or project and summarily at the end.

CONCLUDING THOUGHTS

How can teachers say yes to the standards? Many theories abound. However, from a practical standpoint, an eclectic strategic approach allows teachers to meet student needs as well as align instruction with the standards in the most systematic way. This constructivist approach starts with the standards and student needs. Following those standards that align most tightly with student need and the content curriculum, teachers select the instructional strategies that give the most chance for increased student achievement as teachers develop students' collaboration and communication skills. An extra curriculum is unnecessary. What works best is the integration of these important 21st century skills into the existing curriculum. By integrating instruction that develops the skills with the content and other 21st century skills, teachers can increase the effects on achievement.

CHAPTER 7

All Together Now

How to Use Formal Cooperative Learning to Enhance Collaborative Skills

We sink or swim together.

—Roger Johnson and David Johnson

WATCH A MASTER symphony orchestra as the conductor guides it through its performance. Who could not marvel at the teamwork that binds the orchestra members with the conductor, the other players in their section, and the entire orchestra? When all are in synch, there is no better example of collaboration. The great maestro Lorin Maazel noted the effects: "The collaboration with the musicians of the New York Philharmonic is sheer joy. The Orchestra is so professional, so prepared, so motivated. I float from day to day, concert to concert, masterpiece to masterpiece, supported by the sound of the New York Philharmonic" (http://www.finestquotes.com).

Collaborative-learning experiences prepare students to engage in the type of quality teamwork expected in the modern adult work world. Although they may never reach the zenith of joy that Maazel described, collaboration encourages students of different abilities, motivations, races, ethnicities, and genders to work together to achieve a shared goal. With these sharpened abilities, students will uncover the positive feelings that go with successful collaborations.

Cooperative learning, most especially the formal group structure, has proved to be a one of the most effective tools for teaching students how to work together. Invariably, several generations of research reports describe how formal cooperative learning increases student achievement, garners high-order project and lesson outcomes, and prepares students for positive social interactions in the non-academic work world.

"For today's work," Ms. Schabass said, "I need you in your base teams. After you review these task cards that I will hand to each group leader, I want you to review our guidelines for cooperation and your roles in the team. You will then have all but the last 5 minutes of the period to work together on the tasks."

Tomas replied, "In our last team meeting, we were in a heavy disagreement over our ranking of the most serious diseases in poor countries. Can we resolve that first?"

"Yes," the teacher answered. "But I would have your timekeeper limit how long. I want you to complete this task that will set up the data collection. A lot of the work will be done outside class time and each person will have to be prepared with new data for the next meeting."

Paola nodded her head. "That's a good reason for me to do my work alone. I would rather make sure it's done right."

Ms. Schabass agreed. "In a few years, you are going to have a job. Chances are you will have to depend on others to get tasks done on time and right. You won't have the luxury of working by yourself. Part of what I am looking for in this project is how you give help and get help together. When you see this task, I think you will be very happy that you have a team working together."

TOGETHER OR ALONE: WHAT WORKS BEST?

It is common for young students to sit at a desk and work alone on classroom tasks. Sometimes they are circling bubbles on a worksheet or test; other times they are filling in the blank or circling correct answers. High school students are also most likely to sit at a single desk and take their lecture notes. A new variation at all grade levels is to place solo students in front of a computer screen.

Some academics will argue that working alone is a matter of learning-style or intelligence. If nothing else, it encourages teachers, they say, to individualize instruction. Most certainly, longtime advocates of cooperative learning admit that the highest-performing students may prefer to work alone.

Critics of cooperative learning prefer to strive for the holy grail of individualized learning. In such cases, they will say, "The student should have the opportunity to work alone. This way we can tailor the learning task to each child's unique learning styles, intelligence, or needs." Although this argument supports use of the 19th century factory model with each worker at a workstation, it contrasts with the experiences 21st century students most likely will have when they enter the modern work world, where so many jobs require collaborative teamwork.

Even with this vision of teamwork in the workplace, supporters of learning alone insist on individualization. Even when presented with research to the contrary, the proponents of individualized learning hold fast to their position. They ignore the contrast of their position with the research that stipulates that team goal structures are the most effective in producing high achievement and individualized structures are the least effective. It is the collaborative effort of the team, "all together now, pull 1, 2, and 3," that gets the most effective results (Johnson, Johnson, & Smith, 2007).

THE SOLITARY WORKER

Classrooms are one of the few places in today's society where workers are obliged to work alone. For 5 or more hours daily, teachers go into their classrooms, close the door, and work with the students. Unless a teacher is assisted by an aide, a teacher's contact with other adults is minimal. For many of these teachers, this solitary confinement is all that they have known since they began their first classroom assignment. Their view of how people work is distorted by their limited solitary experiences.

While rowing a single skull in a race is an option, the multiple-person skull races are the most common. There are more races with pairs, fours, and eights to row than singles. Similarly, outside the teaching world, collaborative teams are a more common daily expectation in the work world. In the armed forces, teamwork is often a life-and-death issue. In the film *The Hurt Locker*, the individual who actually defused the bombs was highly dependent on his team. In business, how an employee works with colleagues is evaluated in annual reviews. Many university researchers, especially in the sciences, are joined together in work teams that span physical spaces. On the modern, high-tech assembly line, workers collaborate in a multistep assembly process. In countries such as Israel, Denmark, Singapore, and the United States, most entrepreneurial start-ups spring from teams of friends with a common interest. Even at McDonald's and other fast-food chains, teamwork is more common than working alone.

TEAMWORK IN THE NON-ACADEMIC WORLD OF WORK

If the 21st century school is going to prepare students to work "in the real world," or the nonschool world, collaboration will need to be a strong thread running throughout daily instruction. Working alone won't cut it as the dominant mode for learning; more likely the opposite will be true. Students will need to spend more time in the collaborative mode with single tasks being the exception.

The idea that students must learn to work in teams is not an either-or command: Work alone or in teams. The 21st century work world will require a both-and approach to tasks. Sometimes work will be solitary. The single scientist may stare into his or her microscope, working alone. So too, the lawyer may sit alone at the computer to research case law. More often, future work will happen in teams such as when technology developers interact in the innovation process to create a new brake system or when auto assembly lines depend on multiple workers putting together the common team-made car.

In future decades, students who learn to work well together will need to learn how teamwork is refined and used at appropriate times as well as learning when it is best to work alone. By mastering both skill sets, the alone and the together, the 21st century student will have greater capacity to develop the necessary skills of self-direction and teamwork, but also the capability to work alone as needed.

In addition to fostering greater achievement through purposeful instruction in cooperative work, is not teamwork also a legitimate and necessary tool for fostering the skills of communication inside and outside classroom walls? If it is, then is it not also legitimate for teachers to ensure that students learn how to work well together in such teams? In previous centuries,

---

Collaborative work doesn't mean the end of individual work, especially for highly gifted students like ours. Yes. There are times scientists and doctors work alone. At the Illinois Math and Science Academy, cooperative groupings are our major instructional style. And when the kids need to work alone to write a report or read, they do that well. But we are preparing them for a work world where collaboration is the norm, not the anomaly.

—Dr. Max McGee, education director, Illinois Math and Science Academy, recorded interview, June 22, 2010

the format of the most common work experiences and the shape of the factory influenced the content and format of the school—working alone at a machine, a workstation, or a task. In the 21st century, in which collaboration and communication are highly prized skills, should not the work spaces and the format and process of the teaching-learning experience shape how students will learn and give them the opportunity to work alone when appropriate and together when beneficial or required by the task?

TEAM TYPES: WHAT IS THE DIFFERENCE?

Cooperative-learning skill development occurs in two ways. First, there is the informal way. Such tactics as think-pair-share, peer partners, write-pair-share, and turn-to-a-neighbor are informal tactics. Teachers structure the interaction, but make no attempt to "teach" or develop the skills inherent in the format. Second, there is the formal way. In the formal way, teachers place students in mixed groups of three to five, assign roles and responsibilities, and provide a common goal for the task as well as guidelines for appropriate interactions and tools for each team's self-assessment. The teacher formally or intentionally teaches the students how to interact constructively using these tactics.

The Johnsons' (Johnson, Johnson, & Holubec, 1993) five criteria provide often-used benchmarks by which teachers and students can formally assess their work as a team.

THE BENEFITS OF FORMAL COOPERATIVE-LEARNING TEAMS

Formal work teams in which students learn the skills of working together to achieve a common or shared goal have multiple benefits. Teachers will lose content time when they first prepare students to work in formal cooperative teams. Just as experienced doubles tennis players rely on a special set of skills, so students learn that a group with formal skills is a more efficient way to learn in a team. As a result, they become more efficient with their cooperative skill sets and more effective in learning their content.

Why are skilled cooperative learners more effective learners than those plopped into a group and told to do a task? Note these ten reasons.

1. Collaboration makes group tasks easier to do, especially those necessitated by task complexity and time limits. If nothing else, there is an efficient division of labor.

THE JOHNSON FIVE:
BENCHMARKS FOR COOPERATIVE LEARNING

1. **Positive Interdependence.** Students who work in groups learn how to work in a constructive way with students from different racial, economic, and ethnic groups. They become dependent on one another to accomplish the shared goal.

2. **Individual Accountability.** Students learn together by helping one another understand the material. However, they also learn that all individuals in the learning group will be responsible or accountable for showing what they each have contributed to the group's accomplishment and what they each have understood and can do.

3. **Group Process.** Students learn that there is a cooperative goal structure to each group task. They learn what it takes to function as a member of a team with give and take. In order to accomplish the shared goal, the members assess that process and learn its components.

4. **Social-Skill Development.** Students develop the social skills needed for collaborative work. Facilitated by the teacher, students reflect on the social skills they are developing and devise ways to improve their interactions with one another.

5. **Face-to-Face Interaction.** Students learn conflict resolution skills as they work with each other on difficult tasks and resolve differences of opinion. In a digital age, students learn to use e-tools to substitute for face-to-face work when substitution is appropriate.

2. Collaboration is a significant raiser of student achievement, especially when it is provided in the form of a cooperative-learning goal structure. Listed in Marzano's nine highest-effect classroom strategies list, cooperative-learning groups have a very positive achievement record when appropriately used in classrooms. Individualistic and competitive goal structures are far less effective in helping students learn the curriculum (Johnson, Johnson, & Holubec, 1992).

3. Cooperative goal structures provide teachers with an essential tool to differentiate instruction with students of varied abilities and motivation.

4. Cooperative goal structures provide students with opportunities to think more deeply about the content they are studying.

5. Cooperative groups make excellent "beds" for use of such tools as graphic organizers when students are gathering project data, discussing ideas among themselves, or communicating their thinking to others. When other high-effect instructional strategies are embedded in cooperative groups, the likelihood of even stronger learning effects comes to fruition.

6. A purposefully collaborative learning environment encourages reluctant or shy learners to share ideas that they might not in front of the entire class and to take a more active part in learning and project tasks.

7. Collaborations better develop students' social skills for solving work-world problems.

8. Collaborations better enable students to communicate with each other and with adults.

9. A collaborative learning environment enriches the interactions students must have as they use collaborative e-tools and develop complex projects or solve difficult problems.

10. When used with heterogeneous groups (ability, gender, race, ethnic origin, and so on), cooperative learning increases positive relationships among the group members and breaks down social barriers by building trust and communication.

AN ACADEMIC TOOL WITH A RECORD

Projects and lessons that are structured collaborations provide students with a well-proven tool set. They also provide students with the opportunity to improve the quality of their learning. Cooperative groups as researched by Roger Johnson and David Johnson (1993; Johnson, Johnson, & Smith, 2007), Robert Slavin (2000), and others provide a tool that has proved over and over that it can increase academic performance well above work done alone or in competition with others. This may be the strongest reason for teachers to include cooperative groups in any classroom, but especially in learning groups that highlight development of collaborative-learning skills. In the 21st century context, this research carries even more weight. In a just-completed meta-analysis of cooperative learning in modern-day classrooms, the Johnsons and their colleagues found that cooperative learning is all the more valued as a tool for building positive relationships in collaborative environments (Johnson & Johnson, 2010). Once again, the study corroborated this strategy's high impact on achievement.

DEFINING A COOPERATIVE LEARNING GROUP

By definition, *mixed-ability* groups with a common academic goal are "co-operative groups." Mixed-ability groups may present the greatest challenge to teachers who must structure the cooperative work. However, such heterogeneous groups tend to result in the greatest benefit.

As noted above, cooperative groups have several distinguishing characteristics that make the effective cooperative-*learning* group distinct from other classroom *work* groups. The Johnson five spell out the attributes that distinguish a learning group that has the essential cooperative goal structure. (Some teachers like to use the acronym "PIGS FACE" as a mnemonic device to represent the five elements.) By defining the strategy with these attributes, the researchers signal, "This is what cooperative learning is. Anything less is mere group work."

INSTRUCTIONAL TACTICS AND FORMAL COOPERATIVE-LEARNING GROUPS

To structure learning-group work that promotes on-task behavior, teaches collaborative skills, and leads to the best achievement results in a collaborative effort, teachers can make use of a variety of instructional tactics. These tactics are the tools that students learn to use in a formal cooperative group. Because they help students become skillful with the five attributes, it is these tools that they master to carve out each successful cooperative-group experience.

1. **Promote DOVE Guidelines.** Guidelines remind students of those behaviors that are most likely to promote the engagement of all members of the group in the task.
   Defer judgment. Do not use putdowns or make negative comments about others' ideas.
   Opt for the off-beat. As a thinker, think outside the box. Try different ways. Seek new combinations.
   Vast numbers are needed. Go for a big quantity of ideas from which you can select the best.
   Expand. Piggyback on or hitchhike with others' ideas.
2. **Structure Pairs.** With computers, pairs are an efficient team size. Teachers structure these pairs to share equal responsibility within each task. Pairs also allow for more intense dialogue. Teachers

may arrange larger-sized groups when the task is sufficiently complex to engage all when students have developed the interactive social skills.

3. **Encourage Roles and Responsibilities.** Teachers post a standard set of roles that students can use to facilitate tasks in learning groups. As with cohesive sports teams, each person has a specific role with spelled-out responsibilities. Samples may include

    Recorder: Has the responsibility to fill in the graphic organizer or keep notes that become the official document of the group.

    Reader: Has the task of reading the material and the instructions to the class.

    Leader: Has the task of making sure all understand their roles, the instructions, and the ideas from the group. Keeps group on task.

4. **Assess Cooperation.** From time to time, the team leader uses a rubric to assess the group's positive interactions. All members talk about how they can improve the quality of their collaborations.

5. **Require Shared Tools.** Positive interdependence is enriched when the group shares a single computer, a single graphic on a large sheet of newsprint (butcher paper), or a web tool or other e-device such as an e-portfolio. The members agree on their ideas for using the shared tool together and its value in promoting collaboration and communication.

6. **Use a T-Chart.** Teachers use this graphic organizer to build students' understanding of the collaborative social skills. After naming an essential cooperative social skill such as "good listening," the teacher asks the class, "What does listening look like?" and records the answers in column 1. Next, the teacher asks, "What does listening sound like?" and records the responses in column 2. Teachers post this T-chart for reference throughout the learning-group tasks. In a no-frills classroom, it is important that students generate these ideas. Purchased prelisted charts, no matter how attractive, do not allow for student "ownership" of the ideas generated.

7. **Monitor Groups.** When students are working in the cooperative-learning groups, teachers walk among the students to confirm that every student gets to contribute, that students are using their interactive social skills, that all are doing their assigned roles, and that all understand the material. Teachers intervene if they note a problem that the group cannot solve. Teachers avoid giving

answers, but use turn-back questions to encourage deeper thinking in the group.

8. **Reinforce "Good Thinking."** By taking note of what students are saying as they work in the learning group, teachers can hear the quality of thinking. When teachers "catch students thinking," they tell students what they like. "I'm glad to hear you thinking carefully before your speak" (controlled impulsivity). "I like the way this group started with a plan" (planning behavior.) "Glad to see how you have re-checked your numbers" (precision and accuracy).

9. **Connect to the Goal.** Before students begin work in their groups, teachers make clear the value of group work and its connection to the collaborative goal.

TOWARD A COLLABORATIVE-LEARNING COMMUNITY

Teachers can deepen the positive effects of cooperative learning with the creation of an all-encompassing collaborative classroom culture. In this classroom, teachers interconnect all available resources to give priority to students working together. For instance, by their nature, digital tools structure interactions between students. These same e-tools compound student engagement when the lesson or project connects with other students beyond the classroom borders. E-tools empower students to skip across those borders. Some tools cause students to talk with one another each time the tool connects the students in a common task. Others, such as social networking tools, create long-term interactions. Blogs, wikis, and pods fall into this group. Other e-tools that are used for a shared task such as making a PowerPoint presentation or a multimedia show invite collaboration. Even SMART boards can serve as a natural tool for promoting collaborative communication. In all these cases, however, teachers miss the richest opportunity to enhance student success if they fail to take advantage of formal cooperative learning so that students will have a doubly enriched learning experience each time they communicate using an e-tool.

Cooperative learning is the most proven instructional strategy for enriching connections in the classroom. By taking the time to prepare students to take advantage of this powerful strategy, teachers provide them with a tool that increases learning for all in an assigned task; further, the teacher is able to structure classroom learning experiences so that all the students find themselves helping all other students.

To move students beyond working on a task-to-task basis in cooperative groups, teachers can give students the challenge of learning how to apply the collaborative skills they are developing to the larger goal of a classroom in which collaborative interaction is the norm. To do this, teachers can initiate the following practices:

1. After students have completed their first experience in a cooperative team, make a new mix of students into "base groups." Base groups will meet at least once a month but preferably at least once a week. Use such activities as team motto, team name, team coat-of-arms, and team cheer to build the group's cohesion. If the opportunity presents itself, take the class on an excursion to a team-building sports facility such as Outward Bound for a day's team-building activity.
2. Invite base groups to assess their teamwork and share the results with the class.
3. For each new unit or project, remix the heterogeneous task groups. During the course, seek to have every student work in a cooperative task group with every other student.
4. Facilitate an all-class brainstorm that begins with pairs, moves to groups of four and eight, and eventually arrives at an all-class community discussion. Determine with the class what the shared goal is for this class as a community. Identify ways to achieve that goal and make a chart to show progress.
5. Hold all-class brainstorming sessions to assess how the community of learners is developing. Discuss such questions as, What does collaboration look like in this classroom? How can we improve our communication? What other activities will help us make more positive connections with one another?
6. Facilitate an all-class quarterly assessment of collaboration and communication in this learning community.

TO THE MAX: THE PRODUCTIVE WORK ENVIRONMENT

Nothing works against technology collaboration more than the shallow concept that wiring student computers in a chain is all that needs to be done. Classrooms that line computer stations around the outer walls or block students off in carrels that signal "individual work" create boundaries in the classroom that work against optimal collaboration. Many high tech schools have made that mistake, and many have learned the error of that way. The most productive work areas for collaboration and communication not only network students, but encourage students in work and learning teams to talk face-to-face. This requires only the removal of carrel walls that divide students. Students grouped in tables of three or four can more easily do the face-to-face talking that they may need at any moment in a collaborative project or task. This structure starts with work tables to which students can bring their notebooks or laptops as they share ideas about the work they are doing and evolve toward working together online, both synchronously and asynchronously.

CONCLUDING THOUGHTS

Collaborative-learning experiences reflect the teamwork expected in the modern adult work world. It is the "all together now" spirit put into practice. When teachers take advantage of cooperative learning, a high-effects instructional strategy, to prepare students to work more effectively in learn-work teams, they encourage students of different abilities, motivations, races, ethnicities, and genders to work together to a achieve a shared goal. As a result, cooperative learning has proved to be a very effective tool for increasing student achievement, reaching project goals, and preparing students for social interactions in the non-academic work world. Cooperative-learning groups, mediated to interact and think more efficiently, produce more effective results.

CHAPTER 8

What Were You Thinking?

How to Sharpen Thinking
in the Collaborative Classroom

> The dynamic conditions of modern life require all individuals to be
> ready for flexible change in their behavioral and mental attitudes.
> This can only be achieved through increased plasticity and
> modifiability of our learning and thinking functions.
>
> —Reuven Feuerstein

I N THE MID-20TH CENTURY, the groundbreaking cognitive psychologist Reuven Feuerstein, a student of Jean Piaget, made public his
seminal ideas about learning and thinking. He rejected the notion that
intelligence was fixed. At a national education conference in the United
States, he presented the argument that intelligence was plastic and flexible. Thus, he said, "we can change it." Most in the audience shook their
heads. Some laughed out loud. "Come on," they whispered, "just look at
the bell curve. Some have smarts and some do not. Intelligence is as hard
as a rock."

In the following decades, Arthur Jensen, Charles Murray, and Richard
Herrnstein argued against Feuerstein's basic view (Herrnstein & Murray,
1994; Jensen, 1998). Their case for the fixed intelligence suggested that
schools had little value for any but the brightest. They suggested that it
mattered little how good or bad a teacher was; whatever he or she did
could have no effect on improving the learning of any child. In the time
since, brain research has sided with Feuerstein. In his most recent book,
Beyond Smarter (Feuerstein, Feuerstein, & Falik, 2010), Feuerstein and his
colleagues outline the advances made in mediating changes in intelligence.
He supports the work with research conducted using conventional methods and with advanced brain-research techniques that are able to detect
changes in the brain's physical structure.

Thinking is a generic word, an umbrella term that covers many different thinking operations and functions that adults and students work to improve on a daily basis. Following Feuerstein's favorite metaphor, "connecting the dots" has become a popular way to describe when public servants and others are thinking well, and when they are not. Throughout the curriculum, well-formulated standards specify the cognitive operations, crucial thinking skills, and mental functions that are essential prerequisites for students who are challenged to use their best thinking to master content in any subject area. Although most classroom teachers attend to the content element of the standards, few if any attend to the stipulated thinking operation. Less attend to the implied cognitive functions.

"Look!" the child exclaimed. "The emperor has no clothes. Where are his clothes?"

The crowd looked. A gasp rose to the sky. "Oh, my gosh," said one mother, covering her child's eyes. "The boy is right. The emperor has no clothes. He is walking naked down the road."

Quickly, the rumor spread. "Come quickly," rose the cry. "Come see the emperor without any clothes!"

The teacher closed the book. She asked, "How many of you have heard this story?"

Most of the students in the class raised their hands. "And what do you think this story means?" asked the teacher.

The class sat quiet for a moment. The teacher saw they were deep in thought. After a few moments, several raised their hands.

"I think it means that people are easily fooled," volunteered the first student. "Just because one person said it doesn't mean it has to be so."

"I agree," said the second student.

"Are you agreeing because Maria said so?" asked the teacher. "Or do you have a reason?"

"I have a reason for my answer. I think it is important to have your own facts to back up a claim."

"And what are the facts for your claim?" asked the teacher.

"Do you remember last week when we were supposed to go on the trip to the museum? Some students said we were leaving at 8:00 a.m. By the time lunch came, we all agreed that 8:00 was what you said. But nobody asked. We just took everyone else's word until Ellie showed us the piece of paper that said '9 o'clock.' We were just like the people spreading the rumor about the emperor."

When asking the question "How can teachers develop students' thinking and problem solving skills so they become more efficient learners of prescribed content?" the standards provide the most important clues. When asking the question "How can teachers develop students' ability to transfer these skills across the curriculum and into life?" the starting point is with these same standards.

The "how to" teach "thinking" is no longer a secret. Research about best practices provides ample alternatives for teachers to teach all students how to improve their thinking and how to use their improved cognitive operations to increase their understanding of prescribed content.

WISDOM IN A CHILD'S STORY

The familiar story of the emperor is one among many fairy tales and myths that can hook children of all ages into critical thinking. From kindergarten to graduate school, students can learn how to make cognitive connections between specified critical and creative thinking skills and the stories of the emperor, Tikki Tikki Tembo, Chicken Little, Borreguita, Humpty Dumpty, Icarus, Juno, and Jabu. The more efficient students become as thinkers about the curriculum they study, the more effective they are when they must use critical thinking operations to meet all the problem solving challenges they will face in the world outside the boundaries of the schoolhouse walls.

WHAT IS "THINKING"?

Thinking, like *driving*, can be interpreted to mean many different things. Its possible definitions are legion. In the simplest terms, thinking is any cognitive process that operates in the brain. It may be a macro *operation* such as hypothesizing or comparing. Or it may be a simple *function* such as attending to precise details, restraining oneself from impulsive guesses, or making simultaneous use of multiple data sources. In the 19th century, strong arguments were made for the theory that intelligence was fixed at birth; these have continued to this day. In the 20th century, Reuven Feuerstein (1980, 2001), Howard Gardner (1999), Robert Sternberg (1988), and other cognitive psychologists refuted this theory. Oliver Sacks (1985, 2010), a psychiatrist, neurologist, and popular author, has contributed detail and complexity to our thinking about intelligence.

Feuerstein, as noted earlier, postulated more than 50 years ago that brains are plastic, or malleable, and intelligence is not fixed. Gardner added his voice with the theory of multiple intelligences and Sternberg presented his triarchic theory of intelligence. For those educators who disagree with the fixed-intelligence theorists and follow the thoughts of Feuerstein and other cognitive psychologists as well as the growing number of brain researchers in support of the changeable intelligence, the belief extends to best practices that change children's minds (Brainin, 1987).

Most recently, Gardner (2007) has identified five types of thinking that he hypothesizes will be most important in the 21st century. First, and most relevant to most classrooms, among the five are ways of thinking that spring from what he labels the "disciplined mind." His list of skills for this first future mind characteristic aligns with those critical thinking skills that enable students to think more analytically about their world: compare, distinguish, infer, classify, and explain why.

Under the label *thinking*, there are multiple cognitive operations, each of which activates different parts of the brain. Humans can think in many different ways depending on what they want to accomplish. Some, like Michelangelo and da Vinci, think visually. They can see a problem from many perspectives. Others may think in several modes at once, making combinations and noting differences. Aristotle was noted for comparing two opposite ideas as he looked for the similarities that he could turn into a metaphor. Others, such as Marie Curie or Jonas Salk, posed a hypothesis and set out to prove it with scientific evidence.

Generic action words such as *driving, swimming*, and *cooking* can only hint at the specific skills and operations that lead individuals to succeed with the described action, no matter how different the conditions. Race car drivers need sharp skills of anticipating, steering, weaving, speed control, and reacting, no matter which track or road they drive over. The master chef's list of skills for tasting, smelling, mixing ingredients, determining heat, and presenting is very long but usable in any kitchen.

There are some who contend that schools in the 21st century need to forget these skills and concentrate solely on the content. Taking any time away from content is time off the task of expanding knowledge by supplying students with information to memorize and store. They reject the thoughts of the cognitive psychologists that emphasize the how of learning.

Understanding, as seen by the cognitive psychologists, requires many different mental processes. Although some geniuses may have been born with the facility to use these skills with great facility from birth, most work hard to learn how to sharpen these skills as they grow older. Just as "getting

> Genius is one percent inspiration and ninety-nine percent perspiration.
>
> —Thomas Alva Edison

stronger" is possible for any who work out and push their physical conditioning with a systematic exercise program, "getting smarter" is possible for those who work out their minds with a systematic exercise program. In this paradigm, effective teachers produce the most effective results on the quality of a student's mental conditioning.

WHO THINKS BEST?

Every child who comes through a schoolhouse door "thinks." Thinking is what the human brain does. In school, all children are expected to learn by using their brains to learn the standards-prescribed content. *All children* includes the poor, those with special learning challenges, females as well as males, students of color, and all individuals who have often been deemed "not able to think as well" or "limited in their learning ability." Some children come to school less ready to think as sharply as needed. For those who follow the theories of Feuerstein, Gardner, Sternberg, and other cognitive psychologists and neuropsychologists who believe in the plasticity of the brain, it is the responsibility of educators to sharpen the thinking of all, to develop the mind's capacity to learn more and more, whether they think their students are the ready or the not-yet-ready. Although every child may not become a superstar Einstein, it is not the job of the educator to predetermine how efficient a thinker or learner any child might become; it is to use the best of practices so that all children do make the changes that allow their minds to continue the never-ending process of becoming more mentally skillful.

Just as NASCAR drivers or master chefs can improve their skills, so too can students. Just as it takes years of learning for the car driver and the chef to become "masters," it also takes the student many years to master the important cognitive skills that make up "thinking." The individual's challenge, since the time when Socrates sat on the famous log and asked questions of his student Aristotle, has been to identify the many skills that make up what humans call "thinking" and to find ways to improve their use.

Under the umbrella, the "big idea," called *thinking,* there are many cognitive operations, functions, and tools that students can develop in order to become more skillful thinkers. Throughout history, various students of the mind have taken the term *thinking* and divided it into two or more classes. The attempts continue in the 21st century.

In addition to describing the "disciplined mind," Harvard's Howard Gardner (2007) has proposed four other categories of minds for the future that he believes are important for schooling in the 21st century. His five categories, separate from his multiple intelligences, include the disciplined mind, the synthesizing mind, the creative mind, the respectful mind, and the ethical mind. "Our survival as a planet," he writes, "may depend on the cultivation of this pentad of mental dispositions." He postulates that all these minds are important for global learning in every classroom (Bellanca & Brandt, 2010).

Others, including the Partnership for 21st Century Skills (http://www.p21.org), rely on a more traditional two-category division: creative thinking and critical thinking. Critical thinking includes those cognitive operations that enable students to analyze, compare, separate cause from effect, prove a hypothesis, form general principles, determine the meaning and significance of what is observed or expressed, or decide whether there is adequate justification to accept a conclusion as true. Creative thinking, also called *divergent thinking*, includes cognitive operations that enable students to innovate by generating multiple ideas (brainstorming), varying components, questioning alternatives, expanding concepts, making metaphors and inventing analogies, associating diverse concepts, and seeking possibilities (Williams, 2010). Brooke Noel Moore and Richard Parker (1986) define *thinking* more narrowly. They explain critical thinking as the careful, deliberate determination of whether one should accept, reject, or suspend judgment about a *claim* and the degree of confidence with which one accepts or rejects it. Given any of these definitions, the crowd who "saw" the emperor's new clothes failed to think critically.

In a metaphoric sense, critical thinking may be viewed as thinking "inside the box." In schools, when attention has been given to "thinking," it is usually given so that students improve how they "connect the dots" in the curriculum, using the divergent-thinking skills that Gardner identifies as central in the "disciplined" mind. On the other hand, the creative thinking skills that encourage students to think "outside the box" focus on having students explore ideas, generate possible solutions, find alternatives, and explore associations. They include thinking skills for what Gardner calls the creative mind and are usually reserved for fine arts classes and other classes outside the core curriculum.

WHAT IS SPECIAL ABOUT CRITICAL
AND CREATIVE THINKING IN THE 21ST CENTURY?

Among the 21st century skills, the various frameworks identify critical think-ing as the most important. Innovation immediately follows. In a standards-aligned classroom, development of these cognitive skills is seen as especially important in order to better foster students' standards-aligned learning ex-periences. Most important, these skills are viewed as essential for students to live and learn successfully in the new 21st century work world. In one sense, critical and creative thinking skills are seen as the motor that drives the car forward. They provide the power that determines efficiency and the effectiveness of student learning. Without the motor's forward thrust, the car of learning is perceived as stuck in the mud, unable to move forward.

In a collaborative classroom, critical and creative thinking skills have a special home. This is especially true if teachers are taking advantage of cooperative-learning teams to upgrade the quality of collaborative work. When they are well-structured, collaborative tasks require inquiry or prob-lem solving by students working together as they take multiple points of view, call on multiple talents, and rely on multiple intelligences to solve significant problems. In a well-functioning team, teachers can use coopera-tive learning at its optimum to enrich the process and heighten the chances of a high-quality product or solution. If these teams have sharpened those critical-thinking tools that enable the inquiry or problem solving to func-tion at a high level, it is likely that the students will gain more from their collaborative work than they would without the skills or if asked to apply the skills to a low-level recall task.

However, in most traditional 20th century–style classrooms, few teach-ers had time to attend fully to these crucial critical thinking skills. When teachers presented their prescribed curriculum, more often than not their students *read from textbooks* about the content that the content standards described or *heard* explanations of the prescribed content from the words of the teacher. In this context, the students' challenge was to decipher the information poured into their heads, make sense of factual data, practice repetitive examples on worksheets, select and memorize what they think is most important to know, and pass a final test to show what they can recall. Completing these tasks in well-organized cooperative groups did raise achievement scores, but certainly did not use the strategy for its po-tential full effect.

In the information-heavy 21st century, it becomes all the more impor-tant that teachers have the time and skill to do more than pour informa-

"Thinking skills? My teachers do that," the principal said.

"That's good," the instructional coach responded. "Did you draw that conclusion from the data you collected when your teachers completed the MILE Guide Assessment?"

"Yes. In the instructional session most put themselves in the basic area less than 25% of the time. Some disagreed and rated themselves 'transitional.' And I would agree with them. These are the ones who do some creative teaching. There are others who ask higher-order questions and the science teachers all have lab projects."

"So are they intentional with these?" asked the coach.

"Sometimes yes, sometimes no. I can't find a pattern. It's more 'catch as catch can,' I think. It depends on the teacher."

tion prescribed by the standards into empty noggins. There are very few content-area standards that do not contain at least one critical or creative thinking operation. As noted with the 21st century skills of collaboration and communication, national professional organizations and state departments of education have outlined standards that describe the most important *content*. For the most part, these same content standards enunciate the critical thinking *processes* that apply within each content area, even though formal instruction in these cognitive processes is bypassed in a vast majority of today's classrooms.

CRITICAL THINKING SKILLS IN THE STANDARDS

Operations of the Mind

In any content area or discipline such as social studies, language arts, math, or science, teachers may help students discover that there are specific operations of the mind that are best suited to the challenge of making meaning from the data they gather. For instance, when introducing a lesson with a story of Abraham Lincoln reading in front of the fireplace, the teacher readies the class for an investigation of those attributes that made him a great president. After asking the students to use this incident to predict what kind of work habits Lincoln would show during his presidency, she launches right into her project. With this scenario, the teacher did stir the students' predictive thinking and character analysis. However, she missed the teachable moment. She missed the opportunity to help the students "think about the thinking" they had done. The teacher bypassed the window of opportunity to have the students examine how they analyzed, compared, or drew inferences so they could learn how to sharpen the quality of their thinking skills in future lessons or projects.

Using Content Standards to Guide Instruction for Sharpened Thinking

An analysis of the Massachusetts Curriculum Framework offers a model expression of content standards that include the relevant thinking processes in a subject area. In the Massachusetts exemplar, each standard explicitly identifies the important critical or creative thinking processes that highlight how students should learn to think about the important content.

Consider this learning standard taken from the Massachusetts Framework for high school mathematics (http://www.doe.mass.edu/). The standard asks that "students engage in problem solving, communicating, reasoning, connecting and representing as they select, create and interpret an appropriate graphical representation (e.g., scatter plots, tables, stem and leaf plots) for a set of data and use approximate statistics to communicate information about data and use these notions to compare different sets of data." What is notable is the standards' integration of various thinking skills with math content. When do students learn the meaning of all these mindful commands?

The label "learning standards" used in the Massachusetts Framework replaces the more usual "content standards" label given by other states. This label immediately suggests a necessary link between the content (e.g., graphical representations such as scatter plots) and the thinking skills required to use the various graphical plots: According to the learning standard, students will have to "engage in problem solving, communicating, reasoning, connecting and representing." Additional descriptors such as "select," "create," "interpret" and "use" suggest there is more to the learning standard than asking students to memorize the terms *scatter plot* and *stem and leaf plots* or to practice how to complete a dozen such plots on a worksheet.

A review of commonly used mathematics textbooks, however, undercuts the content-process link in this standard. These texts devote the most space in their pages about "graphical representations" to a definition of each representation (nicely bolded) with additional space reserved for practice procedures using each of the graphs. Little space is provided to the thinking words that this standard explicates.

SAMPLE THINKING VERBS

Analyze	Evaluate	Reason	Develop a hypothesis	Connect
Explain why	Represent	Judge	Use	Compare	Estimate

www.doe.mass.edu

Teachers who were informally interviewed indicated that they had very limited time to "cover" the topic of geometric representations. Time to help students "create, interpret, and use" was a luxury they could not afford. "Lots of them (students) can't even recall the procedures," said one teacher. "Any extra time I have is needed for practicing the multiple problems in the textbook." At best, the teachers suggested, they covered the material as required. "My strong math students will 'get it.'" As for the rest of the students, one teacher commented, "The bright ones can do the practice without me. And I don't have the time to teach all the thinking stuff, which most of my kids wouldn't get anyway."

In contrast to teachers who focus on the "what" or the content as detailed in their textbooks and are happy to "cover" the textbook topic, those teachers who engage in 21st century skills find that the skills' impetus urges them to allot time to explicit attention to the thinking skills identified in these same standards. In fact, if the count of words in a standard were any indication of the value of the thinking process element related to the content described, many more teachers would have the impetus to concentrate at least equally on the thinking processes.

THE NEXT GENERATION: THE CORE CONTENT STATE STANDARDS

With the advent of the Core Content State Standards, adopting states will follow the Massachusetts example, whereby the marriage of thinking skills and content is strong.

"*Analyze how and why* individuals, events, and ideas develop and interact over the course of a text"
(College and Career Readiness Anchor Standard for Reading).

"*Reason about* and *solve* one-variable equations and inequalities"
(Common Core State Standards for Mathematics) (www.corestandards.org).

All standards provided in the Massachusetts Framework, as well as those in the next-generation model, the Common Core State Standards, do link content expectations with a thinking process. The majority call for critical thinking; those that request problem solving include the creative thinking skills as a part of that macro process.

The Forgotten Standards

Because so much emphasis is placed on math and language arts, the standards for other disciplines are often bypassed. However, just as language arts/literacy and mathematics standards include both the thinking process key word as well as important content, those in other disciplines do as well. The following standards are samples extracted from different disciplines and grades. In each, thinking and content are partners.

1. Foreign language: High school cultures strand
    Using sentences, strings of sentences, and fluid sentence-length, paragraph-length, and essay-length messages with some patterns of errors that do not interfere with meaning, students will
    > ***Describe*** the evolution of words, proverbs, and images and ***discuss how*** they reflect cultural perspectives
    > ***Analyze*** examples of literature, primary source historical documents, music, visual arts, theatre, dance, and other artifacts from target culture(s) and ***discuss how*** they reflect individual and cultural perspectives
    > ***Describe*** conflicts in ***points of view*** within and among cultures and their possible resolutions and ***discuss how*** the conflicts and proposed resolutions ***reflect*** cultural and individual perspectives
    > ***Distinguish*** among knowledge, informed opinions, un-informed opinions, stereotypes, prejudices, biases, open mindedness, narrow mindedness, and closed mindedness in literature, primary and secondary source documents, mass media, and multimedia presentations about and/or from culture; and discuss how these presentations reflect cultural and individual perspectives

2. Social studies: Grade 3
    Describe the difference between a contemporary map of their city or town and the map of their city or town in the 18th, 19th , or early 20th century.

3. Literature: Grade 7
   Standard 8: Understanding a Text
   Students will
   > *Identify basic facts and main ideas* in a text and use them as the basis for *interpretation.*
   > Use knowledge of genre characteristics to *analyze* a text.
   > *Interpret* mood in a text and *give supporting evidence.*
   > *Identify evidence* in a text that supports an argument.

Analyzing the Critical Thinking Skills in the Standards

The grade 3 social studies standard above provides a model for selecting an important thinking skill to develop in a lesson or project. In this case, the words "describe the difference" indicate that students will be using the skill of comparing as they focus on differences among the maps. Teachers will need to take very little time to develop this important skill. It is also a standard that students can exceed easily. For that, teachers need only ask a follow-up question that will enable the students to go beyond their classroom walls as they ask peers in other communities around the globe, "How is where you live different from our city or town?"

The lesson example that follows shows how easily teachers can work simultaneously with content and thinking skills. By selecting connected instructional strategies that research has shown will have the highest impact on achievement, teachers get a "two for one" result. In one swoop, they can deepen students' understanding of the prescribed *content* while preparing students to use the targeted thinking skill in other learning experiences and become more effective learners.

The nonrepresentational figure the Venn diagram is familiar to many teachers as a tactic for helping students compare facts or concepts. For early learners, this graphic organizer has been a very effective tool for making comparisons such as "How is an Asian elephant like/different from an African elephant?" "What are the similarities among the three Billy Goats Gruff?"

Often, effective teachers have taken the students beyond comparing the facts that answer these questions to explicating the comparing process. By going a step beyond using the Venn or other graphic organizers for a single comparative action, teachers can scaffold students' understanding of new comparative thinking behaviors. In less than 5 minutes per day allotted to developing the students' mastery of the comparative skill, perhaps the most called-for type of thinking across all curriculum areas, teachers can

Step 1: Ask the launch question.

"Here are two maps. How are they alike? Different?" Seek multiple answers from at least five students. Post the responses for all to see in a list for "alike" and a list for "different."

Step 2: Give feedback to the students' responses and state the objective that focuses on the thinking skill.

Model "comparative thinking behavior" by employing the Venn diagram to help students distinguish between two familiar maps of their community. Project the maps and a blank Venn diagram that you can write on, on a screen or whiteboard. Show students how to pick out the similarities on the maps. Label each and provide alternative vocabulary words such as *likeness*, *sameness*, and so on. Explore how they understand these words. Follow with a similar discussion of "differences." Model how to use the diagram to show the differences.

Step 3: Check for understanding.

Display the completed Venn and check students' understanding of the key thinking terms by asking them to explain the terms, how they used them, and why the words *like* and *different* are important.

Step 4: Guide practice of the thinking process.

1. Break students into formal cooperative groups of three at their computer stations.
2. Assign roles (operator, recorder, asker), review guidelines and procedures, and so on.
3. Send a sample of their town's current map and a sample town map from the last century to each computer. Give each team a paper-printed blank Venn. One student will record the group's ideas as they proceed through the comparison process. Keep the groups' together on each substep in the process. Keep the projected substeps on the screen or interactive whiteboard. Complete each substep before advancing the class.
4. In your team Scan Map 1 for all the items you think are important on the first map (target number 6). Scan Map 2 for the same items as Map 1 (same number).

   - Scan both maps for other ways they are alike (e.g., color, size, shape, placement, function, etc.) (Target six more in each).
   - Enter all items that match under the same spaces on the Venn.
   - Scan both maps for how each map is different (select six items).
   - List in the center space.
   - Check for missing items.

Step 5: Reflecting and reviewing.

Ask students to identify what they have learned about making comparisons and think about how they could follow the seven subsets in other situations. Highlight the "thinking" vocabulary so that students sink the meaning of the "thinking" words into their short- and long-term memory. Review these words on a regular basis by asking students to do quick "like" and "different" identifications of objects in the room. ("Let's take a minute to talk about 'alike.' When is something 'like' something else? Tell me how my desk chair is like yours.")

Step 6: Construct process summaries.

Conclude with a discussion that allows the student teams to write their summaries of the differences between the current time's map and the map examined as called for in the standard. Review the key thinking words and ask students for examples that challenge their use of the words.

crystallize the process and make it a permanent fixture in students' learning tool kit. What helps this process is the teacher's explicit declarations to target the comparing process along with student discussions of what and how they do the comparing.

A Guide for Developing Critical Thinking Skills in Lessons

When a standard identifies a thinking skill such as comparing to accompany the content in a lesson, teachers can adjust their lessons or projects to include the intentional development of that skill. In the example shown in the sidebar, six steps provide a logical progression of activities interspersed over a week's time that take students well beyond the activity (the Venn) and help them learn about and from the thinking they just did using the Venn.

Moving On

On succeeding days, it is important for teachers to keep the target skill in the students' mind's eye. This helps students crystallize the targeted thinking process and form a habit of thinking. For instance, in the 3rd week of focus on the thinking skill of comparing, teachers can ask volunteers to review the meaning of the word *compare*. Next, they can ask student teams to review and check one another's understanding of the substeps for using the graphic Venn to organize the similarities and differences. Finally, having checked for understanding, teachers can invite the student teams to use the Venn as they compare the current map with the map from the next century. If students have their own blogs, they can help each other store completed Venns and summaries. If students are not able to access blogs, they can maintain pen-and-paper portfolios to hold their completed work.

When teachers schedule the third round of map comparisons for the final century in the above example, they have the opportunity to draw back and give students more room to think on their own. The third round of study with the third map allows teachers to step further away from the thinking process and encourage students to increase their self-direction in the management of the thinking processes.

In a step-back role with this map comparison, teachers ask their map-making student teams to review what they understand about how to compare using the Venn as a helping tool. When the teams have finished their reviews, teachers direct the students to use their thinking process with a new map. Teachers walk among the pairs, check student progress, make corrective suggestions, and encourage deeper thinking. Afterward, they conduct an all-class discussion about the comparisons made between these two maps and how students used the Venn to help.

When students show that they understand the skill of comparing as the tool for distinguishing elements of the maps, teachers know they are ready to conduct a final summative task during which students can assess what they have leaned to do with the targeted thinking operation. The teacher can also provide a quiz that will evaluate students' knowledge of the differences among the various maps. A test and the student reflection bring to a close this sequence of tasks related to this standard.

Adapting the Lesson. As teachers pass through their curricula, they can use this model lesson as a guide for development of other standards-embedded critical thinking skills. By starting lessons with a process launch question such as "What does it mean to compare?" or "What does it mean to solve a problem?" or "What does it mean to analyze cause and effect?" teachers raise the possibility that students will jump-start expansion of their critical thinking skills. By using students' prior knowledge, teachers are not assuming that students might develop a critical thinking skill just

---

Crystallize: The mental ability to access prior knowledge so as to increase understanding of a concept or process well enough to put new ideas and skills to daily use.

A CHART OF MATCHED THINKING SKILLS

Web	Generating Ideas	Creative
Radial Web	Generating Ideas	Creative
CMap	Generating	Both

and Connecting Ideas

Venn	Comparing	Critical
Matrix	Classifying	Critical
Sequence	Ordering	Critical
Newspaper Chart	Classifying	Critical

because it is stated in the standards. It will happen because students are given the tools to develop and use their understanding of how to think about the content they are asked to study.

In addition to phrasing a launch question that focuses on a desired skill improvement, teachers can advance the development of the students' understanding and use of a targeted thinking skill by refining their own questioning and cueing skills as they "coach" students' skill refinements. In addition, teachers will want to expand their repertoire of graphic organizers matched to the appropriate critical thinking skill.

Assessing the Lesson. Last, by developing rubrics, checklists, or observation charts for assessing the thinking skills, teachers can enable students to deepen their understanding of the targeted skill. Teachers provide other useful tools that reinforce the fine points of the skill in action. A well-constructed assessment tool not only helps with end-of-lesson evaluation of student performance, it also focuses all students on what is most important to learn about the targeted skill. By posting the assessment tool online or handing out a print copy, teachers provide students with the tool that they can use at the start, the middle, and the end of the lesson to guide their self-reflections.

Lest We Forget

Most standards open the window of opportunity and encourage deep development of *critical* thinking skills such as comparing, distinguishing, analyzing, and differentiating. The other side of the coin, *creative* thinking skills, deserves equal attention for all children, not the just the gifted and

---

SAMPLE CHECKLIST: SUMMARIZING

___ I understand what it means to gather ideas into a summary.
___ I know how to make a thesis statement at the start of the summary.
___ I know how to select examples and list them in a summary.
___ I know how to select transition words.
___ I know how to make sure that I have captured the key ideas or facts.
___ I know how to list the important elements in this thinking skill.

My summary of my responses:

---

talented. Development of creative thinking is too often forgotten. Seldom are skills such as generating ideas, predicting, or developing alternatives mentioned in the standards. However, it is important to recall that the distinction between critical thinking and creative thinking is theoretical and value controlled. It is theoretical in the sense that "experts" have hypothesized the distinction. It is value controlled in the school community because the favored disciplines favor mathematical, scientific, and literary studies that spotlight the critical thinking operations.

However, even in a curriculum in which most standards favor critical thinking, the operations and processes that are called *creative thinking* will play an ever more important role in 21st century schooling. More and more, inside-the-box critical thinking will be interconnected with outside-the-box creative thinking as students are asked to make sense in ever more sophisticated ways.

When teachers identify a creative thinking skill in the standards or need to introduce divergent thinking in a lesson or project, they can follow the same principles and practices they developed with critical thinking skills.

A SAMPLER OF CREATIVE THINKING SKILLS

Expanding Alternatives	Visualizing	Adapting	Composing
Integrating	Modifying	Inventing	Constructing
Analogies and Metaphors	Designing	Developing	

As with critical thinking skills, teachers enrich students' learning *about* their creative thinking by assigning the use of appropriate graphic organizers as a starting point. A popular organizer that promotes creative thinking is the concept map, first made popular by Tony Buzan. He named the process "mind mapping." On his website (www.buzanworld.com), Buzan provides a quick, free tutorial for making a mind map. Other sites will sell and some will give templates, instructions, and courses for making mind maps.

Closely aligned to mind maps are concept maps. Although experts love to debate the distinctions between mind maps and concept maps, for the classroom teacher who wants to develop student's creative thinking, either is a very useful tool. In a digital classroom, the CMap is a free, easily downloadable variation (http://cmap.ihmc.us/conceptmap.html). Students can learn to use it with the provided online tutorial.

Once students have mastered the digital essentials of the CMap, teachers can adapt it in multiple ways. Whichever of the electronic or print concept maps they select, such as the sample map for Thomas Edison (Figure 8.1), teachers must remember that first and foremost, it is a tool for helping students generate knowledge. Second, it helps them organize their

Figure 8.1. Sample Concept Map: America's Premier Inventor

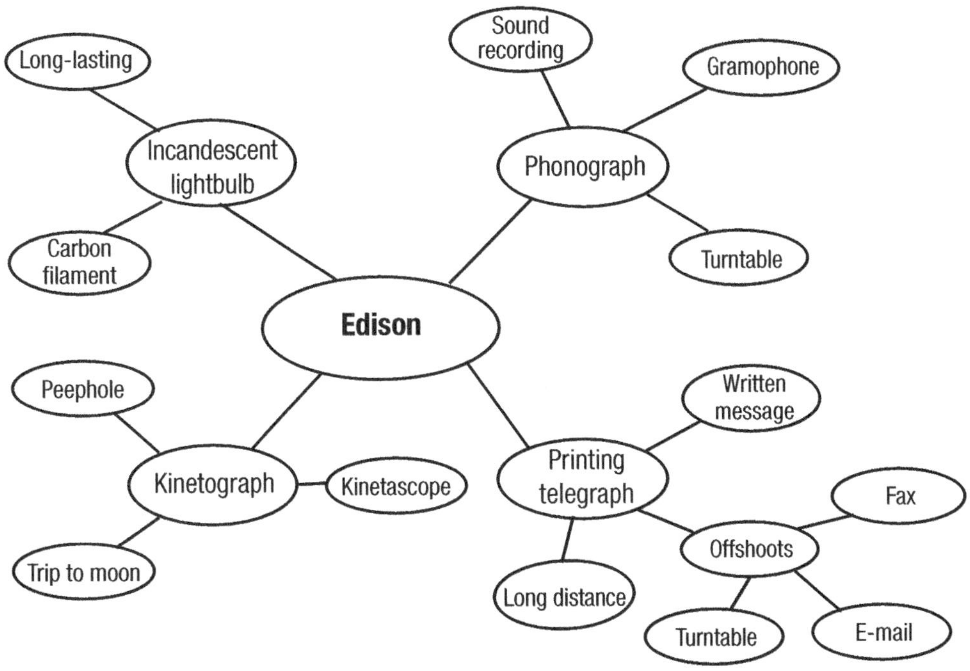

thoughts and see alternative connections among topics and subtopics as they dig into content. In the Edison example, the map starts with his four most famous inventions. Students can add in the next group of circles the next level of detail. For instance, under the phonograph, they might add *cylinders*, *dual needles*, and *wire cylinders*. Off of each of these they could extend their thinking to add more branches. For this map, the branches from multiple uses, students could add *listen to music*, *dictate letters*, *read stories for the blind*, and *a clock*.

Third, teachers can use the tool as a foundation for students to examine the creative thinking they did when expanding their maps. For the Edison map, it would be very appropriate for teachers to instruct students to make a journal entry (Edison filled 3,500 notebooks with ideas and drawings for inventions. His journals that he called his "idea books" contained lists of things he was doing and to be done and notations on what he was thinking about different possible inventions.)

Designing a Start-Up Lesson with Implanted Thinking Skills

When teachers take the time to teach students about a thinking skill enumerated in a standard or to develop the skill through multiple content lessons, they are laying the groundwork for students' metacognition. As students develop the ability to reflect on their own thinking, they increase

---

A STUDENT'S JOURNAL OF INNOVATIVE THINKING

Name: _Zipporah Winthrop_   **Date:** _April 4_

Types of thinking I did today: Creative.

Brainstorm
Predict
Generate
Enrich
Associate

My best thinking today was making idea associations. I used three metaphors in my essay on the Civil War. To do each one I brainstormed a list of ideas. I proved that the two types of thinking are connected because I had to evaluate which metaphors I wanted to use.

their effectiveness as learners. Whether the focus is on critical or on creative thinking, what matters most is that teachers take the time to help students understand the skills they will be using and to develop their abilities to use these skills effectively with the content the standards are asking the students to learn.

The template that follows shows a model for developing the creative thinking skill of "generating variations."

Generating a variety of ideas, commonly called brainstorming, is a creative thinking skill. It shows the innovative characteristics of fluency (a quantity of ideas) and flexibility (many different ideas). When music classes listen to Beethoven's Fifth Symphony, the most recognizable elements are the variation of chords repeated almost as a theme. When art students see the number of colors in a basic palette, they can easily imagine the additional variations that are possible. With this task, teachers can set a target number of variations that students must produce. How many variations? For this task, how many variations can students develop as solutions to the core problem? Not only are the students generating variations, they are also strengthening the fluency and flexibility of their creative thinking.

CONCLUDING THOUGHTS

Thinking is a generic word that describes a class of cognitive operations and functions. Throughout the curriculum, well-formulated standards specify the desired cognitive operations, the thinking skills, that students are expected to use when mastering the content in any subject area. Although most classroom teachers attend to the content element of the standards, few attend to the thinking operation, at least with any depth. Some lack the time to focus on the operations; others don't believe they can change student's minds; the majority simply lack the preparation to mediate student thinking and develop the cognitive operations. They may well believe that they are already "doing that," teaching the thinking skills. In reality they are skimming the surface and missing the chance to enable students to not only learn the required content more deeply, but also develop thinking skills that will enable them to learn more effectively.

The "how to" for teaching thinking is not a secret. Well-researched best practices provide ample alternatives for teachers to teach students how to improve their thinking and how to use their improved cognitive operations to increase their understanding of prescribed content. The challenge is to learn how to integrate the teaching of the thinking skills into the teaching of content, as is called for by most state and national learning standards.

A TEMPLATE:
PROMOTING THE IMPROVEMENT OF THINKING SKILLS

Template: Developing a Thinking Skill: Generating Variations

Targeted Thinking Skill: Generating Variations

Critical _____   **Creative** __X__

Content Focus: Innovation in modern America

Launch Question: How do I generate alternatives for solving a problem, gathering information, or thinking differently about a situation, an event, or a person of importance?

Students will understand (about thinking skill): Several ways to develop a variation; 3 or more tactics for thinking in a different way.

Students will do: Use a radial web to gather information about a famous person or event showing his or her various contributions.

Graphic Organizer: Radial

Instructional Strategies and Tactics: Cooperative Learning (paired partners); nonlinguistic representations (radial web),summaries, questions and cues, objective and feedback.

Assessment Tactics: Checklist

Activity Sequence:

Demonstrate alternative thinking by showing alternate contributions of a famous
    person on a radial web.

Ask students about when in their lives it was helpful to solve problems by
    thinking of alternative solutions.

Present launch question, objective, and rationale.

Review radial web example (first entry in this list) highlighting processes for
    making idea bigger, smaller, different view, different look, outlandish, more
    numerous, etc.).

Pair partners and assign recorder and speaker roles.

Show radial web on each computer screen. Show how to make entries. Check.

Give instructions for task. Prime pump with responses from volunteers.

A TEMPLATE:
PROMOTING THE IMPROVEMENT OF THINKING SKILLS *(continued)*

Allow 5 minutes for pairs to find alternative. Have students select best ideas and put on class blog.

Make a summary radial web. Discuss with students.

Ask students to make second on-screen radial web. What are the ways of thinking you used to generate the different alternatives that developed from the central idea?

Repeat 7–10 with focus on thinking.

End with a summary.

Give students a checklist of what they should review about how to generate ideas.

Day 2. Repeat process with review of thinking needed to generate ideas.

Select new application of this skill, do task, and review thinking processes.

Day 3. Draw back. Ask in what other situations you might use this tool to generate and organize multiple ideas.

Days 4+. Make other assignments for applying this skill in other classes.

Invite each student to summarize what was learned about generating alternatives, using a radial web, being flexible thinkers, and so on and include in e-journal.

Over the next month, continue emphasizing use and improvement of this skill.

Reflective Questions: Scatter reflective questions through the activities: What are my favorite ways to make sure I am thinking flexibly? Where is it important in my schoolwork to generate alternative ideas? Outside of school? Why bother?

Knowledge Check: In a final quiz, essay, or unit test item ask, "What are three tactics I can use to generate alternative ideas or actions?"

Skill Check: In a final summary paragraph present a problem scenario not previously discussed and ask students to provide at least three alternative solutions. Have them fill out a concept map showing the branching of their ideas.

MASTER TEMPLATE: DEVELOPING A THINKING SKILL

Targeted Skill:

Critical _____   Creative _____

Content Focus:

Launch Question:

Students will understand (about thinking skill):

Students will do:

Graphic Organizer:

Instructional Strategies:

Assessment Tactics:

Activity Sequence:

Reflective Questions:

Knowledge Check:

Skill Check:

CHAPTER 9

Sharpened Minds
for Sharper Thinking

> If the past millennium ushered in greater democracy, this one
> should usher in greater individuation—individuation not in the sense
> of selfishness or self seeking, but in the sense of knowledge about
> and respect of each individual.
>
> —Howard Gardner

CRITICS OF THE 21st century skills agenda are already crying "wolf, wolf." In addition to their concerns about abandoning content, these critics fear that the emphasis on collaboration will kill off what they claim are the important 19th century values that promote development of the individual.

Howard Gardner, who is not a member of this group of critics, posits the need for individuation. His work on the multiple intelligences and the multiple minds needed for success in the 21st century world presents educators with frameworks that celebrate development of the individual. It is up to those who teach to translate his and others' mindful theories into sound practice. In his comments about the five minds for the future, he describes the time and work it takes to master a single discipline. However, he is careful to point out that that mastery includes a "way of thinking" about the content of the discipline (Gardner, 2010).

Although those who question the value of including skills that studies have shown most contribute to academic achievement by establishing a positive culture for change and by providing students with the skills to learn content more efficiently, (Johnson & Johnson, 2010), the value of collaboration as a tool for enriching learning experiences stands out as one of the preeminent tools used in schools that are garnering positive results by ensuring that students learn and apply the skills in their daily studies. In collaborative learning experiences such as those provided at Manor New Tech (Texas) and other 21st century–focused schools in the New Tech High

School Network (http://www.newtechnetwork.org), students not only learn *about* skills for working together, they are expected to use these same working-together skills across the curriculum on a daily basis. By the time they graduate, these students are well experienced in the nuances of teamwork. As records are also showing, the students are thriving in the skills-rich environment to a far greater degree than they did in their traditional schools. That thriving is most brightly reflected in their academic records and the high percentage of admissions to colleges and universities.

With collaborative lessons and projects, teachers, not only can raise achievement, but also can improve the sharpness of students' thinking skills. Like skilled mountain climbers, students learn to work in teams helping one another with the challenges all face. The more the team members help one another, relying on the different skills each has, the more likely it is that each individual will reach the peak. Individual triumph is celebrated as each climber fulfills his or her role within the group, all of whom—not just one—plant flags on the mountaintop.

When mediating the development of quality thinking, teachers at Manor take advantage of the collaborative culture, the teamwork they have put in place. In the classroom, teachers can more readily sharpen each student's thinking skills by helping students use the skills to address content through the project model of learning, which requires teamwork skills to a high degree. Yes, it is possible for teachers to mediate individual student thinking. The collaborative approach, however, allows for students to more easily refine their thinking skills through intense cognitive interaction with their peers as well as with the teacher.

Although this cognitive refinement takes place most often within the team context, mediators still expect individual students to demonstrate their own cognitive skill development. As with individual assessment of the content, enriched by the collaborative experience, the assessment of thinking skills is individualized. Each student is accountable for showing how he or she has satisfied all course requirements, including learning the content, using collaborative skills, and thinking more sharply.

Cognitive Mediator: A teacher who focuses questions and feedback to students on the development of students' thinking skills. The mediator uses questions and cues to advance the quality of students' thinking about content, thinking strategies, and metacognition.

THE COLLABORATIVE AND COGNITIVE CONNECTION

Creating a collaborative classroom environment in which students are willing to think together, as opposed to working against the teachers and the other students with disruptive behavior that inhibits teaching efforts in many traditional classrooms, makes it possible for teachers to attend to the sharpening of each student's thinking skills.

In an intentionally created cooperative environment, teachers have the greatest opportunity to promote the full range of 21st century skills, but most notably the cognitive skills. To hone cognitive skills, teachers assume the role of mediators. They begin with a demonstration of targeted operations and functions. They show students how to best refine a specific cognitive operation or function, whether that skill enables students to make keener analyses inside the box or generate more abundant ideas outside the box. With this skill modeling, teachers can focus their mediation on specific cognitive functions such as impulse control, precision and accuracy, or use of multiple sources of data. Teachers also have the option to focus on those specific operations, such as analysis for cause and effect or assessing alternative points of view, that are called for in a particular curriculum.

With the selected skills targeted, teachers then have the opportunity to help students sharpen their use of that skill *within* the content. These are the very skills that the critics so fear new skills infused into the curriculum will eradicate. With sharper skills for mastering the content, as demonstrated in the increasing number of 21st century–style classrooms springing up in such diverse locations as Bloomington, Indiana; Coppell, Texas; Troy, New York; and San Diego, California, students not only dig more deeply into their states' standards-strong curricula, but also walk away with additional skills that make them more valued citizens, employable in many different workplaces. They don't walk away as a group. Each goes his or her own way, walking on his or her own unique pathway into the future, well nourished with instruction that not only expanded his or her knowledge base, but provided the appropriate skills for this generation's survival and success.

MAKING EVERY MOMENT TEACHABLE

Although the phrase *teachable moment* may be a cliché (it received a top-cliché award of the year in 2009), there is no teaching tactic more appropriate or powerful than the immediate, on-the-spot attention of a caring adult to a moment open to learning, a window of opportunity. Alfonso's coach

Alfonso caught the basketball. He turned and dribbled away from his opponent.

"Stop, for a moment. Right there," said his coach. "Let me show you what you just did."

The coach copied what he had seen. He turned from Alfonso and dribbled away. "Now, let me show you a different way. Watch."

This time the coach pulled the ball to his side. In a single motion, he moved his left foot back and turned his shoulder slightly to his side as he dribbled the ball while still facing his opponent. "Do you see the difference in what I did?"

"Yes. You dribbled while still facing Jamie."

"And why do you think I did that?" asked the coach.

"You didn't lose any time. And you were ready to attack."

"Good thinking!" exclaimed the coach, with growing excitement in his voice. "Now, before you try it, tell me how this move is going to help you in a game."

recognized those teachable moments and took every advantage to touch the boy's inner needs.

Following the skill cycle (Figure 9.1), the coach engaged the boy in a conversation. The coach made sure that he had the boy's full attention. With Alfonso reciprocating, the coach made a correction by demonstrating and explaining a different, better way to bounce the ball. With excitement in his voice, the coach asked Alfonso to compare what he saw in the two moves. When the boy made the comparison, the coach became more excited, while not forgetting to ask Alfonso, "Why do you think that?" The coach gave his *enthusiastic* feedback ("good thinking") and encouraged transfer ("tell me how this move will help in a game").

In this brief exchange, the coach demonstrated the key elements that are important for mediating a student's thinking so that every important moment is a teachable moment. Mediation of thinking may be the most powerful tool that teachers have when trying to develop a student's critical and creative thinking skills. Advancing student thinking is the most effective way to help students become efficient users of the content and skills they are trying to learn. Effective mediators not only deepen understanding, but also advance the skills learned. Alfonso's understanding of dribbling strategies and his improved technique marked his "content" advancement. By capturing and retaining Alfonso's attention, by questioning to explore what he understood, and by enabling him to transcend the skills the boy was learning, his coach showed his effectiveness as a mediator. Underscoring the "content" of his feedback, the coach talked with his body and exuded

Figure 9.1. Contrasting Roles: Mediator vs. Teacher

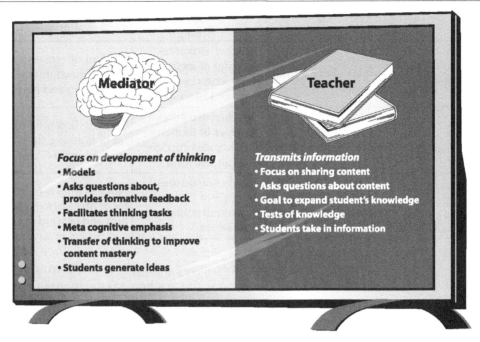

affect in his voice. He never tried to hide his enthusiasm and excitement about the boy's progress. He accented his comments with his emotions.

Effective teachers, like Alfonso's coach, want their students to learn not just for the moment, but for a lifetime; not just content, but transferable skills. These teachers step out of the role of the information giver and into the role of mediators. What is the difference? In the upper grades, information givers lecture about subject matter, occasionally lead discussions or guide practice, and give tests. Just as Moses took hold of the tablets handed to him, students take hold of the tablets of wisdom the teacher hands to them. These teachers focus directly on the content, the knowledge, and subject matter skills outlined in the curriculum. For instance, in geometry, the curriculum calls for students to learn how to measure shapes and forms. After the teacher explains the formula, the students memorize the procedures and practice it on a page of similar word problems. When history teachers want students to learn the causes of a war, they outline the causes and tell students to "know these for the test." When language arts teachers want students to know the high points in a short story plot, they summarize the story's events and label the high points. The discerning student's job is to figure out if he or she should memorize this information.

Figure 9.2. Skill Development 3.0 Matrix

	1.0 Basic	2.0 Strong	3.0 Exceptional
3.0 *Metacognition*	Teacher asks students to think about thinking skills	Teacher structures transfer of metacognition across curriculum and beyond	Student directs own transfer of metacognition across curriculum and beyond
2.0 *Cognition*	Teacher asks about use of thinking skills	Teacher structures transfer of thinking skills across curriculum and beyond	Student directs own transfer of thinking skills across curriculum and beyond
1.0 *Content*	Teacher asks complex questions in content	Teacher structures transfer of ideas across curriculum and beyond	Student directs own transfer of ideas across curriculum and beyond

In the primary grades, the learning paradigm is built around worksheets. In the best of these classrooms, the teachers take advantage of direct instruction, making sure that students are tuned into the lesson objective. In the worst, teachers may skip the objectives as well as any explanation of the task. They send students directly to unguided practice on the pencil-and-paper worksheets or to electronic worksheets at a computer terminal. Even when a teacher may take coaching seriously and isolate the individuals who need additional help, that help is limited to debugging issues related to the content or a content skill. If a student is having difficulties with logical reasoning or mathematical thinking, chances are the teacher is unprepared to respond. If the teacher is prepared to respond to any question, the most likely form of answer will be telling or re-explaining. In a sense, the teacher will hand the student a fish rather than a fishing pole.

To become effective mediators of student thinking, teachers stop giving answers, telling, lecturing, and asking "what" questions. They stop handing out worksheets or using subgroups that banish students to practice at a computer station. Instead, they conduct well-planned lessons in which they ask "why" and "how" questions that cue ways for students to think about a topic. They demonstrate thinking skills such as predicting or differentiating, and they coach students to solve problems with precision and accuracy or by using other cognitive functions. In their role as mediators, teachers encourage students to seek deeper understanding of what they are studying. Like parents who direct a child's attention to a butterfly and explain its special characteristics, mediators sharpen children's focus so they concentrate on the key elements in a learning task. And they never forget to underscore their positive feedback with their emotional accent marks.

CRITERIA FOR A MEDIATED LEARNING EXPERIENCE

When teachers take an active role in developing students' thinking skills, they increase students' efficiency for learning and effectiveness from that thinking. They do this using refined questioning skills for *mediating* a learning experience. Reuven Feuerstein has developed a set of criteria that define what he labeled as a "mediated" learning experience (Feuerstein, Klein, & Tannenbaum, 1991). As Alfonso's coach demonstrated, Feuerstein's set includes three of these criteria in *every* instructional interaction. These three define the mediated learning experience.

Intentionality and Reciprocity

The coach made it clear what he wanted the boy to learn. He grabbed Alfonso's attention and held on to it with additional questions. The boy responded or reciprocated with his attention to the skills the coach intended to teach. If the coach were working with a team, his instruction would follow a similar pattern. At the start of the lesson, the coach's intention would be designed to provoke the responses of the many.

Meaning

The coach continually communicated by word, facial expression, gestures, and tone of voice his enthusiasm for what Alfonso was learning. He made what he was teaching a "big deal" because he wanted Alfonso to understand the value of what he was learning as well as the rules for playing the game. To deepen Alfonso's understanding of what he was being asked to do, the coach probed Alfonso's thinking with "why" questions.

Transcendence

Once Alfonso showed that he grasped the concept the coach was teaching, the coach pushed Alfonso to a new level. With growing excitement in his voice communicating that the next question had great value, the coach asked for Alfonso to think about using what he had just learned "in a game." This question took Alfonso out of the single incident in this practice and challenged him to think about its transfer. This required Alfonso to form a generalization about what he had learned and then apply this fuller understanding in a new, future situation.

Another example shows a variety of ways that the teacher mediated students' mathematical learning experiences. By asking questions and

MEDIATING METACOGNITION

Teacher: This is how I might think about looking for similarities. Let's go one step at a time. We will discuss each step. First, I would say to myself, take your time. Make sure that you get all the information and cover all the bases. . . . Now tell me what is the first step to take in this task? What did I do?

Student A: You checked yourself. No racing ahead.

Teacher: And why did I do this?

Student B: You wanted to cover all the bases.

Teacher: And what does that mean?

Student B: You wanted to get a plan for doing the PMI [the Pluses, the Minuses, the Interesting questions]. What would you do first, second, and third and how would you make sure that you checked all the information you could?

Teacher: That is good thinking. Now, who can tell me from these points, what you are going to do with your PMI?

demonstrating mathematical thinking rather than by talking "about" the mathematics or leaving students to discover the ideas on their own, the teacher helped the student form a conceptual understanding. Although some may criticize this approach by saying it takes too much time ("It is faster," they say, "to just tell the students what to do."), Feuerstein and others such as Grant Wiggins and Jay McTighe (2005) point out that learning is not about "covering" material or finishing teaching tasks more quickly. It is about helping students understand the concepts they are studying and developing the skills that are usable in bridging new concepts.

There is no doubt that "telling" is faster. What "telling" ignores is the need for students to go beyond having a formula or some procedures to memorize. By working with the students' thinking, the teacher ensures that the students gain the cognitive flexibility that will enable them to solve other similar problems and leads them to a result that shows the students' accomplishments.

In the mathematics sample above, note the tactics the teacher uses to gain reciprocity, deepen meaning, and promote transcendence.

1. The teacher used a second equation to demonstrate how to solve the equation:
   Announced her intention;
   Engaged students by structuring desired response; and
   Conveyed meaning with enthusiasm at the accent points.

2. The teacher instructed the students to listen to her thinking about how to complete the equation:
   Checked prior knowledge;
   Made a plan;
   Thought out loud about problem solving steps; and
   Checked the process used against the plan.
3. The teacher asked students to recap.
4. The teacher guided transfer to facilitate understanding of the problem solving method that applied to additional equations (transference).

MEDIATION OF THINKING IN A PROJECT-BASED LEARNING EXPERIENCE

When teachers mediate learning experiences, they call upon the same question-asking skills as they would use in teaching students how to solve an equation, analyze a poem, or paint a portrait. These include use of wait time, higher-order questions, respect, distributions of responses, and the other questioning skills noted in the TESA (Teacher Expectations Student Achievement) research on student achievement (Gottfredson & Marciniak, 1995).

After a demonstration that highlights the refined thinking and productivity that teachers want to see in a project, good mediators ask open-ended questions that require thoughtful responses about a project's "process" (e.g., "What do you think it will take to do this project?" "How will you plan to do this?" "What will make this project difficult for you to complete well?"). Then the teachers wait. They do not answer their own questions. They do not tell the students what to do. A group or a whole class is involved; the mediators are careful to distribute their questions around the class.

To help themselves with longer wait time and greater distribution among those who will answer, creative mediators may use a hat or

---

HIGH-EXPECTATION QUESTION-ASKING SKILLS

Wait Time: Two to three seconds of silence after question.
Equitable Distribution of Questions: All called upon systematically.
Phase-Specific Thinking Operations: Appropriate thinking skill for learning phase.
Open-Ended Questions: Encourage complex thinking and logic.

shoebox filled with the names of all the students in the class. The mediators pull the names randomly out of the hat so that all students know they will have to think. With open-ended questions, the mediators are not searching for one-word responses that give an abrupt yes or no; they want thoughtful answers to "why" and "how" questions about the problem solving process as well as the content.

Strong cognitive mediators also are skilled "cuers." They help students put ideas together by asking clarifying questions, by probing for examples, and by paraphrasing. "Give me an example of a country where malaria is rampant." "Why do you think that poverty level is a good predictor of disease?" "So you are telling me that affluent countries have diseases different from those in poor countries?" "Did you consider . . . ?" "Did you take a look at . . . ?"

When mediators ask in-depth questions that cause students to think more extensively about their answers, these mediators have a reason. The reason is to enable students to take the answers they have generated and to frame valid generalizations about these responses. Such generalizations better enable students to transfer what they have learned to new and unique situations.

METACOGNITIVE MEDIATION TO ENRICH PROJECT-BASED LEARNING EXPERIENCES

Project mediators do not limit their questions to the content that students will use or the products they will make in an investigation or problem-based scenario. They push students "to think about the thinking processes" they have been using as they have worked with e-tools or in cooperative groups to gather and make sense of information for the project.

TWO SAMPLE LISTS: COGNITIVE OPERATIONS AND FUNCTIONS

Operations	Functions
Sequencing	Restrained Impulsivity
Finding Similarities	Goal-Oriented Perception
Hypothesizing	Systematic Exploration
Categorizing	Precise Labeling
Predicting	Conservation of Constants
Drawing Conclusions	Planning Behavior

Ultimately, at least one-third of students' time in a project could center on thinking about their thinking and the transcendent applications of their insights. By selecting specific processes, such as *precise thinking* or *making inferences*, mediators help students refine these prerequisite thinking skills.

- **Example:** *Precision.* "You are telling me that you found it difficult to be as precise in your calculations as you wanted. Let's stop and think about what that means. I want you to think very carefully about what you were thinking as you completed that formula."
- **Example:** *Making an inference.* "When you look at a person wearing a police uniform, what do you conclude?" "When you look at a plant and its leaves are sagging and turning brown, what do you think made it so droopy?"

Mediators of thinking have many opportunities in a project when they can structure students' responses so that they are "thinking about their thinking." For instance, after they finish their analysis of the data gathered in a sunflower-growing project, students can make private journal entries that use de Bono's PMI assessment tactic, to look at the Pluses, Minuses, and Interesting Questions (de Bono, 1989). In this case, the targets of the PMI are thinking operations such as "making inferences" or "making a hypothesis." "What are the pluses of making sure you have a hypothesis?" a teacher would start. After students present their responses, the teacher moves on to the other two questions: "What are the minuses?" and "What questions do you have about making a hypothesis?" Following Mary Budd Rowe's advice, the teacher would become silent and let the students do the talking (Rowe, 2003). Some have commented that "the person who talks is the person who learns." This dictum would encourage the teacher to remain silent—listening and encouraging students to think out loud about their thinking.

Teachers may also use the PMI to facilitate student assessment of the targeted cognitive functions such as "precision," "making inferences" or "using multiple sources of information." With a PMI, a common starter question to elicit the "pluses" is "When you searched for similarities, what did you do well?" Students, preferably working in pairs or in threes, list the "pluses" in the "P" column. Next, they list "minuses" or what they did not do well. Finally, they make a list of "interesting questions" in the "I" column. De Bono contends that use of this format several times a week will turn assessment of thinking into a habit of mind. Brain research reinforces de Bono's contention by describing how the repetition of a thoughtful action encourages dendrites to grow (Ratey, 2001).

WHY MEDIATION IN ENRICHED PROJECTS?

A project is a multiphase learning process that engages students in authentic and meaningful learning experiences that require them to learn from what they do. Teachers enrich projects when they mediate students' thinking throughout a project. The thinking and problem solving that go into the process are more important than the products that emerge. The products, especially those in the final output stage, contain the indicators of the quality of thinking that went into the completed project and its parts. If teachers take time to identify the inherent thinking functions at the start of the investigations, assess students' baseline performance levels, and set outcome targets for improvement, they find it easier to assess both the final product and the thinking processes. Most important, their mediation of the thinking enables students to sharpen the functions. The sharpened functions enable the students to make "better cuts" the next time they have to use the sharpened skills.

To make this final assessment easier and more helpful, teachers can either intentionally plan the inclusion of mini-lessons on thinking at appropriate times throughout the project. They can also take advantage of teachable moments. In both cases, teachers must allot time to focus students on the quality of their thinking throughout the project. Teachers not only want the students to think more critically and creatively as these students tackle the project tasks, but also want the students to demonstrate those cognitive improvements that form a habit of mindfulness in the efficiency with which students will solve future problems.

Increased cognitive efficiency is not something that just happens. Nor is it only an automatic by-product of the learning process. Increased cognitive efficiency is a purposeful act designed to enrich the collaborative project. The mediator's intentional mediation of the thinking processes provides the rigor and robustness that mark collaborative projects as enriched and distinct from other experiences in which students "just do it" for credit.

Students complete enriched learning projects so that they can learn the processes of investigating, innovating, and problem solving and sharpen the thinking skills they need to expand the quality of their thinking skills. The pinnacle of this sharpening task is reached when teachers mediate the students' thinking about their metacognition.

PROMOTING METACOGNITION IN PROJECTS

When teachers add intentional tactics to promote students' metacognition, they raise expectations for student performance to the highest level. All students have the inherent capability to reflect skillfully on the types of thinking they have been doing as long as teachers provide the opportunity and lead with their mediation of the learning experience.

The most effective teachers will create multiple opportunities for students to develop their metacognitive skills in any project.

The Investigation Project

Students are provided a "big picture" framework that outlines the thinking task. For the investigation, students have an opportunity to think about the launch question and how they went about finding answers through research in which they gathered information (e.g., "What types of thinking do I have to use to gather the appropriate information?" "When I couldn't find what I wanted, how did I problem-solve alternatives?" "When I found information how did I decide its quality? Its appropriateness?"), made sense of information (e.g., "How did I uncover the meaning of the material I was examining?" "How did I connect the pieces of information to make a coherent concept?" How did I separate important from unimportant information?' How did I distinguish ideas?"), and communicated the new insights (e.g., "How did I decide what was most important to communicate?" "What did I express well?" "What do I need to improve in my explanations or presentations?").

The Problem-Based Learning Project

In a problem-based learning project, students have the opportunity to assess their understanding and use of the problem solving process. "What tactics did I use to define the problem precisely and accurately? How did I make use of multiple sources of information to set up alternative solutions? How flexible was I in making selections? What tactics did I use to modify my solution? How effective were my questions?"

The Innovative Project

When the mode of the enriched learning project is innovation, students are challenged to look at the familiar in new and different ways as they search for their solution. Most often they start with a commonly used product such as a car battery or decorative clay pot. The question is "How can I make this better?" or "What can I do differently to enhance this ____?" Sometimes that question relates to shape or size; other times it relates to function or another attribute.

To answer the essential innovation-sparking question, students need to gather information about the object. For instance, with the car battery, they may want to improve how long it lasts before it becomes "dead." What acids are used? What metals? Which acid-metal combinations have lasted longest? What other metals, acids, and combinations are possible?

With the basic questions answered, the innovators begin experimenting with new ingredients and new combinations. They take careful notes about their observations and gradually hope to find the best results. To test their hypotheses, they check their best guesses. Finally, they have a new combination, in a eureka moment, that they think will work better in the long run.

In the classroom where enriched learning is a core value, the innovative process doesn't end at the "aha" moment. There is more important work to do. That is the work of metacognition. Teachers who want students to learn from their innovation search will take the time for intense reflection of the thinking that occurred before, during, and at the end of the project. They will help students assess their question framing, their hypothesis making, their generalizations about data sets, and their conclusion making.

TARGETING THE COGNITIVE OPERATIONS

It is the teacher's responsibility to enrich students' thinking by starting with the inclusion of a standards-aligned thinking skill in each enriched project. This means that the teacher will ensure that all students understand the concept of the target skill identified in the standard (e.g., hypothesizing, comparing, predicting, inferring) that they will develop during the project. Once students have a clear picture in their mind's eye of what the skill is, why it is important, and how is it best used, teachers can mediate the skills development in the content or with the e-tools they are using. The most difficult time for a teacher to mediate a thinking skill and encourage students to reflect on its use is in the middle of a project. Thus, effective teachers know to introduce a thinking skill's basics (what? why? how?) at the start of a project. This is similar to practice time in a sport. When the students are immersed in the project and have to use the thinking skill, they are in the middle of the game. At best, the teacher can pull a student aside to coach use of the skill, but time is too constrained in the middle of the project to do so.

After the game's completion, when the project is done, the teacher can ask students to look back and reflect on what went well or not so well with the thinking skill in the project. This post-action reflection time may be the best chance that the teacher and students have to assess the quality of the skill's use.

TARGETING THE COGNITIVE FUNCTIONS

Feuerstein defined 26 cognitive functions, the micro thinking skills that are the prerequisites to all learning. Of these 26, the most valuable for students who are learning to become self-directed learners able to produce high-quality products and solutions from their projects is the cognitive function of reflective thinking. Reflection is characterized by students' ability to control impulsive, unfocused, and random guessing. Teachers can encourage students to concentrate on reducing their impulsive thinking behavior in all three phases of the learning process.

Figure 9.3. The Three Phases of Learning

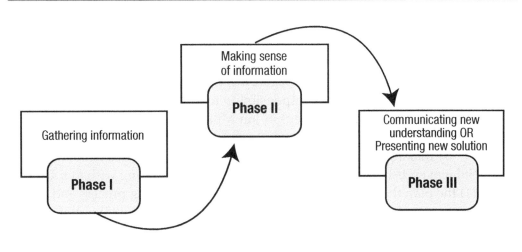

THE CONSTITUTION PROBLEM: A SAMPLE PROJECT

Phase I: Collecting Information

In this first phase of a rigorous project learning experience, students gather information. The two primary sources are (1) their own prior knowledge and experience or (2) new knowledge from print (on- and off-line), oral (face-to-face interviews or podcasts) or visual (multimedia) data sources. Students skilled in searching know how to check their own prior experience by using such tools as the KWL or web graphics. They can gather new information with carefully planned systematic searches that may include note taking, CMaps, cause-effect charts, fact charts, and other information-gathering graphic organizers. They can learn to file their information in life binders, a free open-source information storage site.

Effective teachers will recognize note-taking and graphic organizers (off-line or online templates) as two high-effect instructional strategies (Marzano et al., 2001). They will help students refine the quality of their data search by focusing students on those tactics that make each of the high-effect strategies even more effective. Using journals (on- or off-line) on a daily basis, students develop their reflective habits even as they start the project with tactics that promote planning and self-assessment behaviors.

In the example below, Jon Miller (a pseudonym), the teacher of a U.S. history class, structured his unit on the framing of the Constitution to include a problem-based scenario that would end with a role-play of the Constitutional Convention. For this "performance" project, students would research the various plans proposed for the new Constitution. Each team would determine how they would present their plan (e.g., the Virginia Plan, the New Jersey Plan) to the convention. All students were required to make a plan of their own regarding the particular thinking skills and functions they would take responsibility to develop through the phases of the project. Suleyma, a student in Jon Miller's class, made a plan with an emphasis on the skill of determining cause and effect.

By making a plan that emphasizes a systematic use of a fishbone chart, Suleyma sets herself up to control her impulsive thinking with four tactics: (1) the plan that has her think about her data-gathering process and keeps her aware of being precise and accurate with her entries, (2) use of a chart that puts her thoughts into a visual order, (3) using the reflective journal to keep herself purposefully conscious of how her thinking is improving, and (4) feedback from her work team that focuses on her plan to improve her reflective-thinking behavior.

THE CONSTITUTIONAL PROBLEM PROJECT

Student Name: _Suleyma Diaz_   **Class:** _U.S. History 311_
Date: _March 28, 2009_   **Period:** _4_   **Teacher:** _J. Miller_
Project: _Framing the Constitution_

Problem Scenario: How to select a workable plan for a Constitution that will pass with a majority vote in the convention.

Focus Thinking Skill: Analyzing Cause and Effect

Goal: To use a system to analyze the causal relationships in this problem-based project.

Target Thinking Goals: Cause and effect, impulse control

Topic: The Constitutional Convention

Objective:
1. To use the fishbone chart to analyze the problem.
2. To use the fishbone chart to gather causal data.
3. To double-check my entries.
4. To edit and proofread all final charts for precision and accuracy.
5. To make a daily entry in my journal about how accurately I make my entries.

Information-Gathering Tool: Fishbone Chart; Journal

Action Plan: For each topic in this study I will use the chart to help me organize my data collection. At the end of each class, I will enter a self-evaluation that describes what I think I did well and what problems I am having. My group has the Virginia Plan. I am to research the causes of their insistence on a federalist position.

Feedback: I will ask my project team to review my charts and tell me what I did well and what I need to do better. I will also write a summary of the problem solving I used, highlighting the quality of thinking I did during the data collection. I am especially interested in checking my accuracy when fact collecting.

Suleyma's plan has several advantages in addition to facilitating her self-reflections with a critical eye. First, the plan puts her in charge of improving her own thinking. Second, it is a plan that she can work on over time. Third, she can take advantage of this plan and apply the targeted improvement to accompany her work in other classes. Fourth, it puts her teacher into the secondary role. He can focus on giving Suleyma feedback on what the teacher observes as Suleyma concentrates on the function she elected to improve.

Figure 9.4. A Sample Fishbone Chart

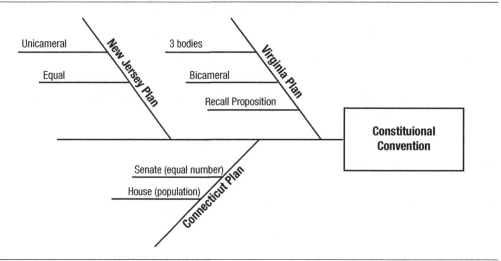

Phase II: Making Sense of Information

As students move from gathering information for their project research, teachers have multiple rich opportunities, multiple teachable moments, to comment on the quality of the thinking behaviors they see students "doing." They do not need to have every student concentrating on the same cognitive operation or the same cognitive function. Neither do they have to keep elaborate scoring systems or notes of their own to track student progress. The recording and tracking tasks fall to the students for "formative self-assessments." The teacher expects that each student concentrates on the improvement of one function by using the e-journal and other tactics. At the end of a project or marking period, teachers need only collect the journals to see the evidence of the work the students have done to refine their targeted thinking skills.

In Phase II, students continue thinking about their thinking as they review the information they have gathered and determine its meaning. For instance, in Suleyma's social studies project, she is working with a team. They had been presented with a variety of statements and documents that showed that the candidates to the convention were far from being in agreement. It was the team's task to figure out a way to bring the "conventioneers" to a consensus and to reach agreement on the basic tenets of the proposed Constitution. In the first phase, they had examined many documents and read books written by experts to give them the background that they needed. Mr. Miller had completed several causal analyses. Other team members had investigated more factual information about the delegates and their positions. There was an abundance of information. How would the team use this information to frame and solve the problem they had selected?

After posting their completed visual organizers for the team to see, members reviewed their information. They decided that they would use the CMap to show the relationships they thought existed. At this point, Suleyma made a slight adjustment to her personal thinking plan. First, she added a new objective as she assumed the role of group recorder. She would concentrate on making each entry precise and accurate. She would question her teammates to double-check all data they provided and she would ask them to make sure she recorded what they said with complete accuracy. When she made her daily journal entry, she would keep her focus on these two emphases.

Phase III: Communicating New Ideas

Suleyma's team spent the good part of every class period for the next week making sense of the information. After they finished their CMap, they concluded that they could divide the delegates into three groups.

Figure 9.5. The Virginia Plan: A Newspaper Graphic

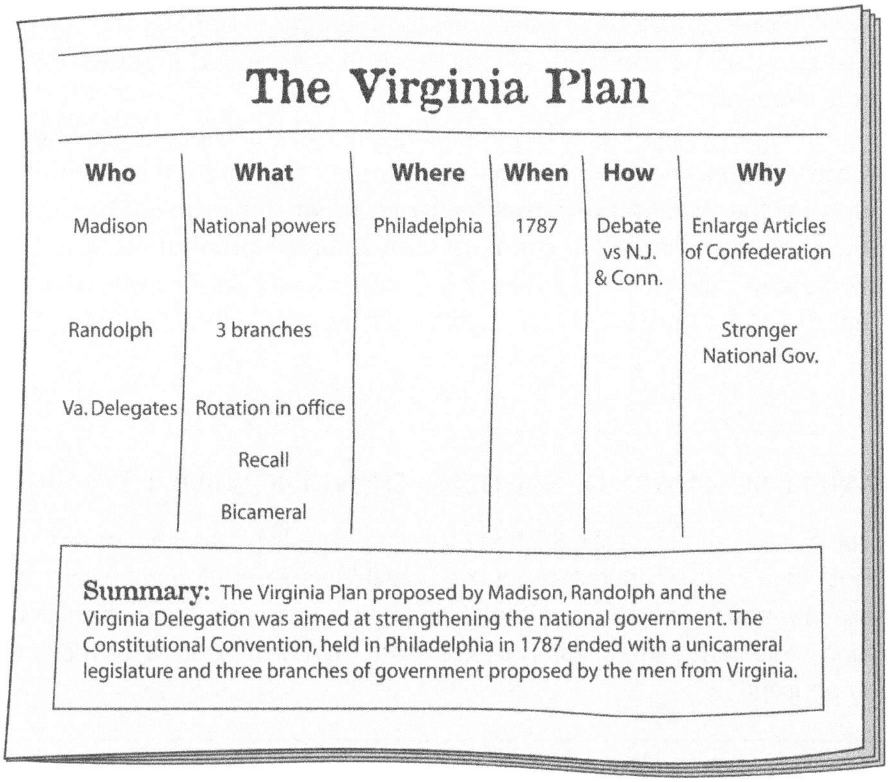

The Virginia Plan

Who	What	Where	When	How	Why
Madison	National powers	Philadelphia	1787	Debate vs N.J. & Conn.	Enlarge Articles of Confederation
Randolph	3 branches				Stronger National Gov.
Va. Delegates	Rotation in office				
	Recall				
	Bicameral				

Summary: The Virginia Plan proposed by Madison, Randolph and the Virginia Delegation was aimed at strengthening the national government. The Constitutional Convention, held in Philadelphia in 1787 ended with a unicameral legislature and three branches of government proposed by the men from Virginia.

SAMPLE JOURNAL ENTRIES

March 4. Today, I had to calculate the amount of our costs for renting the video equipment. It was the school's equipment, but we had to check out the equivalent if we did rent or buy. After I checked numbers from three sources, I rechecked each one and redid the math by hand and on the calculator. I also asked Theresa to check and make sure my placement of figures was precise and I was accurate in my calculations.

March 11. Today, I had the jobs of measuring distance and light for the video in our multimedia presentation about the Virginia plan. I double-checked all readings to make sure I was accurate. I also had Theresa check my entries for accuracy. This job also took me back to cause and effect. I decided to make a fishbone to guide my thinking on the effects of light from different angles.

Each group had its own ideas about the basic principles desired for the Constitution. For each group, they adopted the newspaper organizer to show who was in the group, what the group agreed on, why their position was "correct," and its implications for the new nation. At the bottom, the group created a summary of this position that pulled together the disparate elements.

This newspaper graphic provided one product for the Constitutional Convention project. Its summary expressed succinctly the main information for the sharing portion of the project. For this problem-based project, the team was charged to come up with a shared point of view and to participate in a mock convention. Each team would select three of the original delegates to role-play the making of the case. However, they could do

A SAMPLE SUMMARY OF STUDENT THINKING ABOUT THINKING

This project proved more difficult than I thought. The fishbone had looked easy. But when I really thought about the possible causes, I found I wasn't very accurate in matching my ideas. I had to go back over my fishbone chart several times and recheck my matches. The next time, I will have to do a lot more thinking up front.

A SAMPLE CONTENT SUMMARY

The Virginia delegates to the Constitutional Convention proposed a federalist government. There were three important reasons that drove the delegates to look for a federal system. I consider these the causes for their position: (a) They wanted to be sure that there was a strong national defense, (b) they wanted common laws to protect all citizens no matter in what state they lived, and (c) other centralized bodies that would prevent the strong states from taking over.

---

so with any communication tools they desired. Suleyma's team decided it would make a multimedia presentation that would include shareware and video clips. These would be the team's second and third products.

While working with her team, Suleyma was required to maintain her journal. For the third phase, she elected to make a single entry each day. Each entry would start with the same prompt, "Today, I improved my thinking by . . ." She focused her entries on the continued effort to be precise and accurate.

Throughout the project, Suleyma's teacher specified that student teams discuss the quality of their thinking. As Suleyma had indicated in her plan, she used a summary in her journal after these discussions.

As part of his assessment of Suleyma's project, Suleyma's teacher, Mr. Miller, read Suleyma's journal, just as he read her knowledge test on what she had learned about the convention and its causes. As Mr. Miller read the journal, he was looking for what improvements he could find in Suleyma's cause-effect thinking skills. Mr. Miller wanted to see both the "know" (the convention's causes) and the "do" (cause-effect thinking) that were listed in the project's outcomes.

On other days, Mr. Miller stipulated that journal entries would focus on the content: what the class had learned about the convention. Because he was focusing on causes and effects, Suleyma's content entries revealed her understanding of the topic.

For this problem-based project, the team was charged to come up with a shared point of view and to participate in a mock convention. Each team would select three of the original delegates to role-play the making of the case. However, they could do so with any communication tools they desired. Suleyma's team decided it would make a multimedia presentation that would include shareware and video clips. These would be the team's second and third products. When finished, they would assess their plan.

STUDENT SELF-ASSESSMENT SAMPLE

Name: _Suleyma Diaz_   **Date:** _May 12, 2009_

What did I do well? At the start, it was tough figuring out what categories to make on my fishbone. Then it was hard trying to figure where a lot of the details went. This is where I had to do a lot of thinking to make sure I was accurate. Once I got this down, it was easy for me to fit a pattern. I was also good at cross-checking. I always had a partner double-check my figures. Thus, I think through the project I improved my precision and accuracy and do better seeing cause-effect connections. The clearest connection I saw was the one between the final Virginia plan and the difficulties that the landowners faced.

    Second, I found I was a good leader in my team. I asked for a lot of fact-checking, which helped me and my team stay accurate.

What could I improve? I still need to be more precise with my calculations. Especially with the data that tells whether a factor is really a cause and helps get me out of fuzzy thinking. In the work team, my first measurements for the lighting slowed us down. I also need to work on how I explain my ideas. I messed the team up several time by not being clear.

Summation: Overall, as I look at my plan, I think the tasks I did worked easily. My plan helped most with how I was thinking. I am more careful with my measurements and how I record them. I also am more likely to ask for proof to back up a cause-effect connection I think I see.

    The final phase in this project brought many "products" for assessment: the journal with its various entry/assessments, the graphic organizers, the presentation, and the content-knowledge test. Most important, the assessment of products allowed the teacher to focus students on the thinking and collaborating they did as they worked through the various phases for solving the problem of deciding on a workable Constitution acceptable to the majority of delegates. These same products, measured by rubrics and followed by a culminating test of what the students knew about the proposed plans and the convention itself, ensured that the teacher had multiple snapshots of what the students knew and did as they studied the Constitutional Convention.

THE CHALLENGE OF METACOGNITION

The topic of metacognition has been on educators' lips for many decades. The essential question at this point is "Why don't we see it more in practice?" The answer is both simple and complex. The simple response is that promoting metacognition in an information-packed, information-dumping curriculum is an impossible task, even for the teacher who is skilled and committed to its use. The complex answer is embodied in the skill level that it requires for a teacher to use it well, even in a well-taught collaborative classroom.

The Intentional Skill Development chart applied to a classroom where a teacher is committed to advancing 21st century skills will illustrate the degrees of difficulty. Beyond knowing how metacognition influences thinking about content—the foundation step—the most effective teachers ask students to think about the quality of their thinking, sometimes before the thinking task (e.g., "How will you go about making a prediction about what President Lincoln will do when faced with the question of freeing the slaves?"), during the thinking task (e.g., "Let's stop and think a minute. What is the precise evidence that you are thinking about and how will you use it in this situation?"), and after (e.g., "You have done a lot of predicting in this lesson. What do you think was the best predicting you did and why?"). To prepare for these questions, the best teachers will insert a mini-lesson about "making predictions" in the content lesson. As part of the mini-lesson, she or he will know exactly when and where in the content lesson, in this case the lesson on Lincoln's attributes, and will invite students to use the thinking skill taught.

Figure 9.6. Intentional 21st Century Skill Development

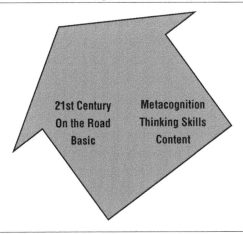

Intentional Skill Development is defined as the purposeful and systematic instruction of a skill. Thinking skills or collaboration skills are no different in this regard. When educators say, "We do that," meaning that they attend to critical thinking or collaboration skills, they usually are talking about use of the skills, but not their purposeful instruction. In addition, they may be noting that it is up to the individual teacher to decide to ask higher-order questions, use thoughtful graphic organizers, or assign projects to the students, usually the gifted ones. Not only does intentional development refer to a teacher's adding a lesson on a thinking skill or collaboration skill as a specific lesson, it also sets the criteria that the skill be formally placed in the scope and sequence curriculum and mandated for instruction to all students.

As shown in Figure 9.1, that development occurs in a cycle. To incorporate intentional development in the daily curriculum requires multiple years of experience so teachers may learn how to promote effective metacognition. A simple graduate workshop or class will not do it. They will need systematic support as they refine the practices in the daily curriculum.

Students who arrive from sponge classrooms, where they are expected to "sit and git" from the sage on the stage may be especially reluctant to think about their thinking. Students who attend highly competitive schools, dominated by Type A compulsive learners for whom quantity of worksheets finished is as good as quality, may be doubly reluctant. In the preteen years, fear of saying the wrong thing, ridicule, or other teenage visions of social catastrophe complicate the challenge. Speaking up in class to talk about the content is tough for any student; speaking up to acknowledge the quality of one's cooperation or to share how one assesses one's own thinking are imagined disasters as horrible as the sinking of the Titanic.

The difficult challenges inherent in promoting metacognitive thought do not warrant shying away. What is warranted is teacher-development time that will assist teachers in the improvement of this invaluable skill. The most helpful pathway to a high skill level for a teacher will involve collegial opportunities that scaffold skill development, in which teachers practice together how to ask questions, respond, and give feedback to students who are asked first to think about their thinking in regard to the content they are studying. Progressively more challenging experiences in how to help students think about their cognitive skills and functions applied to content and eventually to pure thinking help teachers climb a ladder step by step.

CONCLUDING THOUGHTS

In collaborative lessons and projects, teachers draw attention to students' thinking and to thinking about thinking, the embedded cognition and metacognition, by intentionally mediating learning experiences such as Suleyma's problem-based scenario. As a result, they help students learn the material more deeply while developing and sharpening students' thinking skills and intentionally promoting transfer.

Acting as mediators, teachers don't allow thinking skills to improve by chance. They set up learning situations that encourage students to use a specific thinking operation such as analyzing cause and effect. Teachers demonstrate how to best use that operation in a concrete project and refine the operation's quality by fine-tuning students' cognitive functions with specific feedback. This purposeful attention targets the quality of student cognition each day. In all instances, these teachers are proactive about improving specific thinking skills as well as deepening their knowledge of the topic. To facilitate the transfer, the teachers help the students embed the skills in their work with their peers. Finally, these teachers enable students to take responsibility for additional, independent improvement of their thinking as students apply their sharpened skills across the curriculum and in their daily life and lifelong learning opportunities. As a result of their sharpened thinking skills, both operations and functions, students leave the class with increased knowledge *and* with tools to become more effective thinkers across the curriculum.

CHAPTER 10

Soaring Above and Beyond

Power Lessons and Projects

> In describing today's accelerating changes, the media fires blips
> of unrelated information at us. Experts bury us under mountains
> of narrowly specialized monographs. Popular forecasters present
> lists of unrelated trends, without any model to show us their
> interconnections or the forces likely to reverse them. As a result,
> change itself comes to be seen as anarchic, even lunatic.
>
> —Alan Toffler

TOFFLER'S WORDS FROM several decades back into the 20th century predicted the information tsunami that threatened to drown 21st century students. In the halcyon days before the tsunami, teachers still had the opportunity to serve as a funnel of information from their heads to their students. That time has passed. The amount of information that students must digest in a single school year exceeds what their grandparents were expected to know. Yet our teaching methods and content have not changed.

To make the changes required for today's students to take charge of the information tsunami, there is need for a model that will show students how to make sense of the plethora of facts and figures. The model must have increased power to maximize students' learning efforts, making them more efficient learners and effective thinkers. The key question then is "How can teachers design more powerful lessons and projects that will result in all students making significant gains not only in achievement but also in use of those skills that will transform them into more powerful learners?"

The answer comes at two levels. The first relates to the creation of power lessons. The second relates to power projects. Power lessons and projects are those that enrich students learning abilities. The enrichment comes from the introduction of three factors applicable to both lessons and projects: the integration of best practice instructional strategies, the use of technology as a tool, and the assessment of metacognition.

Even when starting with the traditional seven elements that constitute a direct lesson design, teachers can create increasingly powerful lessons that enrich student learning and produce powerful results. This chapter starts with the addition of new ingredients to enrich the simplest of lesson designs and concludes with a sample "Power Lesson" that integrates best practice instructional strategies with the other two elements. These models ensure the simultaneous le development of three crucial elements of 21st century teaching and learning: critical thinking, collaboration, and communication. With these elements combined, teachers are better able to enrich the collaboration and communication that enriches the quality of what and how students learn in a standards-based curriculum.

FROM AN ACCIDENTAL COLLABORATION TO A MILLION-DOLLAR MUSICAL

The story behind the musical *Million Dollar Quartet* is a picture of a remarkable and dramatic collaboration. The musical's name sprang from an impromptu jam session on Tuesday, December 4, 1956, in the Sun Studio in Memphis, Tennessee. Four future musical superstars, Elvis Presley, Jerry Lee Lewis, Carl Perkins, and Johnny Cash, played together in a singular event. In 2008, the musical based on that recording session opened at Chicago's Goodman Theatre.

It is reported that the jam session happened by chance. The four stars walked into Sun Studio at different times on that day. Gradually, the players warmed to one another and to their different musical styles. They soon began blending their music. As the session continued, the collaboration increased. The manager of the studio called a local newspaper, the *Memphis Press-Scimitar*. The following day, an article was published in the paper under the title "Million Dollar Quartet." The article contained the now well-known photograph of Elvis Presley seated at the piano surrounded by Jerry Lee Lewis, Carl Perkins, and Johnny Cash.

The gathering at Sun Studio was accidental. The musical play that emerged more than 50 years later was not. What both the gathering and the musical showed was that collaboration and communication cover a wide spectrum of purposes. The four players who turned into million-dollar musicians had little intention of working together. But they discovered a common bond and their manager made the most of the new connection. In that unintentional collaboration was the seed of the intentional collaboration that resulted in the play.

ADDING HIGH OCTANE TO LESSONS

Like playwrights who create well-designed plays, classroom teachers can create lessons that move collaboration from an accidental incident to a soaring purposeful production. Checking off the crucial elements that make the most difference in the enrichment of student learning, teachers will find that they have many options for writing their "plays," in which single instructional elements are joined together into a single, meaningful lesson that carries students to the highest levels of achievement.

Just as the completed picture is most important in a puzzle, the whole lesson with its integrated parts is most important in an enriched learning experience. Each of the elements is a contributing factor. The final picture is only as effective in producing the desired "understand and do" results as the combinations the teacher makes to form the whole.

INCORPORATING HIGH-EFFECT INSTRUCTIONAL STRATEGIES

In the 1970s Madeline Hunter and others made popular the "direct instruction model." The aim was to use a seven-step model to bring a more systematic system of teaching to the classroom with less "egg thrown against a wall." Since those days, research on effective instructional practices has increased insight into what ways of teaching are the most effective in amplifying student achievement. When teachers take best advantage of the "strategies that work," as identified by the research of and delineated by Marzano and others, they employ a creative thinking process that allows them to blend those strategies into more powerful lessons (Marzano et al., 2001). For instance, a single lesson might well integrate (1) cooperative learning, (2) advance organizers, (3) visual representations (e.g., graphic organizers, charts, and graphs), (4) summary statements as tools to help students attain closure, and (5) retain the stated objective. It makes common sense that an appropriate combination of these well-supported instructional strategies will provide students with much more learning power than any one alone.

In the 21st century, the enriched learning lesson includes as its first attribute what research has said is most helpful for guiding teachers in their construction of high-powered lessons, lessons that will cause student achievement to soar. These are the high-yield strategies (Marzano et al., 2001). It is not unimaginable to see that such power lessons and projects, carefully matched with content requirements, will produce far better results than other models with less built-in power. The power lesson, like the high-octane superperformance of Formula 1 race cars that easily outrun the best of showroom sedans (even BMWs and Mercedes), fast outpaces conventional lessons. This is especially true in comparison with lessons that rely on worksheets and long lectures, instructional strategies that have no research support, or those that are thrown together in a haphazard manner.

SEVEN ESSENTIAL ELEMENTS OF A POWER LESSON DESIGN

There are seven components or elements for teachers to include in a power design. The power lesson's components, however, are more complex and powerful than the elements identified by Hunter and her colleagues, sometimes called the "seven steps to heaven."

The seven power lesson components are the following:

1. The standards
2. The best-practice, high-yield instructional strategies and tactics
3. The backward-design model
4. The use of formal cooperative-learning groups
5. A focus on cognitive operations
6. The purposeful development of cognitive functions
7. Formative assessment with strong, helpful feedback

DESIGN OPTIONS FOR POWER LESSONS

When teachers integrate the five most effective teaching strategies into direct instruction, they are taking positive steps to improve the quality of instruction. However, it is possible for teachers to go beyond these incremental steps and help students make huge leaps forward in their understanding and skill development. The enriched power lesson encourages those leaps.

When it comes time to design an enriched power lesson to best support even the lowest-performing students to learn beyond their perceived or labeled maximums, teachers can select the best mix of the seven elements in a power lesson. With each element teachers have many chances to make mix-and-match options so that strategies and tactics flow, although the formats may differ. Just as a boat and a ship are different basic versions of an object that floats on water and carries people or cargo, the power lesson will have many variations. Like the differences that distinguish the simple rowboat, canoe, and sailboat from a speed racer, a battleship, or a passenger cruise ship, lessons and designs vary by size, function, propulsion, and other factors.

Given the various options available, it should not be difficult for teachers to design lessons so that students can understand the required curricular content and develop the 21st century skills they need to better attain the content standards. This is especially true when teachers must decide how they are going to teach a lesson that covers the material and achieves the desired results, not only for the standards-aligned content, but also for development of the skills for collaboration and communication.

Because good design is more than throwing a set of activities against the wall and hoping that, like an egg, the learning will stick; an effective lesson requires that the cook plan the meal, no matter how simple, so that the diners receive the minimum daily requirements of vitamins and minerals and the most nutritional fuel boost as they enjoy the taste.

NEW DESIGNS FOR IMPROVED LEARNING

Lessons come in many shapes and forms, but school lessons do have a common definition: a single continuous section of formal instruction into which a topic or unit is divided. In the upper grades, the lesson covers 1 or 2 weeks and ends with a test. For instance, a U.S. history teacher may present a lesson about Malcolm X. A middle grade science teacher may present a lesson on buoyancy. Both teachers present their lesson by announcing its title. They then use direct talk or the "lecture" to provide students with the important information that says, "Yes, this will be on the test this Friday."

This time-honored approach contravenes the good advice given more than 21 centuries ago when Plutarch noted that minds were not vessels to be filled, but fires to be lit. The empty-vessel strategy involves pouring information into "empty" student heads so they can fill up the "empty vessel." Others in history have described this approach as "writing on an empty slate." Done well, this method may also involve such tactics as using whiteboard or PowerPoint visuals to show examples and charts, requiring students to take notes; outlines to follow; an occasional discussion; and home study mandated before students memorize important vocabulary words or the key information for a test.

Another lesson design, common in elementary classrooms, is built on a sequence of practice activities. The students are handed workbooks. The teacher explains the task (e.g., how to add single-digit whole numbers), and the students practice a page or two of these problems. The teacher checks the answers, and the students go on to complete the next pages. In this pseudo-lesson, there is much practice time, but no one teaches the students what to practice or the value of what they are learning. Moreover, often little corrective feedback is given along the way.

In the worst-case scenario for this approach, teachers hand out worksheets and then return to their desks to correct completed sheets. These teachers believe that students "doing" worksheets with repetitive problems in the same format (e.g., one step, two step) will produce achievement through repetition and reinforcement.

This antiquated lesson design is a far cry from what the research says "works." At best, when teachers pre-teach concepts followed by worksheet activity and careful monitoring or "guided practice," students refine a targeted skill. More likely, students tune out as they mindlessly circle numbers or fill in blanks, noticing little on the paper and little in the classroom around them. When teachers differentiate the guided-practice options with centers, simple projects, computer programs, and the like, the students' incentive to concentrate may be increased.

In a better scenario, teachers can add power to the direct-instruction lesson. They need to incorporate high-yield strategies such as advance organizers, cooperative groups, graphic organizers, or summary statements to the lesson's mix. By also adding technology tools to enhance communication, they will raise the lesson's octane rating to superhigh-test. The more teachers attend to the addition of these powerful tools, the more acceleration they will get toward the lesson's outcomes.

Certainly, an astute observer who enters an elementary classroom in which the teacher is an active user of high-yield instructional strategies will notice the engagement of the students. The observer is sure to see the teacher using one or more strategies here and there to prepare students so they can achieve more highly on tests that require strong memories. In many textbooks, new teachers' editions support this approach by scattering examples of strong instructional strategies, perhaps talking about cooperative groups and showing a graphic organizer. The text may even recommend some "best practices," such as

- Use an *advance organizer graphic* as an anticipatory set.
- Identify *results* as objectives.
- Use *cooperative groups* with *graphic organizers* to gather information from printed materials or online sources.

- *Check for understanding* with a thumbs-up signal or electronic clickers.
- Analyze information by using *a matrix* or *story chart*.
- Guide discussion by using *higher-order questions.*
- Give *feedback* from formative assessments.

GOING ABOVE AND BEYOND

Let there be no doubt that the *incidental* or *random* use of these strategies as described above can help students achieve more than a bare-bones direct-instruction lesson. But so much more is possible if teachers intentionally design their lessons with the goal of achieving powerful results through students' purposeful use of high-yield tactics and strategies. When teachers use the strategies more purposefully, they transform their students into power achievers. When they teach students to use these strategies, teachers transform the students into power racers.

ON THE WINGS OF A POWER LESSON

A well-designed power lesson encourages teachers to focus on student development in multiple domains so that students more readily understand the prescribed content and develop important skills for thinking and collaborating. When a teacher makes a power design to integrate content standards with best practices of collaboration and cognition, he or she expands the repertoire of possible strategies to include not just in this one incident but for future lessons as well.

Note how the samples that follow enrich the lesson and point to more powerful results:

- A launch question or loosely structured problem serves as an advance organizer of content shown on the whiteboard. Students learn the importance of this essential question and when and how to use it well.
- A blog set up with categories to show evidence of standards-aligned understanding or skill.
- An electronic graphic organizer with student pairs to collect information in response to the launch question.
- An analysis of gathered information in response to a launch question by cooperative groups of four.

- A checking for individual understanding and skill development via quiz, test, or essay along with other formative tactics such as prompt completions in an e-journal.
- An assessment of understanding and skill from each student's written statement.
- The purposeful promotion of learning transfer.

Promoting Learning Transfer: An Example

The Holocaust	Focus Within This Unit	Intentional Transfer to Other Projects	Intentional Transfer to Other Courses
Skill I Cooperative learning	Roles and responsibilities	Do check at end	Do self-assessment
Skill II Cognitive skill	Asking analytic questions	Cause and effect	Do cause and effect
Cognitive operations	Use fishbone	Watch for key cause	Use fishbone in notebook
Cognitive functions	Be accurate	Double-check in notes	Review math formulas
Content concept I	Anti-Semitism in Europe	Analysis of World War II	Analysis of *To Kill a Mockingbird*
Content concept II	The diaspora	Historic causes of other ethnic cleansing	Cause analysis of Macbeth's downfall

These examples are not "either-or" dictates or "it's the one *or* the other" tasks. Teachers may elect to use any of these examples to fit in a power lesson. The teacher selects designs to fit the outcomes he or she wishes to achieve. Similarly, teachers can use their standards to identify the crucial critical and creative thinking skills, technology skills, or the collaboration and communication outcomes that they wish their students to develop. Then, it is easier to blend the development of these 21st century skills into a multilevel power lesson that fits the triple outcome: content, cognition, and collaboration—all integrated, as happens in non-academic-world scenarios, and not isolated, as so often happens in school lessons.

To create this synthesis of content, collaboration, and cognition, the following steps are a guide:

1. Set trifold (three objectives: one for the content, one for the collaboration, and one for the thinking skill or cognition highlighted in the lesson) "understand" and "do" outcomes such as "Students will explain the difference between cause and effect and students will chart causes of a single effect on a fishbone."

A SAMPLE POWER LESSON FOR EXPLICIT PROMOTION OF COLLABORATION, COGNITION, AND CONTENT

Title: The Illinois Constitution
Level of Difficulty: Medium
Grade: 7 or 8

Launch Question: What elements of the Illinois Constitution are most likely to affect our daily lives? (Students use KWL to identify what they know and want to know about these laws. They work together in a two-four-eight grouping strategy to gather their ideas.)

Content Management System: Using Moodle, the teacher sets up individual blogs for each student. Within the blogs, students set up categories for their entries: content, collaboration, critical thinking, and communication.

Explicit Instruction: Schedule days for explicit lessons for each category (4-week unit).

A. Content
   1. Overview of Illinois Constitution. Start with an advance organizer. (Provide teams with current event articles that relate to the Constitution. After teams read, ask each to tell what they think might be the legal issue. Take a day to show them how to use a blog you set up (http://www.blogster.com) to record their ideas and ask question).
   2. Small group jigsaw of the sections. Ask for a written summary on the blog signed by each group member followed by an online poster made on Glogster (http://edu.glogster.com). For the poster, each team must (a) visualize one or more key points from their reading, (b) connect it to one of the scenarios identified at the start of the lesson, and (c) add other samples of events related to the section. For instance, are video cameras at intersections or speed traps a violation? Are bribes to government officials an issue?
      a. Presentation to class of Glogster posters applications.
      b. Feedback from other groups on what they liked about the presenting group's poster.
B. Critical Thinking
   1. Evaluating ideas about the topic. Show samples of prior student work. Demonstrate how to give feedback for evaluating others' work with constructive critiques.
   2. Drawing conclusions about the connections between the incidence in the news and the Illinois Constitution. Show examples and encourage responses from the groups.

A SAMPLE POWER LESSON FOR EXPLICIT PROMOTION OF COLLABORATION, COGNITION, AND CONTENT *(continued)*

C. Collaboration
   1. Blog
   2. Glogster poster
   3. Two-four-eight summary
D. Communication
   1. Summaries
   2. Final essay

Information-Gathering Strategies to Use:

A. Jigsaw
B. KWL

Making-Sense Strategies:

A. Discussion to compare. Use groups of three with reports to class.
B. Class feedback. Circulate among students, observe and give kudos as observed. Summarize feedback on whiteboard.

Checking for Understanding:

A. Give feedback during group work about accuracy and completeness. Circulate, observe products, and comment as needed.
B. Ask questions about criteria used to judge constitutional connections made on posters. Require proof for each idea.
C. Monitor group roles for cooperation.

Assessment of Outcomes:

A. Understanding of Constitution and its applications.
   1. Blog summaries
   2. Glogster posters
   3. Final unit test with question parallel to original essential question
B. Skills (Critical Thinking and Collaboration Outcomes
   1. Observation checklist
   2. Student entry in blog via rubric
   3. Group assessments of cooperation from rubric

Formative Feedback:

A. Use weekly observation checklists for targeted skills (e.g., cooperation, predicting).
B. Use quizzes for checking understanding of content.
C. Hold team feedback sessions so students may discuss progress in teams.
D. Send periodic suggestions to students at blog sites.

2. Provide a "launch question" or a loosely structured problem as an "advance organizer" of content.

3. Set up a Content Management System (CMS) with a blog or another CMS to show categories (e.g., cognition, content, collaboration).

4. Give explicit instruction related to targeted outcomes (e.g., cognition, content, collaboration).

5. Provide strategies to make sense of content information.

6. Check for understanding of content and mediation of targeted critical thinking skills and collaborative skills.

7. Assess understanding and development progress for all targeted skills. (What can students do more skillfully to think critically and collaborate? How do these promote content mastery?)

As this sample lesson illustrates, teachers can teach the required content and foster collaboration and communication simultaneously. The focus is on the Constitution and its applications. Instead of just asking students to read and explain the meaning of the sections in the Constitution, or showing a film and giving a final exam with readily scanned multiple-choice questions, teachers can use cooperative groups and content management systems to foster collaboration and content as means for advancing the students' understanding of the document. By using the two websites, students learn to apply skills they may already have in manipulating a blog. However, by adding to their natural interest in e-tools and their intuitive knowledge for making the tools work for an educational challenge, teachers increase the chances of engaging even the most reluctant. The blog gives a new medium for developing their writing skills and the glogster site stimulates their creative thinking. At the same time, by asking the students to look for everyday applications of the law, teachers enable students to use their complex thinking skills, especially the critical thinking operations of comparing, applying, and making judgments and the creative thinking skills for generating ideas and designing new products. Teachers also foster critical thinking by expecting students to be precise, accurate, and thorough in their use of evidence. They do this most when they purposefully monitor the students in their work-learning groups. Finally, by scheduling time for explicit instruction of the collaborative and communication skills, the teachers prepare the students for those strategies and e-tools they will have to use during the lesson so they can be more efficient in how they work together. At the end of the lesson, teachers have a multitude of data from their observations and a rubric that focused on observations of how students thought and worked together with the Constitution content. To go with the observation of what the students showed they were able to do, teachers in this three-level integrated unit have test results, essays, or other assessments of knowledge gained.

Yes, it is possible for individual teachers to integrate collaboration, communication, and other 21st century skill development into any traditional lesson. Yes, it may require more time to complete the lesson and arrive at the final knowledge tests for the content. And yes, teachers will have also strengthened their students' ability to use and transfer the thinking and collaborating skills. Given how much they accomplished by stretching the lesson's allotted time by 10%, for the students they have enriched learning by 25%.

THE PROJECT: A MODEL WHOSE TIME HAS COME

As much as power lessons will help teachers introduce 21st century skills into the curriculum, the lesson model does not attain the heights of change to which Toffler alluded decades back. The model that does that is the enriched-learning project.

Like the power lesson, the enriched-learning project is a superhigh-octane instructional model. If the comparison that fits the power lesson is the high-octane NASCAR, the comparison that is more apt for the project model is the stealth fighter plane. Both rely on high-yield instructional strategies explicitly taught and integrated into the daily curriculum, technology tools for instruction, and assessment of students' metacognition.

If the ingredients are the same, why is the enriched-learning project thought to be more powerful? The most important answer is that the project model frees the teacher to be an observer, a mediator of process, and a facilitator of assessment. Several other conditions of this model allow the teacher to focus his or her energy on student learning for more sustained and deeper learning experiences, rather than being the dominant transmitter of information:

AN ENRICHED-LEARNING PROJECT DEFINED

A project is a collaborative enterprise involving research. Its aim is to produce a product that reflects the information and ideas gathered from research. In a school, the students' learning through this model of instruction is *enriched* by use of high-yield instructional strategies, Web 2.0 tools, and formative assessments that target content and 21st century skills.

1. *The project puts greater emphasis on the process of learning.* By following the three phases of learning (see Figure 9.3), teachers are able to devote more time to refining students' learning of skills in each of the phases. Although a teacher will start with the same standards, the interdisciplinary nature of the project model allows her to mix and match outcomes with increased opportunity for students to apply their thinking and collaborating skills. For instance, in the investigation model, a school could ask that all 4th- or 9th-grade teachers design strong research practices into the projects. Some may assign online research and teach the techniques; others may use print resources at the local library; yet others might emphasize surveys or interviews. The sum total says, "This year's courses are about learning how to locate, make sense of, and evaluate information from multiple sources."

In the next year, teachers may highlight the innovative project with the focus on divergent thinking. In the following years, teachers would focus on the problem scenario, able to spend considerable time in facilitating students' problem-identification skills in multiple projects.

2. *Collaboration is reinforced more intensely.* Students not only are able to develop skills in cooperative-learning groups, but also can work with teachers to build collaborative-learning communities in each class. They can work in internships off campus to apply the skills they are learning.

3. *There is increased time and comfort for teachers to use metacognitive reflection in multiple learning domains.* They can structure formative assessments and give formative feedback on critical thinking (week 1), collaboration (week 2), and content (week 3). For each target, teachers have the time to walk among the teams at work, observe, conference, and

---

A PROJECT'S INGREDIENTS

- The Advance Organizer
- The Essential Question
- The Know and Do Outcomes
- The Student Tasks
- Intentional Collaboration and Communication
- Intentional Thinking and Problem Solving Multiple Assessments

ask students for self-assessments that are focused on that week's target. With a blog, students can more easily check in and record their assessments and take note of the teacher's feedback

4. The classroom environment is structured architecturally to align with the various types of tasks inherent in project-based learning. There are permanent small-group and private workspaces, permanent wall space for display, permanent presentation space with set-in-place presentation media, access to Internet sites, other communication technology, and connections for multiple computers.

CONCLUDING THOUGHTS

It is more than likely that students who have improved their collaboration and communication skills in one lesson will apply these improved skills in the next, especially if teachers plan to scaffold all three elements and make sure they close with a tactic to heighten transfer of learning. Transfer of learning reinforces the notion that learning is not for a test but for a lifetime. What students learn about collaboration, content, or cognition in a lesson doesn't stop when they walk out the door on the last day of a project or lesson. It should carry forward. Teachers help students carry forward what they learned in each of these dimensions by planning for purposeful reflections in a journal, a test question, or a round-robin discussion. They may use a prompt such as "From this project, the most important lesson I can carry to other classes about collaboration is . . ." or "This week in my other classes, I will concentrate on [cognitive function] by . . ." and provide each student with time to reflect in a think-pair-share or write-pair-share activity. Such reflections not only encourage a look back at what was learned in the project, but also reinforce that learning and the importance of learning transfer for content, collaboration, and cognition.

CHAPTER 11

An Internet Investigation Project

Climate Change

> Our generation has inherited an incredibly beautiful world. We must
> not be part of the generation responsible for irreversibly damaging
> the environment.
>
> —Richard Branson

A N INTERNET INVESTIGATION is a collaborative inquiry project. In this sample project intended to stimulate both collaboration and critical thinking, middle or secondary students collaborate to investigate two sides of the debate regarding climate change. After gathering data from online sites, they make contact with peers at other schools in other districts or nations and gather additional information. After judging the information by assessing the different points of view, students prepare an electronic communication that summarizes their final agreements and disagreements.

THE INTERNET INVESTIGATION

An investigation project springs from the inquiry model of learning. It is grounded in a search for an answer to a significant question. The search is grounded in content standards but raises larger issues and confronts broad thematic concerns. Neither Internet nor other technology resources are necessary to complete the investigation, which can take many forms. However, when teachers ask students to use Web 2.0 tools and micro hardware to enrich their search, they enhance the collaborative spirit, expand communication opportunities, and sharpen critical thinking and problem solving skills.

Teachers can use a variety of formats for the investigations. There is the classic scientific inquiry with its well-established format. There is the discovery format that relies on the artichoke strategy of peeling away

One sunny day last June, four American teachers sat together in a bright café garden in the British Cotswolds. They had just completed a day of touring and were waiting for their traditional cups of tea.

As they reflected on the day's garden visits, a gray-haired British gentleman leaned to the tourists' table. "I say, are you Americans?" he asked.

"Yes, we are," responded the senior member. "But we are from different states. I am from New York."

"Well, I just wanted to ask you one question," he stated. "What is wrong with your country? It has changed so much."

The four Americans looked at one another quizzically. They were unsure how to respond. Finally, the New Yorker broke the silence.

"I don't know what you mean."

"Why, of course you do," he said. "The Kyoto Treaty—America used to be the leader on global issues. Why did you sabotage one of the most important issues in the world?"

Needless to say, the four American tourists found themselves quickly immersed in a feverish discussion of global warming and climate change with a citizen of the European Union at the end of a day's touring devoted to gardening. Unsurprisingly, there was no consensus. Some sided with the Briton; others disagreed. One took the position that global warming was a myth, overblown by the media. Another joined with the British questioner in challenging the "current administration's political motives for avoiding the treaty." A third, well-versed on the issue, quoted facts and figures about global warming's impact on our environment. The fourth, totally uninformed on the issue, listened silently.

layers of ideas and information. And there is the debate format that organizes a project around opposing points of view. The debate format is the most readily adaptable.

WHAT IS THE DEBATE FORMAT?

The debate format is a way to organize a project around two opposing points of view. It is a format that is familiar to secondary school debate teams who enter school-school competitions. In classroom projects, this format is built on the intentional development of students' abilities to compare and contrast, recognize and challenge different points of view, and seek out a meaningful synthesis of opposing ideas.

WHAT IS THE VALUE OF THE DEBATE FORMAT?

The debate format is not a new way of teaching and learning. It goes back to Socrates, Plato, and Aristotle. This format was the familiar way to discuss the Constitutional Convention. Abraham Lincoln and Steven Douglas debated the ethics of slavery. The 20th century saw the arrival of TV debates for the presidency. Today, public debates rage between conservatives and liberals over social issues such as stem cell research, environmental protection, and reproductive rights. In less serious scenarios, families debate trips to the grandparents' house, college choices, birthday presents, and holiday dinners. At the worst, they argue. At the best, they use their skills to examine both sides of the issue, explore alternatives, and analyze options, listening carefully to each other and clarifying points of view.

In the debate project format, students select a point of view regarding an identified issue. Young student teams may prepare to debate a local issue such as "Does the Little League baseball park need a home-run fence?" High school students might debate "expansion of the teen center" or "increase of police patrols in the school."

Each side is given assignments and resources to gather information for their point of view, analyze it, and prepare their case. When access to the Internet is available, teachers can build in online-research skill building and tasks for the research and analysis phases. Teachers may also give teams a selection of e-tools such as shareware, blogs, and websites as the tools to communicate their ideas during the actual debate.

This format is an easy-start project that allows inclusion of all elements that are important in a 21st century collaborative project. Teachers can organize according to the three phases of learning: gathering data, making sense of data, and communicating new ideas. This process encourages the teaching of thinking skills, such as examining points of view, analyzing arguments for bias, comparing, cause-effect analysis, and judging relevant data. In addition, it allows teachers to target such cognitive functions as precision and clarity, impulse control, using multiple sources of data, and connecting ideas that are not obviously related. Finally, the team format allows for incorporation of formal cooperative-learning tactics such as four square and jigsaw (Bellanca & Fogarty, 1991).

When teachers take advantage of these elements and incorporate them into a debate project, they are increasing the chances that students' mastery of the content investigated in the debate and the learning-thinking methods used will yield strong achievement results. When teachers tie the debate content to grade-level or course standards, they will see higher engagement and interest among the majority of their students.

THE CLIMATE-CHANGE ISSUE: A TOPIC WORTHY OF DEBATE

Climate-change debates have grown over the past decade, not only during informal conversations, but also in houses of government, scientific forums, and other gatherings around the globe. When browsing for the two-word phrase on the Internet, it is easy to find statements that damn the issue as a liberal conspiracy perpetrated by bad science. Likewise, it is easy to find a similar number of passionate political statements calling for urgent action to control the doomsday factors that are seen threatening Earth's environment. Is climate change fact or fiction? Whom do we believe?

The Basics of the Issue

To study the issue of climate change, an easy question to pose for students as they start their investigation is the one of "fact or fiction?" What do the data say? How strong are the arguments for and against the existence of global warming? What facts can they verify? What position do they want to take? With whom must they side? How do they judge the accuracy and validity of what they are reading and hearing from "experts"?

Two Points of View

Global warming is the greatest hoax ever perpetuated on the American people.
—Senator James Inhofe, Oklahoma

The science of global warming and its impact is overwhelming and unequivocal.
—Representative Nancy Pelosi, California

The issue of global warming has strong voices on each side. It is directly related to the issue of climate change. Some voices are scientific; others are political. Each set of voices uses data to support its case. Some say that the two sides are not so far apart. "It is," they say "a matter of interpretation. If you are an advocate of free trade and big business, you will argue either that there is no such thing as global warming, or, if there is, it is not something we have to worry about for decades or centuries." The others say "No. It is coming fast. We have to act now." With statements like these, who is the most believable? Are their data equally valid? How do we analyze the data for bias? For accuracy?

This particular debate provides rich fodder for student inquiry of the best sort. It not only enables teachers to teach students how to conduct research, but also gives them an issue that has at least two points of view and many nuances for students to consider. Thus, the issue is ripe for teachers to create teachable moments that will enable them to develop students' critical thinking skills. In short, this is a hot topic that will challenge students to do their best thinking and problem solving.

Preparing for the Project. This project emphasizes the development of students as skilled questioners and good challengers of assumptions. It provides teachers with the opportunity to teach students how to ask sharper questions so as to gain more precise and complete information, enabling them to better challenge different points of view and to question assumptions. It also emphasizes the development of their online collaboration and communication skills in assessing points of view and the drawing of logical conclusions from sound data.

To facilitate the flow of the project, teachers prepare online samples of questionnaires, spreadsheets, organizers, letters, and e-newspapers. Teachers may use these with rubrics so that students may know better what is expected as quality work. The rubrics can also target students' critical thinking with an emphasis on evaluating sources and checking facts.

A SAMPLE INVESTIGATION FOR SECONDARY STUDENTS

Title: Climate Change: Fact or Fiction?

Overview: Upper-grade students working in pairs will search online for answers to basic questions about climate change. With the answers, the groups will take an initial position in the debate: "Climate change: Fact or fiction?" Based on their position, the teams will construct a survey to send to peers in other areas of the country, other nations, or both. They may want to include the perspectives of a nation within a nation, our Native Americans (see www. wisdomoftheelders.com). These questions will encourage them to use their "respectful minds" as they solicit data responses from peers in other countries with other points of view (Gardner, 2007). After gathering this information and before they complete the final project phase, a digital product that communicates both sides of the debate (e.g., a WebQuest or an electronic newsletter), they will use a spreadsheet to analyze the information received and to compare it to data from their own community. What is similar and different in the points of view?

> ## THE PHASES OF LEARNING IN AN INVESTIGATION
>
> 1. Gather information through Internet dialogue and research.
> 2. Make sense of the information by comparing data and seeing another point of view.
> 3. Communicate new understandings in a new way.

Advance Organizer.

1. Using a projector connected to the classroom computer (or a substitute such as an interactive whiteboard), teachers take students to a search engine page on the Web under the key phrase *climate change*. Earlier information and perspectives will also be found by searching for *global warming*, the term that was first in use as scientists began to find evidence of change. They select one previewed page and open it. They ask the students to read the material silently and to think about their responses until the teachers signal them to turn to a partner and share.
   A. "What do you think is meant by 'climate change'"?
   B. "Why do you think it is an important or not important issue?"
   C. "What questions come to mind as you think about climate change?"
2. Teachers seek several responses to each question. They listen to each response but do not discuss. They do not call upon any one student more than once.
3. For all students to see, teachers note the differences of opinions heard. They explain that there are many differences on the topic of climate change.
4. To end the discussion, teachers share the project's purpose: "To evaluate the positions taken about the reality of climate change."

Phase I: Gathering Information

1. This phase helps students dig immediately into the data-collection tasks in which they will sharpen their skills of electronic information gathering and evaluating. Teachers review the purpose of the project, their expectations, the phases and tasks, and how they will assess students' performance. Teachers conclude by pairing students for the first task.

2. Students sit at computer stations or with their own laptops. The teacher uses a coin flip to determine the starting role for each student. For each new computer task, the pair will trade off this role. If students do not keep an electronic journal, the additional role of recorder will maintain a written log. It is important for teachers to maintain individual accountability and equity of work done.

3. Each pair will gather its initial data 100% online. They will review school policies about Internet use. (It will be helpful for each student to have a written copy of this policy to send home with a letter to the parents). This letter will describe the project and the policies. If you have students whose parents speak little or no English, translate the letter into the appropriate languages.

4. Students review the use of the various tools they will use in the project. If students are sophisticated in the use of word processing and the other e-tools, a quick run-through at this point will suffice. If not, they complete a review prior to each task that requires use of any electronic tool unfamiliar to them.

5. Students access the school's search engine. If the school does not have a preferred engine, the teacher selects one (e.g., Yahoo, Google, MSN, Bing) so all students are using the same engine. If the school has special firewalls, teachers remove these according to school practice.

6. Once the engines are open, students enter *climate change* into their browser. They are to search for sites that argue for climate change as a problem and sites that say that it is not a problem. Once they have picked the sites, they are to preview the information on each so that they can answer the following questions as seen by each author. A two-column chart will help them organize the answers they find. Because of the large volume of information on this topic, teachers can use the jigsaw cooperative learning structure to shorten the time for research.
   A. What is climate change?
   B. Why is it important to know about it?
   C. What is the position of those who say it is a problem (with evidence)?
   D. What is the position of those who say it is not a problem (with evidence)? Do they seem biased or impartial? Why or why not?

7. Students review the following rubric so the pairs can know how they will evaluate this information-gathering step when they do their self-assessment. (This example includes an optional grading scale).

A SAMPLE RUBRIC: INFORMATION GATHERING

To what degree have you answered each question

1. Clearly?

           1————————2————————3

        no   OK   well done

2. With specific examples?

           1————————2————————3

        no   OK   well done

3. In an organized manner?

           1————————2————————3

        no   OK   well done

Grading Scale	
Points	**Grade**
11–12	A
9–10	B
7–8	C
5–6	D

8. As they find responses to each of the questions, students can bookmark the pages they wish to use. If the first articles selected do not have all the information they want, they can return to the master page for climate change and find additional sites to help.

9. Encourage students to check accuracy by going to www. factcheck.com and determining the validity of the details.

10. If there are sufficient printer capabilities in the classroom or computer lab, students may print the pages they selected to help answer the questions. At this time, they should open a new document, enter the four questions in bold, and then proceed to construct their answers.

11. After pairs have completed this task, they will email it to you with their electronic signatures and place a copy in their own project file. Review and grade responses before returning them by email.

12. Teachers will invite each student to open a special electronic file in a classroom blog. In this file, their journal, they will retain all their own documents and data. A special section will hold journal entries made at the end of each class period. They may use the stem starter "Today in this project I learned . . ." or another stem starter of the teacher's choice, such as "I have a question about . . . ," several times a week.

Phase II: Developing the Conversation

1. In this phase, learning pairs will set up a conversation with students in other schools. Using the list of prearranged, approved school partners, it is best if each team uses the Internet and search engines to select a school in a different geographic region with a different climate. If teachers have not already done so, students can select the schools, write letters to the principals and teachers, and explain their project to students in potential partner schools. After selecting the school, they may write a sequence of email letters that will acquaint them with the other school, the region of the country, and the issue of climate change in that region. Time allotted for the start-up conversation integrates development of letter-writing skills, electronic search skills, and geography.

2. After students have returned the completed information sheets from Phase I, teachers will conduct a classroom discussion for each of the questions. After the class has discussed the last question, teachers can ask for a show of hands to the following questions:

    *   How many strongly believe that climate change is a major environmental problem?
    *   How many believe it is a solvable problem?
    *   How many strongly believe it is not a problem at all?

3. After the vote, move the students to different parts of the classroom, according to their vote. In each section, have the students form learning groups of two with one person in each group selected as the recorder. Encourage all to express their ideas. Provide index cards on which the recorders will write the pairs' reasons for their vote. Insist that responses tie back to their Internet research and initial conversations.

4. After each learning pair finishes its cards, each group will address a second pair. Select one person from the four to record the ideas on newsprint (provide markers and paper). They may use written words, symbols, graphs, or pictures. Encourage visual diversity.

5. Each group of four will display its completed responses. Each group will select a presentation team. This team will present to the class.

6. Encourage all listeners to ask clarifying questions and to press for examples and specifics of source investigation from the presenters. Note that this is not a time for disagreement, only understanding of each learning group's position.

SAMPLE CLIMATE-CHANGE SURVEY

Team names: _____, _____, _____

School: _____ Grade: _____

Email address: _____

Fax: _____

City: _____ State: _____ Country: _____ Zip: _____

Dear Friends:

We are studying climate change and its impact on our community and other communities around the world. We would like to obtain some information from you about the effects of climate change on your community. We would like you to answer the questions below in our survey. After we receive your responses, we will have additional questions to ask you by either email or fax. We prefer email. We will keep all answers confidential.

Your names: _____

Your school: _____ Your grade: _____

Your city/town/village: _____

Your state: _____ Your country: _____

Your email: _____ Your fax: _____

1. How large is the town, city, or village in which you live (number of people)?
_____

2. What type of vehicles are most commonly driven?
_____

3. What fuels are most commonly used?
_____

4. How do most people heat their homes?
_____

5. How do most businesses heat their stores? Offices?
_____

6. How would you rate the quality of air in your town?
_____

7. Leave the newsprint posted for all to see.
8. Via email, distribute "Three-Story Intellect" (a modified version of Bloom's taxonomy) to all as a guide for asking questions. Review the guide and encourage teams to take their questions from the upper stories. This model will help students ask thought-provoking questions on the survey they are going to construct. Check for student understanding of the question vocabulary.

Figure 11.1. Three-Story Intellect

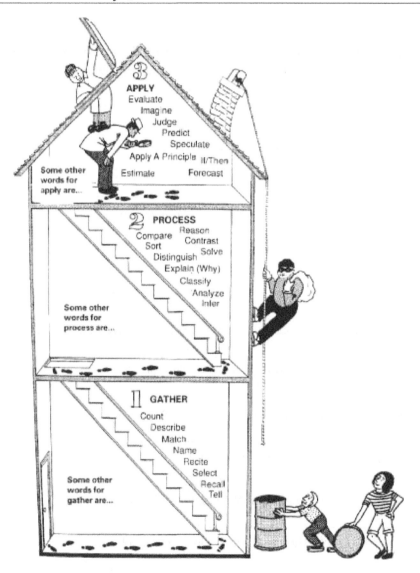

Used with permission by Bellanca & Fogarty, 1991

9. Email students a copy of the survey form. Be sure they save it into their document folder for this project. They may use these questions, change them, or add others. They may also choose to make checklists for each question.
10. Facilitate the school contacts and instruct groups in how to send the surveys.
11. The responses they receive may motivate the students to ask other questions about climate change and to engage in further electronic dialogue. Remind them to focus on the community and the school about which they are talking. Advise them to stay away from emailing personal information or personal questions as they talk to the students in other schools.

Phase II (Continued): Understanding and Interpreting the Information

1. In this phase, students will make sense of the information they have gathered from all sources (websites, libraries, dialogues with partner schools). Ask the students to work in this phase to monitor their logical thinking skills as well as their electronic skills. Help them analyze data and look for biased interpretations.
2. Teachers instruct each learning group to set up a file in which they can store responses as they arrive. While waiting for responses (about 1 week), take this time to teach as needed the use of the following electronic tools. Select content that relates to global warming and climate-change issues.
    A. Electronic spreadsheets
    B. Electronic newsletter format
    C. Electronic file management
3. Once each learning group has collected sufficient data in its electronic file folder, teachers assist them in using the spreadsheet to classify the information from the responses. After students have finished this task, they highlight the similarities and differences they see. Ultimately, they will answer the question "Is climate change fact or fiction?" perhaps in an essay or a verbal or multimedia product.
4. Each learning group partners with a second group. Each pair shares its spreadsheet and discusses what it observed. Each of these new, larger learning groups will combine data into one spreadsheet.
5. When this task is completed, the groups draw conclusions from their data. They respond to this deliberately open-ended question

with the purpose of enabling the students to develop logical generalizations from the data they have. They provide one or two examples, if needed, and highlight the questions "Why?" and "Why do we think that?" They may also comment on their logic.

6. Each group uses sheets of newsprint and markers so it can record its conclusions. Secondary sheets can display data relevant to each conclusion. Teachers monitor discussions without providing clues, judgments, and so on.

7. When all have completed their sheets, one team of four at a time stands before the classroom and shows its conclusions. Each team needs to be prepared with at least three conclusions and readiness to explain from its data how it arrived at the generalization.

8. The groups are to divide the defense in such a way that every member is involved in some part of the presentation.

9. The students may modify statements that are too broad or two narrow in relation to the data they have.

10. When all groups are finished, they respond to the "fact or fiction" judgment. Note that there is not a preordained answer. Teachers will insist that the conclusion reached by the total of data gathered is valid, accurate, and precise.

Phase III: Communicating New Understandings

1. Students reform into new groups of three.

2. Note that there will be three roles in the new groups: editor, reporter, and copyeditor. Each role identifies the leader in completing one part of the task of developing an electronic newsletter based on what students have learned from the investigation of global warming.

    *   **Editor:** directs the first phase of this task. The editor will guide the discussion of what stories and articles the newsletter will include and what the layout will look like.
    *   **Reporter:** directs the second phase. The reporter will lead the decision making about who will write what, timelines, and details of the content.
    *   **Copyeditor:** directs proofreading and final layout of the newsletter.

3. Each group will create its electronic newsletter. (If teachers allow options, apply the same criteria to each option.) Teachers select tools from the websites that might facilitate students' e-work (e.g., formatting palette, tables, and borders) or provide a newsletter

template (browse *free newsletter templates*). Monitor the work so that students include the following:

- Name of newsletter and layout
- Headline: captures conclusion about answer to fact-or-fiction question on global warming
- Feature story
- One editorial that takes a position on the key question: Fact or fiction?
- At least one other news or feature article
- Grammatical and spelling correctness (spelling and grammar check)
- Pictures or graphs optional
- Visually attractive

4. Each group will email the completed newsletter to the others in the classroom, to the teacher (for grading and feedback), to the partner schools, and to others in the school community selected through approval of the class. The newspaper's editorial will focus on the debate of fact versus fiction and reflect on a position agreed upon by the three members.
5. As with other news methods, students may wish to offer "Pulitzer prizes." The class will create a rubric prior to step 3 above and announce (a) the categories and (b) the judges for a "blind competition." Prizes may go for any of the areas identified in step 3 above.
6. If time allows, students will conduct an all-class debate. Teachers monitor the discussion so that everyone gets a chance to speak and debates with civility. (Start by dividing the class seating arrangement as "fact," "fiction," "both and undecided." Group together all who believe climate change is fact, all who believe it is fiction, and those in the middle. Encourage active listening and respect for others' ideas. Discuss how participants can maintain civility in the discussion.)

Assessing Performance. There are several levels for assessing student performance. They include assessing use of electronic tools, group contribution, understanding of topic, thinking, and the final project. Using one or more rubrics provides students with guidelines for the learning they do as well as feedback on the quality of their work. Students may complete rubrics for their peers as well for themselves. The sum total of the rubrics used can equate to a final grade.

SAMPLE RUBRICS FOR ASSESSING AN INVESTIGATION

1. Assessing Use of Digital Tools

Name of Electronic Tool: _____ Student Name: _____

Date: _____ Name of Investigation: _____

To what degree did this student

	Not Yet			Excelled
Use a new e-tool appropriately?	1	2	3	4
Use the tool with increased skill?	1	2	3	4
Make appropriate use of the Internet?	1	2	3	4
Gather information from several sites?	1	2	3	4
Analyze information for bias?	1	2	3	4
Communicate clearly and respectfully?	1	2	3	4
Assess own skill development?	1	2	3	4

Comments:

2. Assessing Collaboration

Student Name: _____ Period: _____

Date: _____ Name of Investigation: _____

To what degree did this student

	Not yet			Excelled
Take responsibility for a specific role?	1	2	3	4
Contribute thinking?	1	2	3	4
Encourage other group members?	1	2	3	4
Facilitate group success?	1	2	3	4
Show respect for others' ideas?	1	2	3	4
Challenge faulty thinking with constructive feedback?	1	2	3	4
Contribute innovative thinking?	1	2	3	4
Seek advice and feedback?	1	2	3	4

Comments:

SAMPLE RUBRICS FOR ASSESSING AN INVESTIGATION *(continued)*

3. Assessing Thinking

Student Name: _____ Period: _____

Date: _____ Name of Investigation: _____

To what degree did this student

	Not Yet			Excelled
Compare?	1	2	3	4
Frame a problem statement?	1	2	3	4
Reflect on learning?	1	2	3	4
Summarize key ideas?	1	2	3	4

Comments:

4. Assessing Understanding of the Issue

Student Name: _____ Period: _____

Date: _____ Name of Investigation: _____

To what degree did the student

	Not Yet			Excelled
Grasp the core idea?	1	2	3	4
Understand the subideas?	1	2	3	4
Know relevant supporting details?	1	2	3	4
Connect ideas and details?	1	2	3	4
Take and prove a position on the topic?	1	2	3	4

Comments:

SAMPLE RUBRICS FOR ASSESSING AN INVESTIGATION *(continued)*

5. Assessing the Final Project

Student Name: _____ Period: _____

Date: _____ Name of Investigation: _____

To what degree did this student

	Not yet			Excellent
Contribute ideas?	1	2	3	4
Follow instructions?	1	2	3	4
Complete one story or equivalent?	1	2	3	4
Proofread?	1	2	3	4
Critique others' ideas?	1	2	3	4
Prove a position on the argument?	1	2	3	4
Add to the presentation?	1	2	3	4
Show both creative and critical thinking?	1	2	3	4
Improve problem solving skills?	1	2	3	4

Comments:

Sample Grading Scale

A = 3.5 +
B = 3.0–3.49
C = 2.5–2.99
D = 2.0–2.49

CONCLUDING THOUGHTS

This chapter showed an investigation project in the debate format. Students found data to support one side or the other regarding the debate and learned to question the points of view and how to present civil arguments. The debate format allows students to analyze different points of view, question bias, and call for supportive evidence in an argument. It also allows them to develop other 21st century skills with a project that stirs their interest.

CHAPTER 12

The Problem-Based Project

> We can and must make sure that our societies have effective laws
> and functioning institutions in place so that every child can enjoy an
> environment that is free of violence.
>
> —Anders Johnson, former U.N. Secretary General

- Around 51 million births go unregistered every year in developing countries.
- Approximately 158 million children aged 5–14 are engaged in child labor.
- In developing countries, more than 60 million women aged 20–24 were married/in union before the age of 18, of whom over 31 million live in South Asia.
- An estimated 1.2 million children are trafficked every year.
- At any given time over 300,000 child soldiers, some as young as 8, are exploited in armed conflicts in over 30 countries around the world. More than 2 million children are estimated to have died as a direct result of armed conflicts since 1990.
- More than 1 million children worldwide are detained by law enforcement officials.
- Approximately 143 million children are orphaned by one or both parents.
- 2 million children are believed to be exploited through prostitution and pornography.
- 40 million children below the age of 15 suffer from abuse and neglect and require health and social care.

THESE ARE GRIM STATISTICS. They are facts that are delivered daily by the media. Are they appropriate material for preteens and teens to study as problems to be solved? Certainly, the issues are meaningful and relevant. Certainly they pose the type of significant questions that challenge young people to do their best thinking and problem solving.

The international nonprofit organization Fire and Ice has built one of its most successful Internet-based learning projects around the theme of violence against children. That project aligns with the United Nations' Millennium Development Goals and reflects the Public Broadcasting Service's recent programs that highlight violence against children in this country.

The second model of project-based learning is the problem-based scenario. In this model, students begin their project with a loosely structured problem. Sometimes, that problem is called a *messy problem*. The first part of the students' challenge is to clean up the mess and find the essential question or issue that is at the heart of the problem.

In the problem-based scenario, students can find a messy problem in several places. The teachers may pose a messy problem drawn from a major international or national difficulty, such as the number of children who are abused or trafficked each year. To make such a problem relevant, teachers may have students focus on some segment of the issue reflected in

---

"Mom, do I have to go to school today?" Rosette asked.

"Of course you do. What kind of a silly question is that?"

"I am scared," the girl answered.

"Of what?" her mother asked.

"What I just saw on *The Morning Show*. A kid was killed yesterday at Fenger."

"No way. Where did you hear somethin' like that?" asked the older woman, now paying attention.

"Look here," the girl said pointing to the TV. "They are talking about it."

As she watched, Ms. Smith's jaw sank lower. It didn't take her long to grasp why her daughter was frightened. What she saw made her choke—four boys with railroad ties were beating, stomping, and kicking a fifth boy, who lay curled on the ground. The announcer described the incident, caught on video by a cell phone as it happened before adults stepped in. No words came to her mouth.

Along with Ms. Smith, residents of Chicago, especially those who lived close to Fenger High School, watched the TV news in amazement and horror that morning of September 29, 2009. Many were used to the violence of gangs. But this was worse, much worse. One mother of a son who wielded the wooden tie cried as she apologized in disbelief as she watched the video with the beaten boy, an honor roll student, who wasn't in a gang. He was an innocent bystander caught up in an inexplicable attack. "I don't know what to say," she wept.

local statistics. Teachers may also rely on other professionals to provide the messy problem from their own experiences in a local social service agency, business, or nonprofit organization. The Illinois Math and Science Academy's project team draws on business professionals to identify messy problems in their own companies. They prepare the problem for student teams to generate worthwhile solutions to real-world problems that involve sewage runoff, chemical pollution, mosquito abatement, voter fraud, space habitation, and other authentic issues.

THE MANY FACES OF MESSY PROBLEMS

Teachers who want to use problem-based learning can adapt the grim statistics that tell the international story of violence against children around the globe. For the most part, however, they don't have to look that far. There are more telling stories closer to home.

Teachers, parents, and the students in today's middle and high schools are often shocked by the violence that springs up almost daily. Gangs attack gangs. Boys verbally abuse girls. Girls wrestle with and scratch girls. Preteens text-bully one another. Drive-by shootings hit innocent young children. Young teens send reputation-killing emails across the Internet. Angry young drivers scream obscenities to passengers in passing cars. Rude girls push through crowds talking trash to any who can hear.

In other societies, the problems are no less severe. Some are mind-boggling. In Haiti, after the horrendous 2010 earthquake, gangs roamed the streets stealing and hoarding food, beating any child, woman, or man who crossed their paths. In Somalia, pirates kidnap sailing families and large freighters, holding their crews in frightening captivity. Beyond borders, terrorists slip through tightly drawn defenses to try to blow a hole in an airplane or to destroy a mosque. In multiple nations, children are kidnapped and sold as slaves. The scenes of violence, watched daily around the world by young and old, leave no place for many young people to hide. Violence has many faces. In local communities, real incidents occur, as seen in sobering statistics on violence against children.

WHAT IS A PROBLEM PROJECT?

Problem projects start with a messy or loosely structured problem that connects an authentic problem to students' experience. Unlike the neat problems students find in math class, where procedures for solving problems are designated step by step, the messy problem has no predetermined answer and no one right way to find it. Unlike tight math word problems ("If Sally has one cookie and Jane two, how many cookies do they have together?") or science text problems ("How long can a 1-pound ball float on a body of water with a density of 7?"), familiar to generations of students, the messy problem emulates what students are more likely to face in the streets outside school and sometimes in the hallways within. Some incidents may present problems, such as drug use, street crime, mean girls, or gang pressure, that students see daily to, from, and during school. Others, such as global warming, global health, and poverty, may be further removed and more abstract.

The key to an effective messy-problem project is the messy problem itself. The best problems reflect a real situation. The parts are loosely connected; the situation is cloudy. Like an octopus, it has many arms waving around, each one ready to do lethal damage.

With this information, students in problem solving teams are asked to "be Thomasina" (see sidebar). "How will you solve this problem?" The teams are told they will have no other information provided. They must sort out the mess and come up with a plan to get "themselves" out of a bad situation.

Other messy-problem scenarios may be further removed. One may identify a situation in the local district in which some residents want to shut down the teen center. Another may identify the details of a challenge facing senior citizens who can't pay their heating bills. A third may reflect laws being broken by local adoption agencies in search of babies to adopt from other continents. The situations are always messy, never simple and clean.

Thomasina is the most popular girl in the junior high. She has a plethora of friends. She is a cheerleader, class officer, and A-student who smiles and laughs and plays two sports. She never makes fun of others, and she is known for her inclusive, caring attitude. Suddenly her world changes from sunny yellow to dark gray. Her friends, even her very best friend, shun her in the hall. Text messages call her nasty names: "whore," "slut," "pile of manure." In the halls, she gets bumped and pushed. One girl she doesn't know picks a fight. No more sleepovers. There are giggles behind her back. Obviously, she is devastated, especially as the anonymous, mean text messages continue.

SAMPLE MESSY PROBLEMS

Two young Senegalese girls wanted to advance their education by enrolling in high school. They were told that to qualify, they would need written parental permission (their parents had never learned to write) and that the only available spaces were in schools a half day's walk away. They would also have to buy their own books; however, they lacked the funds to do so.

Two friends in a coffee shop discussed the rumor of a large boa constrictor believed to be present in the town's sewer system. They thought that the city inspectors had decided to let well enough alone. The friends, both mothers, were concerned with this response. They had also heard that a neighbor's cocker spaniel had disappeared.

General George Washington was faced with a choice. He could take his troops across the semifrozen Delaware River and march toward Trenton. Or he could stay camped in Pennsylvania, where food supplies and water were running out. If he crossed the river, he would have to use fewer boats, since the oars for many were missing.

The primary purpose of a messy-problem project is not to come up with the single best solution. It is to teach the students how to define the problem so there can be an effective solution. One former project officer from the National Science Foundation and current Dean of the Graduate School at the University of Illinois, Dr. Debashis Dutta, contends that teaching students of all ages how to define and solve messy problems may be the major challenge of 21st century teaching and learning. He believes that content knowledge, especially in science and engineering, is changing faster than our society can learn it. What he wants to see is that all students, including his graduate students, know how to problem solve. He has gone so far as to set up a program for faculty in the Graduate School to make the teaching of problem solving to graduates and undergraduates the central focus of their assignments (Dutta, 2010).

Inherent in the identification of the "real problem" in a messy situation is the need for students to ask questions—the right questions—that will help them peel away distractions and find the central issues. These are the essential questions necessary to define and solve the problem.

In the problem project, teachers focus on helping students learn what questions to ask. This question-asking focus continues in all three phases of the project. Not only will students learn which questions to ask about the problem, but also which questions to ask in order to find the added information that is not readily apparent. Once they have their clear definition, students will learn how to use questions to make sense of the sub-issues and find solutions that will eradicate the problem.

WHY IS MESSY-PROBLEM SOLVING IMPORTANT?

Messy problems are authentic, loosely structured problems that have the most potential to engage students. These problems are relevant, interesting, and motivating. They provide students with the opportunity to dig their teeth into issues and challenges that they may see in their communities or that raise their concerns. They are problems that probe students' empathy. For whichever of these reasons, loosely structured problems give the students a messy situation that they have ideas about cleaning up.

Every day, young people see the ugly face of youth violence pop up on their TV screens. What is happening? Down the street? Across town? In Chicago, youth from different neighborhoods beat one another to death. Mean girls on the streets of Los Angeles are reported on TV news to seek one another out to fight. Young gangs in Haiti battle adults with sticks and stones for looted food. Suburban teenagers race cars until they crash and kill one another.

On the international scene, TV broadcasts other incidences of child violence. Global TV connections often focus sustained attention on the issues. The World Conference on Human Rights, held in Vienna in 1993, drew the world's attention to this problem. Noting that domestic violence is a public health and civil rights issue that is widespread across the globe, the World Health Organization (WHO) conducted an extensive study on worldwide domestic violence (Shrader, Sagot, Pan American Health Organization, & World Health Organization, 2000). That study provided evidence of the atrocities committed annually against children. WHO estimated that 53,000 children are murdered each year and that the prevalence of forced sexual intercourse and other forms of sexual violence involving touch, among boys and girls under 18, range from 73 million to 150 million incidents per year. In another study, WHO found that violence against infants and younger children is a major risk factor for psychiatric disorders and suicide and has lifelong damaging effects, including depression, anxiety disorders, smoking, alcohol and drug abuse, aggression and violence towards others, risky sexual behaviors, and post-traumatic stress disorders (WHO, 2009).

A SCHOOL-BASED RESPONSE

Although the United States and other governments have devoted an abundance of funds to help nations combat this violence, little of the monies go directly to the education of the young at school. Few dollars are awarded directly to schools to address prevention of school-related violence. Most of the funds provided under the federal Violence Against Children Act of 2007 went to law enforcement agencies and little to the empowerment of young people to find alternative ways to solve daily problems.

A Novel Approach to Prevention

The award-winning international Fire and Ice project by Elluminate, Inc., of Calgary, Canada (http://fireandice.elluminate.com/), brings the issue of violence prevention and the skills of problem solving to students in a way to which they can relate. Fire and Ice is an example of a project that has import in their lives. This international project on violence against children is one small endeavor to educate young people from countries on diverse continents, including North America, about violence, its causes and ways to reduce its prevalence among their peers. Most important, it is a problem-based project that empowers students to find solutions to act against violence in nonviolent ways.

An International Internet Resource

Elluminate delivers 21st century distance education programs to rural schools in developing nations. It uses web-conferencing technology that leaps across low bandwidths. In poor countries it creates Internet conditions to connect these schools with schools in more affluent nations. Its school division, Fire and Ice, connects schools from remote rural communities in the Southern Hemisphere (the "Fire") with partners in the Northern Hemisphere (the "Ice"). Students from both hemispheres have collaborated in projects about issues of mutual concern such as global climate change, organic gardening, peace, poverty reduction, and recycling. Its most serious endeavor is to build a collaboration across continents on the shared problem of youth violence.

Elluminate's project provides participating schools with the needed collaboration and communication tools through two safe and password-secure online platforms, TIGed and Elluminate Live. Fire and Ice's regional coordinators provide a 1-hour online training session to prepare teachers in how to use the tools. To overcome possible language barriers, schools are first matched by first languages; schools may also be matched by second languages being learned. In addition, Fire and Ice conducts graduate-level courses to help teachers learn the ins-and-outs of a collaborative project and how to start up a collaboration across the borders.

What is a school's first step of the process for starting this project? Typically, the process begins as follows:

1. A school signs a Project Commitment Letter.
2. A Fire and Ice regional coordinator and participating schools review the project outline in an introductory online meeting.
3. Teachers participate in a 1-hour training session on two platforms: TIGed (asynchronous) and Elluminate Live! (synchronous).
4. Students sign Internet Safety Contracts.

Elluminate staff sometimes match schools that do not share a common language. They find this promotes a more interesting cultural experience for the students. For any asynchronous collaboration that occurs in TIGed, Elluminate encourages the partnering schools to use free online translation resources wherever possible, including www.freetranslation.com and http://es.babelfish.yahoo.com. This match-up with a school that does not speak English as a first language allows your students to participate in an authentic multilingual dialogue.

Fire and Ice staff will try to match schools in the direction of North/South, as opposed to East/West. For example, North American schools are typically matched with South American or West African schools, while European schools are matched with East African schools and Australian schools are matched with Asian schools. Sometimes, students are matched with peers from different cultures on the same continent such as Colombian students with Brazilian students.

For schools that cannot afford the minimal cost of a project, Fire and Ice waves the usual $500 annual fee that underwrites the communication costs. The annual fee enables Fire and Ice to deliver the interactive and collaborative experiences of the project. The fee covers the school's technology-platform usage; the cost of the regional coordinator to manage the project; and translation and interpreter costs, which are also available at other sites (see above). The fee also helps to enable one school from the developing world to join Fire and Ice on a scholarship basis.

As Fire and Ice teachers, educators will have a number of responsibilities. They will also have the opportunity to work with an experienced facilitator as they do their first project. Fire and Ice recognizes that teachers are some of the busiest people in modern society and have many demands placed upon them. Therefore, the Fire and Ice regional coordinators will do their best to provide outstanding support to all project teachers from the project's start to finish. In return, Fire and Ice expects the teacher, the principal, and the students to show a serious commitment by

- Ensuring that permission letters are signed by all participating Fire and Ice students
- Paying the annual fee (if applicable) in a timely manner
- Being responsive and accessible to the regional coordinator
- Attending all training and orientation sessions and practicing using the collaboration tools outside those sessions
- Actively participating in all planning meetings, test runs, and live events
- Giving reasonable notice to the regional coordinator if plans change and a meeting or event needs to be rescheduled
- Actively encouraging collaboration amongst their students in the two platforms with their partner schools
- Delivering creative and inspiring project outcomes, to the best of the class' abilities

Each teacher is also responsible for facilitating the project with his or her students. Each class in the project typically prepares a short PowerPoint presentation and a script. In the presentation, all students will introduce themselves, their communities, and their first studies of the violence theme. Using the project's advance organizer, students will have gathered some data about violence in their community, perhaps by using a Google Docs survey. They will present that data and have questions to ask about the partner school's community. In preparation for the event, the coordinator will encourage everyone to rehearse, as well as simulate, questions to ask. If bandwidth permits, some teachers may also wish to use some of the more advanced Elluminate communication features, such as the webcam or the video launch, to show pictures of the students and their community.

GLOBAL INTERNET TRAVEL: A NEW LEARNING DIMENSION

Because most are novices at using an Internet project (or at least an Elluminate project), the coordinator-supported Fire and Ice project provides many benefits to help students travel around the globe, not the least of which is a safe and secure introduction to global collaborative learning.

- The project provides an experienced facilitator who supports and guides the students through the project.
- The students get to engage in a project that will take them to a world they have never experienced to visit peers in a culture they have never known. It is immediate travel beyond the classroom borders on a highly secure and safe journey.

All students get to study the same theme or challenge, in this case, violence, with students from another world, another continent. The globe shrinks and the students get to develop new friendships and gain new insights, made possible only by the Internet's international connections.

A START OF SOMETHING NEW

Using a starter project managed by a professional group such as Elluminate in which teachers can depend on the assistance and guidance of an experienced "pro" with Internet projects, this first, getting-started step will be the most difficult. This outline provides the basic plan and sequence of events, which becomes easier as school teams work through the tasks.

1. Identifying the outcomes
   A. All students will understand many of the causes of violence in the two communities and recognize the similarities and differences.
   B. All students will identify the many different types of violence that occur in both communities.
   C. All students will understand how the cultural values of each community are related to the violence that occurs.
   D. All students will complete research about the causes of violence and the most common solutions.
   E. All students will portray violence as it is experienced and communicate their portrayals to peers in another school.
   F. All students will collaborate with students from a different culture with the common goal of finding a significant solution to the violence issue.
2. Getting ready
   A. Make contact with Fire and Ice and follow their guidance in preparing the logistics for the project.

    B. Introduce the project with a letter to the parents of students. Share excitement, the rationale, and the benefits for the students.

    C. Introduce the project to students with a well-prepared advance organizer.

    D. Build in time for discussion in the classroom about the project's outcomes, its timelines, and the e-tools the students will use.

Consider the project's three phases. The first phase will include the Fire and Ice connection, discussions with the partner school, surveys, and sharing of new ideas. After the Fire and Ice stage is finished, all will have the opportunity to go into a deeper study of the violence problem.

Prepare an advance organizer. Find a current event story about violence that may have occurred in the community. With a think-pair-share or a write-pair-share, have students reflect on how they think violence affects their lives. In the discussion, ponder ways to enrich communication and collaboration in an international discussion.

Present a loosely structured problem scenario. For instance, research the Fenger High School (Chicago) story, describe the mayhem that was occurring and say, "You are the first to arrive on this scene. How you act may well mean life and death for the victim. How are you going to stop the attack?"

Encourage students to ask hard questions about the event. List and discuss all questions.

3. Going beyond the walls with Fire and Ice

    A. Introduce the problem project. Review its outcomes (what the students will know and do as a result of this study) and describe how the project will work on an international level. Discuss the special challenges in trying to collaborate and communicate outside the classroom boundaries.

    B. Make connections as arranged with the Fire and Ice coordinator.

    C. Facilitate the project as planned with the other school(s).

4. Coming home again

    A. Prepare an assessment of the problem-based project. Ask the students to work in pairs and respond to these questions:

What did we learn about violence against children from this
    project?

What were the advantages of working "without borders"?

What did we contribute to the project?

What did we learn in the project that we could use to solve the
    problem scenarios we discussed?

How well did we achieve the outcomes of the project?

What did we learn that will help each of us deal with violence
    that may seep into our lives?

What did we learn about problem solving that will help us in
    other situations?

B. Ask the students to share their assessments with the class.
    Pick a medium for them to use, such as a digital picture show,
    a shareware presentation, or a mini-movie production. Allot
    time for the sharing and discussion of these assessments.

In this sample project, teachers who are novices in using projects can
see or employ a model for making international connections on the Internet. By working with project-experienced staff who facilitate the international connection, the teachers can more easily establish the project way
of teaching in their classrooms. By folding technology use into the project,
they take the first step in enriching projects for international collaboration
and communication as well as provide many opportunities for students to
develop their cognitive skills.

AN EXPERIENCE NOT FORGOTTEN

After teachers connect students in an international Internet experience such
as provided by Fire and Ice, it is highly likely that students will leave that
classroom more able to define and solve problems, more insightful about a
significant worldwide issue, more appreciative of other cultures, and more
able to collaborate and communicate in an in-depth manner. Further, it is
likely that they will long remember the conversations and cooperation that
this project enabled. Unlike their parents or grandparents, whose schooling was limited to the neighborhood boundaries, they will have traveled
around the world, via the Internet, to experience learning in a whole new
21st century dimension that even today, few students have the chance to
experience.

Here are some other avenues, other problem scenarios to include:

Birth Registration: Around 51 million births go unregistered every year in developing countries.

Child Labor: Approximately 158 million children aged 5–14 are engaged in child labor.

Child Marriage: In developing countries, more than 60 million women aged 20–24 were married/in union before the age of 18, of whom over 31 million live in South Asia.

Child Trafficking: An estimated 1.2 million children are trafficked every year.

Children in Conflicts and Emergencies: At any given time, over 300,000 child soldiers, some as young as 8, are exploited in armed conflicts in over 30 countries around the world. More than 2 million children are estimated to have died as a direct result of armed conflicts since 1990.

Children and Justice: More than 1 million children worldwide are detained by law enforcement officials.

Children Without Parental Care: Approximately 143 million children are orphaned by one or both parents.

Female Genital Mutilation/Cutting: An estimated 70 million women and girls alive today have been subjected to some form of genital mutilation/cutting.

Sexual Exploitation of Children: 2 million children are believed to be exploited through prostitution and pornography.

Violence Against Children: 40 million children below the age of 15 suffer from abuse and neglect and require health and social care (www.unicef.org/protection/index_violence.html).

A LIST OF SAMPLE MESSY-PROBLEM SCENARIOS

Increases in mosquito population

Dying plant species

Public dumping of chemical waste

Increased number of pregnancies in school

Restrictive school law regarding time per subject

Insufficient library materials

Internet blocks

Dying maple trees on campus

Travel restrictions for internships

Teachers who desire to take a piece of their curriculum not generally allowed in the *coverage* sweep can take advantage of the problem-based learning scenario. The practices described in the Fire and Ice scenario are easily modified. They can serve as a model set of procedures for designing a project based on the curriculum and local resources. What these home-grown projects will lack may be the expertise of an established organization to facilitate the international connection. However, use of the lists of possible agencies (Chapter 4) can solve this problem.

Teachers who have elected to go forth with a problem-based scenario can take one of two roads. They can ask their students to brainstorm and select the messy problems from their own communities or they can brainstorm possibilities with their colleagues. In either case, a set of pre-determined criteria will enrich the selection process. These criteria may include affordability, Internet partners' availability, prep time, relevance to students, authenticity, inclusion of higher-order thinking, hidden solutions, no right answer, and so forth.

CONCLUDING THOUGHTS

Problem projects begin with students learning how to ask the crucial questions that will help them solve a messy problem. Teachers can provide the problem scenarios or guide students to generate their own. The problem scenarios need to match as closely as possible to a set of criteria defining *messy* or *loosely structured*. In this way, the selected problem scenario may come from an international, national, or local issue.

As they proceed through the project, students work together to further define and refine their ideas via improved questioning skills about a significant and authentic messy problem. Teachers can introduce this model by referring to existing Internet programs that will facilitate students' learning how to communicate and collaborate beyond classroom walls and apply the process to a significant issue such as violence prevention or local wetlands destruction.

CHAPTER 13

The Innovation Project

> Innovation is not the product of logical thought, although the result
> is tied to logical actions.
>
> —Albert Einstein

WHAT IS AN INNOVATION PROJECT?

INNOVATION AND CREATIVITY are the two 21st century skills most highly valued by those who are outside the school walls and interested in a closer alignment of school curriculum with post-school career opportunities. Their interest focuses on innovative schools with the ability to develop future students who can think outside the box, as did Edison, Guglielmo Marconi, Henry Ford, and so many other innovators. They want to restore American leadership in the development of innovations and inventions that will enable American society to continue its worldwide leadership in this field. In this final format for projects, the emphasis is on enabling and encouraging students to think innovatively about solutions to the problems they identify.

WHAT IS THE INNOVATION PROJECT'S FORMAT?

Innovation is the process of making a new "thing." It results from many trials and many risks. It may be a new phone such as the cell phone or a new version of the same thing such as the iPhone or the BlackBerry. Often, it is the novel combination of two familiar things, such as a suitcase and wheels. As Bill Gates has pointed out, "Never before in history has innovation offered promise of so much in so short a time" (www.thinkquotes. com/innovation).

Innovation springs from a pattern of thinking that leads to inventions. *Inventions* are objects that have come into existence for the first time in history. These two words describe slightly different patterns. The term

Dr. Gottmind stood in front of his electronic microscope. He had finished explaining how he had used a small laser beam to dissect a breast cancer cell. He smiled.

"Why does this please you?" the reporter asked.

"Because it is our first surgical success with this particular laser beam. We had used it for other surgeries, but this cancer was very troublesome," the scientist responded.

"And how long did this take?"

"For this result?. . . Almost two years."

The reporter's eyes widened. "That is a very long time."

"Not so long," Gottmind said. "Not when you consider the different options we had to try. Many times I thought we were at a dead end."

"What will you do now?" another reporter asked.

"Start on the next step. We want to know how we will use this new tool in other ways. The exploration goes on."

"And how long will this next trial take?"

"I would predict about 2 or 3 more years. Innovative thinking takes time, persistence, and patience, as well as looking at the problem from all sides."

innovation describes a novel variation of an existing idea or product. For instance, when the Chicago restaurant firm that owns Pizzerias Uno and Due gave the pizza world the Chicago deep-dish pizza or when Domino's initiated home pizza delivery and developed the first traveling heated pizza boxes, both firms were called innovative.

On the other hand, *invention* usually describes an object that is brand new or takes such a big leap from its predecessor that it is not kept in the same class. Edison's lightbulb was a big leap from the gas lamp. Ford's carriage was a giant leap from the horse and buggy.

In either case, the axiom "There is nothing new under the sun" applies. What matters with both processes is that "the new kid on the block" is different in appearance, constitution, or function from its predecessors and provides more convenient services or a very different result. With the lightbulb, there was no more weekly filling of the gas lamp; with the warmed pizza box, the pizza arrived hot and palatable rather than cold and mushy.

The United States has long prided itself as being the king of innovation and the queen of invention. The names McCormick, Colt, Edison, Wright, Ford, Jobs, and Gates are recognized worldwide for their owners' novel contributions. IBM, known for technology; General Mills, known for cereal; and DuPont, known for chemicals, are but a few of the many hundreds of American companies noted around the globe for their innovative thinking, which resulted in many inventions.

With the advent of the 21st century, many business and government leaders have expressed two concerns about the perceived loss of the United States' innovation crown. They are looking to American education as the principle tool for restoring that crown. The Partnership for 21st Century Skills, assembled by corporate leaders, especially from the technology sector; government agencies, especially from state education departments; and other education leaders with an appreciation of the potential of technology in the classroom, have created a national lobbying force to address the need for innovative thinking in schools. The partnership not only lobbies for the adoption of a framework for 21st century skills, it also publishes on its website model lessons, units, and projects that illustrate best practices for integrating 21st century skills into curricula, and keeps a growing number of members abreast of new developments.

In the center of the Partnerships' recommended 21st century skills framework sits the skills of innovation and creative thinking. Schools such as the New Tech High Schools and the High Tech High Schools have made innovation and invention the center of their change efforts. Not only do these new schools use innovative architecture that adopts Frank Lloyd Wright's principle of "form follows function" to create internal classrooms that spring from multiple modes of instruction (individual work spaces, small group study centers, etc.); also, their buildings contain a variety of learning spaces of different sizes and shapes. There is none of the boxed classrooms in long hallways typical of the traditional American school.

The innovation format stresses the final phase, the making of a product, as the most important phase in a project. Other formats, such as the comparative format, problem-based learning format, or investigation, may put more emphasis on the first and second phases (data collection and data analysis), with the product more often than not being a way to communicate about the results arrived at mostly through logical thinking processes. These others put more emphasis on convergent thinking; the innovative format highlights divergent thinking and the inventing of new products, especially ones related to technology.

When one reviews the project results in these technology-centered high schools, it is clear that the curriculum favors the inventive thinking skills of the divergent thinker. Although there is ample evidence that students in these new schools use an abundance of logical thought, the use of divergent thinking in the production of an innovative solution or an invention of a new product is primary. In the investigation format, students may be challenged to engage in logical thinking (What conclusions can we draw from the data?) to solve a scientific or social problem, but the greater emphasis is placed on the formation of the hypothesis (What if we approach the solution from direction x rather than y?), so that students learn how to form a hypothesis and gather the data to test it (What if we change the metal in the battery.). The teacher not only helps the students conduct the experiments, but also highlights the divergent, outside-the-box, "how to" thinking for framing the hypothesis.

In the innovative format, a second distinguishing feature is the emphasis placed on discovering a solution. As would a lab scientist employed by a battery company or a bioenergy company, students would use their creative thinking to generate many hypotheses. The teacher would focus instruction on learning how to think divergently or outside the box. The students would explore different metals before turning, for example, to a systematic sequence of experiments to find the metal with the longest survival rates in various acid combinations. The teacher would focus the students' metacognitive reflections on the dispositions of patience, persistence, and attention to detail that the innovation process requires.

Although more attention is given in the technology-rich new high schools to innovations in science and technology, innovative thinking need not be restricted to the creation or adaptation of new technology tools. The development of innovative thinking is just as valuable for solving social issues, such as poverty with microeconomics, developing creative writers and artists, or working with modern media as done in the film *Avatar*.

WHAT IS THE VALUE OF THE INNOVATIVE FORMAT?

Because the innovative format emphasizes divergent thinking, students have a rich opportunity to develop skills that challenge them to think outside the box. Yes, students must do analytic research, wrestle to draw logical conclusions, and match causes with effects—all convergent thinking processes. In the innovative project, they can pay more attention to their search for alternatives, the development of options, and how to seek out different points of view—all divergent thinking processes.

In the innovative format, students seek to produce inventions or make innovative products similar to what an observer would see happening in a high-tech company that is attempting to adapt a cloud environment for hospital data storage or developing a new application for Google or Apple. From the replication of these thinking processes, they learn better what it

> You know the mantra "Give the man a fish, he'll eat for a day. Teach a man to fish; he'll eat for a lifetime"? Maybe the mantra should be "Give the man a fish, he'll eat for a day; give the woman microcredit, she, her husband, her children, and her extended family will eat for a lifetime."
>
> —Edward de Bono

takes to think beyond the walls and borders with skills that school systems have not often promoted in the curriculum. More important, they are encouraged to develop the dispositions of divergent thinking for use in whatever field they enter.

POVERTY: A MIDDLE GRADES INNOVATION PROJECT

In this project, students create variations on the microcredit microbanking system of Nobel Peace Prize–winner Muhammad Yunus. It was Yunus who revolutionized the fight against poverty when he created the Grameen Bank in Bangladesh (www.grameenfoundation.org/). Students will create their own fund-raisers for projects by creating their own innovative adaptations of the microbank.

Preparing the Project

1. On the scheduled day for the project start, form students into cooperative groups of three. Assign roles and responsibilities and review the cooperative guidelines. Roles may include a technology specialist, the banker, and the teller.
2. Communicate the project's goal and outline the intended outcomes. What will students understand and do as a result of this project? When outlining outcomes, present the rubric to be used for each objective. Handing out a copy of the goals and outcomes for students to include in their notebooks for the project will allow reference to each outcome as needed.
   A. The goal: To use the Internet as a tool for studying effective ways to combat global poverty.
   B. The outcomes
      Students will understand the ideas of Muhammad Yunus as a tool to fight global poverty.
      Students will use a variety of Internet and Web 2.0 tools in the project.

Students will develop and carry out an action plan for contributing to the fight against global poverty by making their own local adaptation of the microbank concept.

3. Review the distinction between convergent and divergent thinking with a special emphasis on the thinking operations of searching for options and weighing alternatives. After explaining each of these divergent thinking skills, ask students to think of the many different ways they could travel from home to school. Ask for different means of transportation and different paths. Select a few and ask students to weigh the alternatives by assigning pluses and minuses to the proposals.

4. Review the tools to be used in the investigation. Be sure that all students have sufficient facility in the use of both convergent and divergent thinking tools, especially the CMap (http://www.cmap.org). (If you don't have access to the CMap, use the standard pencil-and-paper concept map printed from the internet by searching "concept maps." The following e-tools will facilitate the student's thinking in this project:

   Word
   Email
   PowerPoint, PREZL, streamed video and still photos, or a
      combination of these
   Spreadsheets
   CMap
   Blog with e-journal

5. Identify the standards (process and content) that will guide the project. Include technology standards and the various content standards included in this interdisciplinary project, especially social studies, mathematics, finance, reading, and writing.

6. Gather equipment and materials needed for the project.

   Computer stations with video cameras and mikes
   Student journals (if not using e-journals)
   Newsprint, markers, tape
   Fake money
   Skype or other VOIP option
   CMap and its tutorial

7. Obtain permissions and make arrangements with the other schools selected to be involved. Connect with other schools via the suggested organizations recommended in Chapter 4.

8. Present students with a schedule for the project. Include due dates for all products.

Advance Organizer

1. Form groups of three. Give each group $27 in Monopoly-like money. Tell them that they have this money as an interest-free loan. What they must do is think how they can use the talents of the group to make this loan earn additional money for them in a start-up business. This $27 is an interest-free loan that they must return when they have completed their plans. Provide 15 minutes for the groups to brainstorm and select an idea, write a goal for their plan, and determine what steps they next must take. *Note:* The class will select one plan that all will actually implement to raise the "real money" for this project. The money actually raised can go as a donation to the Grameen Bank (www.grameenfoundation.org/).

2. Send the trios to the Internet to find the story of Muhammad Yunus, the 2006 Nobel Prize winner and the founder of the Grameen Bank. Before each group starts its search, solicit a list of key words they can use with their search engine (e.g., *Yunus, Grameen Bank*). Brainstorm a list of questions to ask for an information survey. You may also want to consider using SurveyMonkey (http://www.surveymonkey.com) or Doodle (http://www.doodle.com) This survey can be an introduction to the idea of microfinance or an introduction to the larger concept of poverty.

SAMPLE QUESTIONS TO ASK IN A SURVEY

Who is Muhammad Yunus?

What is his occupation?

Where does he live?

What innovation did he make in banking for the poor?

What problem did his innovation solve?

How did his innovation help?

Why do you think his innovation has spread so far?

When did he start his work on the microbank?

Why is the prefix *micro* used with his bank?

How well has his innovation worked in other countries?

Why is the word *innovation* used with his bank?

Phase I: Gathering Information

1. Give the trios each a copy (scan for online use) of this survey to guide their gathering of information about Yunus. If you use an online tool such as SurveyMonkey you will download it onto each computer.

2. After students have located this information, guide a discussion with the whole class. Use different groups to report each response. (Designate a speaker for the group.) When a response is inadequate, seek multiple ideas by asking a second or third group to add on.

3. Draw a large concept map on the board or overhead for all to see. Invite students to make a replica in their e-journals by using CMap or scanning a free online concept map master or the sample in Figure 13.1. If you are using a blog, show the students how to access the blog for their own e-journals. If you are using a wiki, show the students how to respond to a question. If the peer schools are using the same e-tool (blog or wiki), they may make their responses at their own site. However, you may elect to have a shared blog or wiki in which all schools respond.

4. As students provide data from their surveys, expand the concept map.

5. After the concept map is finished, it will be a good time to introduce or reinforce the writing of summary statements. According to Marzano's research, among the instructional strategies that have the strongest impact on student achievement, advance organizers, cooperative groups, and summarizing are in the top nine. Later in this lesson, students can use graphic organizers, form hypotheses, compare, and give each other feedback. These strategies are also in the top nine listed by Marzano and his colleagues (Marzano et al., 2001). Review the components of a summary.

    A. The topic sentence that answers the key or essential question or presents the "big idea" that will unify the paragraph (the center of the map

    B. The supporting sentences that answer the supporting questions or ideas (the next row of entries) and the facts (the outside items)

        Provide a sample summary such as "George Washington was the first president of the United States. He was elected to head the 13 colonies. During his years in office, his major accomplishments were . . ."

        Collect and write feedback about the summaries guided by a rubric.

Figure 13.1. Sample Concept Map

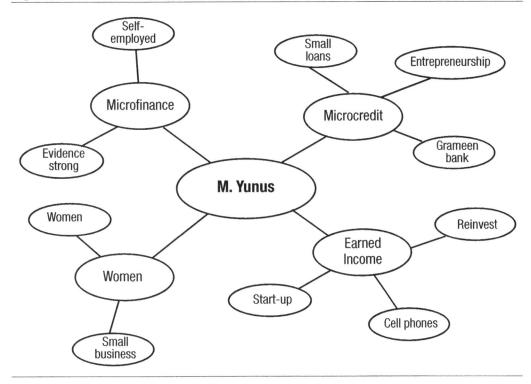

6. Make arrangements for raising the money for the bank via the selected project.

Phase II: Developing the Conversation

1. Provide students with the other school contacts for which you have made arrangements via the Internet. Review the school's guidelines for Internet use and the principles of E-netiquette and cross-cultural courtesy. (Consider connections via E-Pals or Global Kids.) If you wish students to talk face-to-face, you can have them set up Skype or another VOIP on their computers. Skype is free among its members.

2. Brainstorm with the class how the members could best go about starting the conversations that will lead to a discussion of global poverty issues. Items might include
   A. Introducing ourselves, our school, our community, and so on
   B. Finding out about the students in the partner schools
   C. Introducing the project and talking about the Grameen Bank project

SAMPLE QUESTIONS FOR SUMMARY RUBRIC

How thorough was the information gathered?

How accurate was the information gathered?

How well was the information organized?

How strong was the bond established over the Internet?

How well was an understanding of each school's life made?

How creatively was the information gathered communicated?

How clearly was the information gathered communicated?

    D. Providing the questions for discussions about the bank.

    E. Encouraging the peer school to conduct its own project. (If the partner school is in an impoverished community, the students might send the money directly to the partner school as a no-interest loan for the class to use. Obtain information from the Grameen Bank that can serve as guidelines for managing the project.)

    F. Review the most helpful brainstorming tips and techniques used.

3. Invite each group to make notes on its conversations. Planning for this conversation will take place over several weeks. Allot at least 1 day per week for email talk. If the other school elects to run a project, plan sufficient "lag" time for those students to complete its project.

4. Ask each student group to assess this experience. They can exchange responses by email and include responses in their e-journals. (Invite the partner school to contribute.) In this experience

    A. "We learned . . ."

       about the Internet

       about our partner school

       about the Grameen Bank method

       about global poverty

       about brainstorming

       about divergent thinking

    B. "We were most pleased that . . ."

Phase II (Continued):
Understanding and Interpreting the Information

1. With the class, build a second concept map based on the assessment data.
2. Ask, "What does this information tell us about poverty and ways to fight it?" Build a list of the ideas. Encourage students to explain each response as fully as possible. Also ask students to compare/contrast the points of view made by each school's students, and ask the students to speculate about the differences. Note that this is a critical moment in the innovative process. Be sure to return to the outcomes to highlight innovation.
3. Decide with the teachers in the peer schools when and how long students will discuss their findings with one another. At any or all steps in this phase, you may want students to interact.
4. Again ask the students to construct a summary of these responses. Review summary making from the earlier map in this project. Provide a rubric to guide the students as they write their summaries. Highlight divergent thinking with concept maps.
5. After reading and providing feedback for the summaries, select two or three summaries to read anonymously to the class.

Phase III: Developing an Application

1. Prepare the class to make its own application to a local problem using the Yunus model. Require the use of the CMap and other tools that will promote divergent thinking as each team designs its own "innovation" based on what they have learned in the project. The outcome should be the identification of a local problem with an innovative solution parallel to the bank identifying the lack of loan money to start new businesses and then developing their own solution.
2. Allow design time scheduled over several weeks. Present the criteria for evaluating each idea.
3. When designs are finished, prepare the teams to make persuasive presentations to a selected audience (e.g., parents, community members, other students, Board of Education). Encourage use of multimedia technology tools for these presentations.
4. Share the final presentations among the partner schools and encourage discussions of the reactions they received from other audiences.
5. As an optional follow-up, design the next unit around the implementation of the projects in the community.

Assessing the Results

1. Use one or more rubrics to assess the results of this project.
   A. What students learned about innovation
   B. What students learned about using the Internet in new ways
   C. What students learned about thinking outside the box
   D. What students learned about working together for a creative solution
   E. What students learned about students from another part of the world about collaborating in new ways
2. To construct the rubric, follow these steps:
   A. Identify the criteria that will best enable you to assess the students' knowledge or skill for thinking divergently. For instance, can the students explain how to use a CMap? Can they identify the criteria for creating a successful innovative project? Can they determine how well their use of the Grameen Bank's approach meets these criteria? Can they assess how well they met the criteria in their own class's project?
   B. Refer to the relevant chapters for ideas on constructing the benchmarks.
      Internet use (Chapter 3)
      Thinking (Chapters 9 and 10)
      Teamwork (Chapter 7)
3. Make a scale with benchmarks for each criterion. For instance, "To what degree did you show how well you could select from alternatives?"

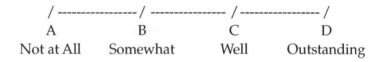

A	B	C	D
Not at All	Somewhat	Well	Outstanding

4. Determine who will complete the rubric: teacher, student-self, student-peer, other, or several.
5. Determine a grading scale for each benchmark and rubric.
   A. Benchmark: 1–4 points each.
   B. Sample Grade Scale: A = Top 10%
                               B = Next 10%
                               C = Next 10%
6. Write summative feedback (e.g., "Marion, I was very pleased to see how far you have advanced in your divergent thinking skills.

I especially like the way that you added figures and color to your PowerPoint presentation with the finished map. Your simple lists of items were very clear. I would like to see you make your lists a little shorter by eliminating some of the less important examples.")

7. Close the project with a discussion among the students at the participating schools. Use the Internet for Skype or email discussions that focus on the creative solutions and how divergent thinking helped with the innovation process.

CONCLUDING THOUGHTS

Innovative thinking is the most desired outcome of the innovation project format. That is a process outcome and rubrics are reasonable tools for the task. When discussing 21st century schools, many outside the school walls who are promoters of 21st century skills give preference to the development of innovative thinking and innovation. Some new school models are designed to emphasize the innovative project model with creative thinking being considered essential.

CHAPTER 14

No Doubt Here

A New Frontier for Teaching and Learning

I believe in helping people and I think that if we can help this one
school, we can help the whole country.

—Shantora Perkins, student,
Thornridge High School, Dolton, Illinois

THE MANY FACES OF PROJECTS

P ROJECTS THAT ENCOURAGE collaboration and enhance communication take many forms. When well planned and enriched with
technology and high-yield instruction, the rich learning that ensues
from such projects carries students beyond the gathering of information,
the predominant mode of instruction they experience in school. Rich projects not only encourage the students to construct deeper meaning from
the enriched-learning experiences inherent in projects, they also allow the
students to transcend the limits of the conventional curriculum and apply
their knowledge in more meaningful ways.

Whether students work on an elaborate project, such as Thornridge
High's biodiesel experiment, on a preset website such as ThinkQuest
(http://wwww.thinkquest.org) or Fire and Ice (http://fireandice.ellumi-
nate.com/), or on an innovative construction of a geodome or a electric
race car, it is more valuable when their teachers take the time to make
sure that students are not just doing a fun task, but that they are learning from what they are doing. Such learning from doing is at the heart
of these new models of instruction that not only have students fill their
own brains to the brim, but also motivate and excite them to engage their
brains in full gear.

STUDENT'S BIODIESEL PROJECT GOING GLOBAL

Brian Sievers teaches science at Thornridge High School in Dolton, Illinois. In his prescribed courses, the mandated curriculum does not allow for students to make sense of the material or to apply it in any meaningful way. To overcome this restriction, Brian formed an after-school Biodiesel Club. Initially, Brian helped his students build a biodiesel lab to convert cooking oil from local restaurants into diesel-like fuel.

The Biodiesel Club won a $10,000 prize in the Lexus Eco Challenge. With this money, Brian and his students have seeded a project to use the technique for providing electricity at a small rural school in Haiti. Partnering with the University of Illinois, Michigan State University, and several nonprofit agencies, they are raising funds to add solar panels to the biodiesel processor.

Knowing that there were no restaurants to provide cooking oil, the students searched for a substitute. Their research turned up the tropical Jatropa plant. This plant, already used as a biofuel in other countries, grows throughout the island of Hispaniola. Additional research told the students how to convert the seeds of the plant to oil. The process, they discovered, was similar to the process they used with the cooking oil.

In the final stages of the project, the students are incorporating solar panels so that they can run the processors for delivery to the Haitian school.

There is no doubt that students can learn by doing projects. Many will attest that they learn more this way than by sitting in a conventional classroom doing conventional tasks. Many are the students who have learned from doing in all subject areas, learning alone and in groups. In this new century, educational research and rapid advances in educational technology have provided rich resources to propel projects from being single-classroom events or after-school activities into the mainstream of engaging and enriched-learning experiences that occur at the heart of classroom instruction. MIT's Seymour Papert believes it is technology that will free teachers to use projects more readily (Edutopia, http://www.edutopia.org/project-based-learning). Teachers can incorporate high-yield instructional strategies, e-learning tools, and the opportunity for students to reflect on the information they research and on their Internet adventures beyond school walls. Then, the sense they make and the products they invent constitute a model of teaching and learning that is seldom equaled by other models in its power to motivate and in the results that appear.

A DIFFERENT WAY TO LEARN

Let there be no doubt that the big advantage of the enriched-learning model ensconced in projects adds a dimension that no other model of teaching does: high student interest and active engagement of the mind for all, not just those who may come to school eager to learn. These powerful motivators push the collaboration and communication inherent in enriched projects not only to the completion of a product, but also to the deeper metacognitive understandings of how and why so many students become so readily attached to learning in this way.

Collaboration is built into any digital learning task that involves two or more students. There is no escape as the student's work becomes locked in the software, demanding from the start that the collaborators communicate with one another about goals, tasks, and outcomes. Even if they "speak" at the lowest level through their hardware, they must speak to one another if they are to succeed.

There are some who grow up in schools as isolated learners, able to hide with their technology. Accompanied only by their e-tools, they prefer to stay isolated in their projects. However, an examination of the 21st century work world indicates that collaboration and communication will be a far more prevalent work style and a far more practiced way of helping all students develop these two crucial 21st century skills.

A NEW WORK WORLD

For those who truly appreciate the collaborative power of e-tools as the soon-to-be-predominant communication and work tools in 21st century societies, wherever their work partners may be around the globe, these same tools give all teachers the ability to create new learning worlds that far exceed in their power to teach anything previously known to humankind. Collaboration and communication are the new basics for the new work world of the 21st century.

To take advantage of this promise and to help students stay on top of the all-too-rapid changes in teaching and learning created by these collaborative-cooperative tools, teachers can support the process by making sure that students are developing the other 21st century skills that their new tools demand: critical thinking, problem solving, innovating, and creating and developing self-direction. Teachers fall short of their responsibility if they simply stand and watch, hand out materials, or make observations and checklists to satisfy accountability requirements. Teachers serve best when they are encouraged by thoughtful administrators to develop their skills to mediate student thinking and problem solving; to use these emerging cognitive skills to better understand rich and rigorous 21st century content; to produce products that show not just new knowledge but also demonstrate the ability to apply that knowledge in useful, beneficial ways.

WHERE IS THE STARTING LINE?

The starting line is immediately in front of any teacher, principal, parent, school, or community leader. As the saying goes, that start line is "as clear as the nose on the front of your face." It doesn't require a single red cent to step up to the line. It does require the individual to know the race is not a snap. It will be a challenge. It will require a giant paradigm shift that challenges the interested person to think in new and different ways about every element of instruction. Anyone ready for the challenge need only wait for the starter's voice to say, "On your mark."

Communication and collaboration are already in the curriculum. So too are most of the other 21st century skills celebrated by the partnership and other advocates. Although there are many schools with a shortage of the types of technology that allow all students easy access, there are few students, even the poorest, who lack access to cell phones and a working computer. On a larger scale, there are schools that have a bounty of technology sitting around, waiting to be used more effectively.

THE NO-FRILLS MINDSET

No matter what a person's formal status in a school might be, that person can initiate a 21st century plan. Any of the plans can be formed with a no-frills mindset. That mindset is built on the principle of making use of what already exists with the minimum of cost. It includes a personal vow of refusing to buy any hardware, software, or professional development being pushed by a sales professional or lauded by a publisher's ads without first having a plan in place. After the plan, budgeted purchases can follow.

Consider the no-frills challenge for a solitary classroom teacher intent on integrating formal collaboration and communication development into lessons relevant to any discipline or course.

1. Read the state standards for your grade or course. One subject area is sufficient. Look for the key words in the standard, the verb that indicates the type of thinking that students are expected to do as they master the core content. Ask yourself, "How can I make sure that my students can improve the quality of their thinking in a specific lesson without any technology?"
2. Redesign one lesson. Include the new communication or collaboration strategy and provide a way to check for the result.
3. Assuming the worst, you have no technology that you can use, ask, "What digital tools do my students own and use? Do they have cell phones? Can they go to the local coffee shop, the town library, or their parents so they can send an email? How can I incorporate that email into a lesson? Can students find a computer that accesses the Internet? Can I have them research on the Internet to find the facts about an author, a historic figure, or a current issue? Can I have them work together, talking with one another via the technology about the assignment?
4. Redesign your lesson and include a simple technology task that begins to develop the students' collaboration and communication. Be sure to assess how well they did that content task by talking together (e.g., How well did they write the formal email request for an interview? Grammar? Punctuation? Sentence structure? Spelling? Meaning?). Use the students to tutor one another on the application of these e-tools to your subject matter.
5. Look for other ways you can integrate technology tools into your projects so that you heighten communication and collaboration. Just remember: Structure the lesson or project so these 21st century skills are an integral part and so that you will assess these skills as much as you assess the content.

If you are a principal who is bringing or expanding 21st century skills in your school, a 21st century mini-plan is your challenge.

1. What is your 21st century vision? Find a quiet time (the first tough step) and review the concepts of communication and collaboration in earlier chapters. Write out or sketch your big idea. What is the pinnacle you dream of for your school?
2. Set a manageable 1-year goal. Use the backward-design process; determine your most achievable results for the year and how you will measure them. Keep in mind your faculty's strengths and go

with volunteers. Sample goals may include that all faculty will understand the what and the why of 21st century skills by the end of the first quarter or that volunteer faculty teams will have designed a simple project to embed in the first quarter's curriculum.

3. Find your volunteers and put them in a spotlight. Communicate and collaborate with them on the strategies that will work best. Look at the Partnership's *MILE Guide* and use the assessment as a tool for starting your collaborative planning to expand from a single project to a reorganization of the whole curriculum around projects (The Partnership for 21st Century Skills, 2009).

4. Schedule study groups throughout the school year. Once a month read and discuss a chapter from *21st Century Skills: Rethinking How Students Learn* (Bellanca & Brandt, 2010). Take one section of the *MILE Guide* and ask each faculty member to vote on where they are in implementing 21st century skills. Tabulate and chart the results for a repeat vote in 10 months.

5. Provide encouragement and support through the year. Hold monthly share-and-support meetings to measure progress and adjust. Listen, listen, listen.

6. At the end of the year, go back to your quiet place, review the results, and start on the 2nd year. In the 2nd year, encourage all teachers to work in pairs so they can construct and assess projects in their classrooms.

If you are in a district leadership role, you have the opportunity to strengthen your district within the 21st century framework. Communication and collaboration can inform your planning process at many levels.

1. Educate yourself about 21st century skills and form your vision for transforming your district over 5 years. To capture the big idea quickly, study the partnership's documents and key publications such as *21st Century Skills: Rethinking How Students Learn* (Bellanca & Brandt, 2010).

2. Encourage your school board to attend 21st century skills workshops at key national or state professional conventions that they favor. Start a reading circle so they can discuss key ideas.

3. Integrate their ideas into a district document. Try to go so far as to make 21st century skills, especially communication and collaboration, part of the district's mission statement. Encourage the board to encourage the administration to carry out the plan.

4. Set the budget parameters to go forward only with existing funds aligned to this mission.
5. With key stakeholders, develop a 5-year plan with an emphasis on professional development. What results are desired? How will we get these results? Examine the many free online professional-development sources that teachers and administrators can use together to put ideas into practice (search for *project-based learning*, *problem-based learning*, *high-yield instruction*, and other key terms).
6. Start the plan with multilevel awareness programs. What are these skills? What is our plan? What is your role in the plan? Start the plan with awareness for all district-level personnel to be followed by principals and key teacher leaders. Don't forget parents and community leaders.
7. Call for volunteers with ideas they would like to pursue. Create spotlight schools and spotlight classrooms. Encourage these teachers and principals to develop their own 21st century projects that they will use later in professional-development efforts.
8. At the end of each year, assess and adjust. In the 2nd year, plan with your spotlighters how to shine the light more broadly on 21st century collaboration and communication.

Literally, the no-frills approach allows you to lead your students, school, or district into the 21st century without being dependent on money. The move may go more slowly, but doesn't have to be any less successful. The success springs from your intentionality and skill in moving step by step at a pace that challenges comfort zones, but allows for more and more involvement by more and more of your colleagues. Equally important are the opportunities for teachers and administrators to become more comfortable in going online to find information and guidance for introducing 21st century resources. Like students, you can make this an investigation.

Step 1: Gather information about the topic (no charge).
Step 2: Discuss and make sense of how you and your colleagues can develop projects and lessons to enhance communication and collaboration the 21st century way (no charge).
Step 3: Design projects and test them out in the classroom (still no charge). The total cost for your no-frills approach? Zilch.

Let there be no doubt. The crystal ball is clear. Today's students need to improve their 21st century skills for tomorrow's academic and work worlds. The only cloud that can cloud your crystal ball will be the tendency of some teachers or administrators to overrate what they think they are already doing with 21st century skills.

As an experienced educator, you know to what degree you and your colleagues are purposefully and systematically developing communication and collaboration. As called for by the partnership, now is the time to increasingly direct your attention to the outcomes called for by the framework. You can build on what already exists to expand the development of these skills and see that every student leaves your classroom with an increased ability to collaborate and communicate. And, here we leave concluding thoughts to the reader. The challenge is to envision the resources and platforms made possible through technology to move knowledge, skills, and relationships beyond the traditional classroom walls and to transform education with our students.

References

Association of American Colleges and Universities (AACU). (2002). *Greater expectations: A new vision for learning as a nation goes to college* [National panel report]. Washington, DC: Author.

Association of American Colleges and Universities (AACU). (2004). *Taking responsibility for the quality of the baccalaureate degree.* Washington, DC: Author.

Association of American Colleges and Universities (AACU). (2005). *Liberal education outcomes: A preliminary report on student achievement in college.* Washington, DC: Author.

Association of American Colleges and Universities (AACU). (2007). *College learning and the new global century.* Washington, DC: Author.

Bellanca, J. A. (2009). *Designing professional development for change: A guide for improving classroom instruction.* Thousand Oaks, CA: Corwin Press.

Bellanca, J. A., & Brandt, R. S. (2010). *21st century skills: Rethinking how students learn.* Bloomington, IN: Solution Tree Press.

Bellanca, J. A., & Fogarty, R. (1991). *Blueprints for thinking in the collaborative classroom* (2nd ed.). Palatine, IL: IRI/SkyLight.

Brainin, S. S. (1987). *The effects of instrumental enrichment on the reasoning abilities, reading achievement, and task orientation of sixth grade underachievers.* Ann Arbor, MI: University Microfilms International.

College Learning for the New Global Century. (2007). *Liberal Education, 93*(1), 36–43.

Crocker, S. D. (2009, April 7). How the Internet got its rules. *New York Times*, p. 29.

Davis, S., Jenkins, G., & Hunt, R. (2002). *The pact: Three young men make a promise and fulfill a dream.* New York: Riverhead Books.

Davis, S., Jenkins, G., & Hunt, R. (2006). *We beat the street: How a friendship pact led to success.* New York: Puffin Books.

de Bono, E. (1989). *de Bono's thinking course.* London: BBC Books.

Dede, C. (2010). Comparing frameworks for 21st century skills. In J. Bellanca & R. S. Brandt (Eds.), *21st century skills: Rethinking how students learn* (pp. 51–77). Bloomington, IN: Solution Tree Press.

Dede, C., Honan, J. P., Peters, L., & Harvard University Graduate School of Education. (2005). *Scaling up success: Lessons learned from technology-based educational improvement.* San Francisco: Jossey-Bass.

Dutta, D. (2010). *Problem solving's priority in the 21st century classroom.* Chicago: University Center.

Feuerstein, R. (1980). *Instrumental enrichment: An intervention program for cognitive modifiability.* Baltimore: University Park Press.

Feuerstein, R. (2001). *Instrumental enrichment* (2nd ed.). Jerusalem: ICELP.

Feuerstein, R., Feuerstein, R. S., & Falik, L. H. (2010). *Beyond smarter: Mediated learning and the brain's capacity for change.* New York: Teachers College Press.

Feuerstein, R., Klein, P. S., & Tannenbaum, A. J. (1991). *Mediated learning experience (MLE): Theoretical, psychosocial, and learning implications.* London: Freund.

Gardner, H. (1983). *Frames of mind: The theory of multiple intelligences.* New York: Basic Books.

Gardner, H. (1999). *Intelligence reframed: Multiple intelligences for the 21st century.* New York: Basic Books.

Gardner, H. (2007). *Five minds for the future.* Boston: Harvard Business School Press.

Gardner, H. (2010). Five minds for the future. In J. S. Bellanca & R. S. Brandt (Eds.), *21st century skills: Rethinking how students learn* (pp. 9–33). Bloomington, IN: Solution Tree Press.

Gewertz, C. (2008). Chicago students to play lead role in dropout project. *Education Week, 28*(13), 4.

Gottfredson, D. C., & Marciniak, E. M. (1995). Increasing teacher expectations for student achievement. *Journal of Educational Research, 88*(3), 155.

Harris, J. R. (2009). *The nurture assumption: Why children turn out the way they do.* New York: Free Press.

Hart Research Associates. (2009). *Trends and emerging practices in general education: Based on a survey among members of the Association of American Colleges and Universities.* Washington, DC: Author.

Herrnstein, R. J., & Murray, C. A. (1994). *The bell curve: Intelligence and class structure in American life.* New York: Free Press.

Jenkins, H. (2008). *Convergence culture: Where old and new media collide.* New York: New York University Press.

Jenkins, H. (2009). *Confronting the challenges of participatory culture: Media education for the 21st century.* Cambridge, MA: MIT Press.

Jensen, A. R. (1998). *The g factor: The science of mental ability.* Westport, CT: Praeger.

Johnson, D. W., & Johnson, T. T. (1990). Cooperative learning and achievement. In S. Sharan (Ed.), *Cooperative learning: Theory and research* (pp. 23–39). New York: Praeger.

Johnson, D. W., & Johnson, R. T. (1998). Cooperative learning and social interdependence theory. *Social Psychological Applications to Social Issues, 4*, 9–36.

Johnson, D. W., & Johnson, R. T. (2010). Cooperative learning and conflict resolution: Essential 21st century skills. In J. A. Bellanca & R. S. Brandt (Eds.), *21st century skills: Rethinking how students learn* (pp. 201–221). Bloomington, IN: Solution Tree Press.

Johnson, D. W., Johnson, R. T., & Holubec, E. J. (1992). *Advanced cooperative learning* (Rev. ed.). Edina, MN: Interactive Book.

Johnson, D. W., Johnson, R. T., & Holubec, E. J. (1993). *Circles of learning: Cooperation in the classroom* (4th ed.). Edina, MN: Interaction Book.

Johnson, D. W., Johnson, R. T., & Smith, K. (2007). The state of cooperative learning in postsecondary and professional settings. *Educational Psychology Review, 19*(1), 15–29.

Katz, I. R. (2007). Scholarly communication—ETS research finds college students fall short in demonstrating ICT literacy—National policy council to create national standards. *College and Research Libraries News, 68*(1), 35.

Kerfoot, B. P., Masser, B. A., & Hafler, J. P. (2005). Influence of new educational technology on problem-based learning at Harvard Medical School. *Medical Education, 39*(4), 380–387.

Kinzer, C. K., Sherwood, R. D., & Bransford, J. (1986). *Computer strategies for education: Foundations and content-area applications.* Columbus, OH: Merrill.

Loveless, T. (2002). A tale of two math reforms: The politics of the new math and NCTM standards. In T. Loveless (Ed.), *The great curriculum debate* (pp. 184–209). Washington, DC: Brookings Institution.

Marcus, S. A., & McDonald, P. (1990). *Tools for the cooperative classroom.* Palatine, IL: IRI/SkyLight.

Marzano, R. J., & Kendall, J. S. (1995). The McRel database: A tool for constructing local standards. *Educational Leadership, 52*(6), 42.

Marzano, R. J., Pickering, D., & Pollock, J. E. (2001). *Classroom instruction that works: Research-based strategies for increasing student achievement.* Alexandria, VA: Association for Supervision and Curriculum Development.

McGregor, D. (2007). *Developing thinking, developing learning.* Berkshire, UK: Open University Press.

Moore, B. N., & Parker, R. (1986). *Critical thinking: Evaluating claims and arguments in everyday life.* Palo Alto, CA: Mayfield.

National Institute of Child Health and Human Development Early Child Care Research Network. (2005). A day in the third grade: A large-scale study of classroom quality and teacher and student behavior. *Elementary School Journal, 105*, 305–323.

The Partnership for 21st Century Skills. (2009). *MILE guide: Milestones for improving learning & education.* Retrieved July 7, 2010, from http://www.p21.org/index.php?option=com_content&task=view&id=800&Itemid=52

Prensky, M. (2006). Listen to the natives. *Educational Leadership, 63*(4), 8–13.

Ratey, J. J. (2001). *A user's guide to the brain.* New York: Pantheon Books.

Rhodes, C. (2009, October 1). U.S. eases grip over web body—Move addresses criticism as internet use becomes more global. *Wall Street Journal*, p. B4.

Roseth, C. J., Johnson, D. W., & Johnson, R. T. (2008). Promoting early adolescents' achievement and peer relationships: The effects of cooperative, competitive, and individualistic goal structures. *Psychological Bulletin, 134*(2), 223–246.

Rowe, M. B. (2003). Wait-time and rewards as instructional variables, their influence on language, logic, and fate control: Part one—wait time. *Journal of Research in Science Teaching, 40*(S1), S19–S32.

Sachs, J. D. (2005, October 26). The end of poverty. *Time*, p. 47.

Sacks, O. W. (1985). *The man who mistook his wife for a hat and other clinical tales*. New York: Summit Books.

Sacks, O. W. (2010). *The mind's eye*. New York: Alfred A. Knopf.

Shapson, S. M., Wright, E. N., Eason, G., & Fitzgerald, J. (1980). An experimental study of the effects of class size. *American Educational Research Journal, 17*, 141–152.

Shrader, E., Sagot, M., Pan American Health Organization, & World Health Organization. (2000). *Domestic violence: Women's way out*. Washington, DC: Pan American Health Organization; World Health Organization.

Silva, E. (2008). *Measuring skills for the 21st century*. Washington, DC: Education Sector. Retrieved October 28, 2011, from www.educationsector.org/usr_doc/MeasuringSkills.pdf

Slavin, R. E. (2000). *Cooperative learning: Theory, research, and practice*. Boston: Allyn & Bacon.

Springer, L., Stanne, M. E., & Donovan, S. S. (1999). Effects of small-group learning on undergraduates in science, mathematics, engineering, and technology: A meta-analysis. *Review of Educational Research, 69*(1), 21–51.

Sternberg, R. J. (1988). *The triarchic mind: A new theory of human intelligence*. New York: Viking.

Stolberg, S. G. (2009, May 27). Sotomayor: A trailblazer and a dreamer. *New York Times*, p. 1.

Stewart, S. (2009, August). Will you want to hire your own kids? (Will anybody else?): A conversation about workforce readiness. *Executive Action Series*, report number A-313-09-EA, pp. 1–8.

SurveyMonkey. *Free online survey software and questionnaire tool*. Retrieved July 1, 2010, from http://www.surveymonkey.com/

Voices of Youth in Chicago Education (VOYCE). (2008, November). *Student-led solutions to the nation's dropout crisis* (1).

Walsh, B. (2010, June 23). The electrifying Edison. *Time, 176*(1).

World Health Organization (WHO). (2009). *WHO global health risks*. Retrieved January 6, 2010, from http://www.who.int/healthinfo/global_buredn_disease/global_health_risks/en/index.html

Wiggins, G. P., & McTighe, J. (2005). *Understanding by design* (expanded 2nd ed.). Alexandria, VA: Association for Supervision and Curriculum Development.

Williams, F. (2010). *Williams' taxonomy of creative thinking*. Natick: Massachusetts Arts Education Collaborative.

Index

About the Authors

James A. Bellanca has taught, mentored, and inspired thousands of educators to take the practical path to instructional improvement. As founder of Sky Light Publishing, he mentored many author-consultants in how to put best practice at the core of their work on instruction and assessment. Adding to his pioneering insights on "how to" use powerful strategies such as cooperative learning and graphic organizers into practice prior to the research on effectiveness, Jim has provided school leaders with insights on use of professional development for changing the quality of teaching and learning for all children, especially those that resist change. In the past few years, he has woven the theories of cognitive psychologist Reuven Feuerstein on "changing children's minds" into classroom practice especially related to 21st century skills. The current book, his third focusing on bringing best practices of 21st century skills into the classroom, marks him as one of the premier voices leading that agenda for all children.

Terry Stirling is Associate Dean of Education and Associate Professor of Educational Leadership at Northeastern Illinois University in her native Chicago. She began her career in education working for the New York Urban League in a program for high school dropouts. She taught history and social studies in public schools in New York and Colorado and conducted professional development programs for teachers and school administrators. Her current interests include leadership, urban education, and educational technology.